W9-CSL-239

THE
BARCELONA
A D D R E S S B O O K

Text: Alex Scott
Research: Pro-Barcelona
Editors: Kathryn-Jane Müller-Griffiths,
Phil Harriss
Photography: Darius Koehli, Vision Agency (pp. 42, 56, 106, 140,
164, 202),
Claude Huber (pp. 8, 64, 178, 192, 210)
Cartography: Falk-Verlag

2

We would like to express our thanks to the following for their invaluable help in the research and preparation of this address book: Ana Figueras and Christiane Bünge of Pro-Barcelona.

We have made every effort to ensure the accuracy of the information in this book. But Barcelona is changing very quickly. A shop might close its doors, a museum undergo renovation, a nightclub lose its charm; prices, addresses and telephone numbers are the most susceptible. We cannot therefore take responsibility for any factual errors of this kind.

Your opinion matters. If you find a change, or a gem of a place we should know about, our editor would be happy to hear from you. Be sure to include your name and address, since in appreciation for a useful suggestion, we'd like to send you a free travel guide.

COPYRIGHT© 1992 by Berlitz Publishing Ltd., London Road, Wheatley, Oxford OX9 1YR, Great Britain.

All rights reserved. No part of this book may be reproduced or transmitted in any form or by any means, electronic or mechanical, including photocopying, recording or by any information storage and retrieval system without permission in writing from the publisher.

Berlitz Trademark Reg. U.S. Patent Office and other countries—Marca Registrada.
Printed in Switzerland by Weber S.A., Bienne.

CONTENTS

INTRODUCTION   7

SIGHTS   9

Monuments   9

*The Universal Exposition of 1888 and
the International Exhibition of 1929*   10

Churches   20

Town Houses   25

City Squares   28

The Olympics   31

      The Cultural Olympics   39

MUSEUMS   43

Art and History Museums   43

Scientific and Thematic Museums   51

ART GALLERIES   57

Commercial Art Galleries   57

Exhibition Halls   62

SHOPPING   65

Department Stores and Shopping Malls   66

Fashion   67

Discount and Second-Hand Clothes   76

Antiques and Collectors' Items   77

Books   79

Jewellery   84

Perfume and Cosmetics   86

Music   87

CONTENTS

Design	88
Gourmet Shops	91
Markets	98
Food Markets	98
Flea Markets	99
Other Markets	99
Florists	100
Gifts	101

4

RESTAURANTS — **107**

Catalan Cuisine	108
Extravagant	109
Excellent Addresses	113
Economical	118
Extra Special	120
Ethnic	125
American	125
Argentinian	125
Asian	126
French	126
Indian	127
Italian	127
Japanese	128
Mexican	128
North African/Middle Eastern	128
Exclusive	129
Easy Going	130
Eating Late at Night	132
Tapas	135
Outskirts of Barcelona	137

NIGHTLIFE — 141

Cinema	142
Theatre	143
Classical Music, Opera and Modern Dance	146
Pop and Rock Music	150
Discos, Bars and Nightclubs	152
Cabaret, Variety and Flamenco	161

5

HOTELS — 165

Up to 8.000-pts	166
Up to 16.000-pts	167
Up to 25.000-pts	171
Top Price	175

CHILDREN — 179

Interesting Things to See and Do	180
Planetariums	181
Workshops and Leisure Activities	182
Magic and Puppet Shows	183
Cinema	184
Theatre	184
Books	185
Toys	186
Boutiques	187
Teenage Fashion	189
Baby-Sitters	191

WALKS AND TOURS — 193

| Leafy Retreats | 193 |
| Leisurely Walks | 196 |

CONTENTS

Boat Rides   199
Coach Tours   199
Other Means of Transport   200

DAY TRIPS   **203**
The Outskirts   203
Further Afield   206

6

PRACTICAL INFORMATION   **211**
Consulates   211
Emergencies   211
Local Transport   211
Money Matters   212
Post and Telephone   213
Tourist Offices   214

MAP SECTION   **215**
Metro Network   (facing page 247)

INDEX   **247**

I t does not take long to discover that Barcelona is a city different from others in Spain—not as different as its natives would have the world believe, but nevertheless far removed from the typical and often clichéd view that visitors have of Spain. Much of this is due to the rich and varied, and above all independent, role in history played by Catalunya.

As the capital of Catalunya (a nation if no longer a nation state), Barcelona has been the centre of a mini-empire which at one point stretched right around the northern Mediterranean coast and included possessions in Italy, Sardinia and beyond. A large chunk of Provence and other parts of southern France are still referred to as "Northern Catalunya". But over the centuries, the Catalans often have suffered from being on the "wrong" side in the many wars that have taken place in Spain and the rest of Europe.

7

This history goes some way to explaining the character of the city and of its people. Most importantly, it helps explain why Barcelona has so often been in the vanguard of Spanish society—most recently in design and art, and on many occasions in social and political fields—and why the city continues to fight so hard to maintain its separate identity.

After the years of dictatorship, during which Franco followed historical precedent and tried to keep Catalans under the Spanish thumb, the opportunity has arisen once again for Barcelona to establish itself on the world stage. The 1992 Olympic Games have been used as an excuse to carry out one of the most radical reforms of the city in its history, with the result that Barcelona has become reputedly the largest construction site in Europe.

But although past visitors to Barcelona will find that several physical aspects of the city have changed beyond recognition, they will be comforted to see that many familiar places have not altered. New visitors will discover a city with a rich history gearing up for the realities of the 21st century, a city in which medieval palaces contain offices filled with computers.

Visitors to Barcelona, whether they come as part of a wider tour taking in the Costa Brava, on an extended business trip, or specifically to explore the city thoroughly, leave with the lasting impression of an exciting metropolis with a character distinct from all other cities in Spain.

Above all, Barcelona is full of people on the move. And you cannot fail to sense that the city, and its inhabitants, are "going somewhere".

B arcelona is not a city full of monuments, and many of those there are have not been allowed to remain simple tourist attractions. Most of the palaces are still used for one purpose or another, in a spirit of Catalan practicality, and medieval buildings such as the town hall and the Generalitat's palace are very much working areas, where sculptures share offices with computers. The town houses designed by Barcelona's favourite sons during the modernist period are testament to the wealth of the city at that time, when businessmen commissioned something special to show off.

The Church has had a rocky past in Catalunya as a whole, and Barcelona in particular, and these days Catalans give the least in tithes to the Church of any people in Spain. Nevertheless, some magnificent places of worship have survived—even Gaudí's Sagrada Família might one day be finished.

City monuments are being created all the time, of course, the latest as a result of the Olympic Games. Many of Barcelona's finest buildings were created for other major world events—such as the 1888 and 1929 Universal Expositions.

9

MONUMENTS

AJUNTAMENT
DE BARCELONA   29 J4

Ⓜ Jaume I
🚌 Via Laietana

Pl. Sant Jaume s/n; tel. 302-42-00.
The Ajuntament or city hall has been home for the municipal authorities of Barcelona since 1372, but though significant portions of the building remain from that period, the frontage dates from the middle of the 19th century. A tourist information office is just inside the main gate (together with a local police post), and some other parts of the Ajuntament are regularly open to the public. The Saló de Cent, dating from the 14th century, was where the 100 citizens of Barcelona met to sort out the city's affairs; next door is the hall where their modern descendants do much the same thing. The walls of the Saló de les Cróniques are decorated with murals painted by Josep Maria Sert during the first half of this century.

Gaudí's weird and wonderful Sagrada Família.

Universal Exposition of 1888 and International Exhibition of 1929

Much of Barcelona's finest architecture from the past 100 years owes its existence or at least its inspiration to the celebration of two key events in the city's history—the 1888 Universal Exposition and the 1929 International Exhibition. Both events provided an excuse for wholesale destruction and remodelling, rather like 1992's Olympic Games. The trend started in 1851, when the "Great Exhibition" was held in London and produced the famous Crystal Palace. Several other European cities copied the idea, their leaders seeing it as a way of celebrating the growing industrialization of Europe and its accompanying major changes in society and culture.

Barcelona's élite saw that an exhibition would put the city on the world map, and confer a new and modern identity on Catalunya's capital. The Universal Exposition also provided a spur to the growing modernist movement in the city, consolidating a golden period of inspiration and innovation so much admired by today's visitors to Barcelona. The Exposition was centred in the Ciutadella Park. Its site was formerly occupied by a hated fortress, built by the Bourbon rulers of Spain in the 18th century to keep the Catalan population subdued. The Ciutadella Fortress stood there until 1869 and became a symbol of the dominance of "outsiders" over Barcelona and its people. Many of the pavilions and buildings erected for the 1888 show—such as the Arc de Triomf, the zoo, the geological museums (housed in the Expo restaurant), and the Hivernacle—remain in the park as testament to the project.

If the 1888 Exposition led to the renovation of the Ciutadella area, the 1929 International Exhibition produced many of the buildings on the mountain of Montjuïc—the original and now-transformed Olympic Stadium, the Poble Espanyol, and the Palau Nacional among them. Once again, Barcelona wanted to show off the best in Spanish industrial innovation, art and design, and to re-establish itself after a bleak period in its history. If it succeeded, the renown was short-lived, as the country was plunged into civil war just a few years later, sending Barcelona into obscurity for a further 40 years.

Only approved exhibitions held since the signing of an international convention in 1928 can legitimately be called Universal Expositions, a term that is intended to indicate the breadth of theme rather than the number of participants. Since World War II, only three such Expositions have been held—in Brussels (1958), Montreal (1967) and Osaka (1970). The latest, and last this century, was accorded to Seville, for six months in 1992.

ANTIC HOSPITAL
DE LA SANTA CREU   **28** H4

Ⓜ Liceu
🚎 Rambla

Hospital 56.
The hospital in which the architect Gaudí died in 1926, was for centuries a sanctuary where weary and ailing pilgrims could get rest and treatment. The building which stands here now, behind the Boqueria market, was started at the beginning of the 15th century, and a significant amount of the original structure remains. Although no longer used as a hospital, the buildings house several institutions, including the Institute for Catalan Studies and the Biblioteca de Catalunya (the regional library, see below). The chapel and cloisters house regular exhibitions of art, while the adjoining courtyard, where patients used to convalesce among the orange trees, is an equally suitable resting place for visitors in better health.

11

ARC DE TRIOMF   **21/22** L4

Ⓜ Arc de Triomf
🚎 Pg. Lluís Companys

Pg. Sant Joan.
Built for the 1888 Universal Exposition, along with the rest of the sites in the Ciutadella Park, the Moorish-style Arc stood at the entrance to the exhibition site. It has recently been restored to some of its former glory, as has the wide Passeig de Lluís Companys, which is flanked by the Palace of Justice and other judicial buildings.

BIBLIOTECA
DE CATALUNYA   **20** H/J4

Ⓜ Liceu
🚎 Rambla

Carme 47; tel. 317-07-78. Daily except Sunday 9 a.m.–8 p.m.
The 15th-century building housing this vast collection of books and documents is the former Hospital de la Santa Creu (see above). The large vaulted hall in which the pilgrims and patients once lived now forms the library, which is used by students and scholars of Catalan history and literature.

CASA
DE L'ARDIACA   **29** J4

Ⓜ Jaume I
🚎 Via Laietana

Santa Llúcia 1; tel.318-11-95. Daily except Saturday 9 a.m.–9.15 p.m.
Once the residence for the archdeacon, this building right next to the cathedral is now the site for the Municipal History Institute. The marble swallows and tortoise panel outside the entrance was designed by Domènech in the 19th century. After a hot walk around the cathedral and other sights, it is a pleasure just standing inside the small patio, which is decorated with colourful floral tiles, a fountain and a shady palm tree.

CASA
DELS CANONGES   29 J/K4

<M> Jaume I
<tram> Via Laietana

Pietat 2.
This fine example of a 14th-century house, just behind the cathedral in Carrer de la Pietat, was formerly the chapter house for the canons. It was restored for official use in 1929.

CASTELL
DE MONTJUÏC   27 F2

<M> Espanya
<tram> Av. Miramar

Castell de Montjuïc s/n; tel. 241-68-09. Daily except Monday 9.30 a.m.–1.30 p.m. and 3.30–7.30 p.m.
The fortress sitting on top of Montjuïc had a varied history between being built in 1640, and being handed over to the city authorities in 1960. In 1940, after the Civil War, the President of the Generalitat (Catalunya's government) Lluís Companys, was executed here, as were many other Catalan patriots. That area is now grassed over, but echoes from the firing squad's rifles seem to persist (possibly because of the shooting club further down Montjuïc). The very solid walls and fortifications have also seen action during other periods, mainly in providing protection from the citizens of Barcelona during various rebellions in the 18th and 19th centuries. These days, the military museum (see Museums) is housed here. The fortress can be reached by cable-car or by more conventional motorized transport.

COL-LEGI OFICIAL D'ARQUITECTES
DE CATALUNYA   29 J4

<M> Jaume I
<tram> Via Laietana

Pl. Nova 5; tel. 301-50-00.
Opposite the cathedral stands the headquarters of the Catalan architects' association or guild, its distinctive frontage decorated by Picasso in 1962. At the time, the artist was in voluntary exile from Spain while Franco ruled, and when his design and the building were completed, they caused a fair amount of controversy in the city. The design represents children at play, singing and dancing, together with representations of the Three Kings or Magi, in keeping with the traditional Christmas market held in the square in front of the cathedral.

ESTADI
OLÍMPIC   27 E3

<M> Espanya
<tram> Av. de l'Estadi

Av. de l'Estadi 54; tel. 426-40-19. Weekends and public holidays 10 a.m.–6 p.m.
Built originally for the 1929 International Exhibition, the stadium was allowed to decay until the city was nominated to host the 1992 Olympic Games. Now, only the façade remains of the original structure. The

12

stadium will be the venue for the opening and closing ceremonies and most of the track events. In order virtually to double the seating capacity, the ground level has been dropped several metres; some 60,000 spectators can now be accommodated. As well as hosting sporting occasions, the stadium provides a setting for the bigger rock concerts (see Nightlife: Rock and Pop Music).

FONT DE CANALETES   **21** J4   Ⓜ Liceu 🚌 Rambla
Rbla. de Canaletes.
This 19th-century cast-iron fountain gives its name to the Rambla, and used to spout water from Montcada. Legend had it that whoever drank from the fountain would certainly return to the city; so travellers from other parts of Catalunya used to meet up here. These days, it tends to be supporters from Barcelona Football Club who meet here before, or more often after, a match to begin a loud and triumphant salute to their team. It is therefore best avoided on match days.

13

FONT MÀGICA   Ⓜ Espanya
DE MONTJUÏC   **19** E4   🚌 Av. Reina Maria Cristina
Montjuïc.
The "Magic Fountain" dominates the site of the exhibition grounds between Plaça Espanya and the Palau Nacional, and provides a regular and spectacular display of colour, light and water, involving up to 260 combinations of jets of water and lights, set to music. The blend of nighttime illumination of the central avenue from the Plaça, the Palau and the Font Màgica transforms this area into a spectacle in itself.

GRAN TEATRE DEL LICEU (See Nightlife: Classical Music, Opera and Modern Dance)
Weekdays 11.30 a.m. and 12.15 p.m. with guide.
Built in 1846 on the site of a former convent, and opened the following year, the magnificent Liceu opera house is in the process of a controversial expansion, taking over neighbouring buildings. The five tiers of seating within can seat up to 4,000 people, making it one of the biggest opera houses in the world. The plush interior is the result of several renovations, the most radical of which was undertaken in 1861 after a fire almost completely destroyed the theatre. The other most notable event in the Liceu's history was the bomb attack in 1893 by anarchist Santiago Salvador, in which 20 spectators were killed. Visits are possible outside performance times, and are probably an easier way of getting in than trying to obtain the very scarce tickets.

HIVERNACLE 29/30 L3
Ⓜ Ciutadella 🚊 Zoo

Parc de la Ciutadella s/n; tel. 310-22-91. Monday to Saturday 9.30 a.m.–6 p.m., Sundays until 1 p.m.

Built for the 1888 Universal Exposition in the Ciutadella park, the elegant steel and glass building now houses exhibitions and other cultural events.

HOSPITAL DE LA SANTA CREU I DE SANT PAU 15/23 N7
Ⓜ Hospital Sant Pau 🚊 Independència

Sant Antoni Maria Claret 167; tel. 347-31-33. Guided tour only. Reserve in advance.

The modern site of the Hospital which used to stand just off the Rambla (see above). The newer buildings designed by Domènech are north of Diagonal, near the Sagrada Família.

14

LLOTJA DEL MAR 29 K3
Ⓜ Barceloneta 🚊 Pla del Palau

Pg. Isabel II 3; tel. 401-35-55. Book in advance.

There has been an exchange here since the 14th century, and the city's stock exchange still operates from this site. In the 1300s, city merchants came here to make their deals with shipowners using the port. The area was soon enclosed, with arches supported by three naves of slim columns. Further building, including a façade, a staircase and more floors came as the building developed its role in maritime and city life, serving over the years as the Chamber of Commerce, and as a fine arts school attended by Picasso.

MERCAT DE LA BOQUERIA (See Shopping: Markets)

This central food market was established just off the Rambla at the end of the 1830s, after the nuns of the Carmelite convent on this site were expelled and the building demolished. Taking as inspiration the style of architecture current in Britain at the time, Francesc Daniel Molina designed the edifice which stands on the site to this day, while the iron and glass design of the roof is the work of Josep Mas Vila.

MONESTIR DE PEDRALBES 4 E11
Ⓜ Reina Elisenda 🚊 Pedralbes

Bda. Monestir 9; tel. 203-92-82. Monday to Friday 9.30 a.m.–2 p.m.; Saturday until 1 p.m.

The original convent was founded here in 1326 by Queen Elisenda de Montcada, and she is buried within its walls. The main feature of the building is the superb Gothic church and the three levels of cloisters. But also worth a visit is the exhibition of art, notably the murals in the chapel by 14th-century artist Ferrer Bassa, showing the influences from Sienna.

MONUMENT A COLOM   **28** J3   Ⓜ Drassanes 🚌 Rambla
Pl. Portal de la Pau.
Sceptics have suggested that, in this monument to the famous explorer, the statue of Colombus is pointing in the opposite direction to the Americas. But though he may have discovered the continent by accident, while looking for a route to the Orient, he must certainly have known his way out of the port to the sea. The monument was erected for the 1888 Universal Exposition, and has lately been through many indignities while infrastructure changes have carried on 87 metres (287 feet) below Colombus's feet. The stone, bronze and iron monument had to be restored in 1979, after rust took its toll on key parts. The lift to the top, inside the monument, provides a spectacular view of the port and Montjuïc, and the traffic a long way below.

15

PALAU
BERENGUER AGUILAR   **29** K3   Ⓜ Jaume I
🚌 Via Laietana
Montcada 15; tel. 319-69-02. Daily except Monday 10 a.m.–7 p.m.
A 13th-century mansion which, along with the Palau Castellet and adjoining buildings, forms the Picasso Museum. Among the modifications made to the mansion, those carried out during the 15th century are considered the most important, giving it the look it has today (including the patio in its centre). Before expanding to take over the neighbouring houses, the Picasso Museum was housed entirely in the Berenguer d'Aguilar Palace (see Museums).

PALAU D'ESPORTS
SANT JORDI   **27** E4   Ⓜ Espanya
🚌 Av. de l'Estadi
Pg. Minici Natal 5; tel. 426-20-89. Weekends and public holidays 11 a.m.–6 p.m.
Described as the "jewel in Barcelona's Olympic crown", the spectacular sports hall, named after Catalunya's patron saint, is a masterpiece of modern architecture, quite in keeping with the complex of installations built for the 1992 Olympics. Designed by Japanese architect Arata Izozaki, and completed in 1990, it can seat up to 17,000 people in the main hall, thanks to its technologically advanced elevating roof. Destined to be used as the regular home for Barcelona's major basketball team, the hall also serves as a venue for rock concerts and other big sports gatherings.

PALAU DALMASES **29** K3 Ⓜ Jaume I 🚊 Via Laietana
Montcada 20. Book in advance.
A 17th-century palace, near the Picasso Museum on the impressive Carrer de Montcada. These days it houses the Omnium Cultural, dedicated to preserving the Catalan patrimony.

PALAU Ⓜ Jaume I
DE LA GENERALITAT **29** J4 🚊 Via Laietana
Pl. Sant Jaume 4; tel. 402-46-00. Book in advance.
Completed in 1359, this is the seat of the Government of Catalunya, the Generalitat. The upper patio of the building, the Pati de Tarongers, was added in 1526. It is planted with orange trees and is these days used for receptions and other major occasions. The Capella de Sant Jordi (Saint George, the patron saint of Catalunya, complete with dragon), and the Saló de Sant Jordi (from the 17th century but lined with modern murals of historical scenes) are equally impressive parts of this entirely functional building. Between 1714 and 1908, the palace was used as a court, but until the Generalitat returned in 1977, the building only performed its traditional role as seat of the autonomous government of Catalunya for a brief period, from 1931 to 1939.

16

PALAU DE LA MÚSICA CATALANA (See Nightlife: Classical Music, Opera and Modern Dance)
Built by the famous architect Lluís Domènech in 1908, the Palau has been and is still used for all kinds of music, from chamber to jazz to rock, since it was commissioned by Orfeó Català. Recently modernized and renovated, the concert hall is a perfect place in which to hear a performance in air-conditioned comfort. And this is the best way to see the interior, since visits are not normally possible. Buying a ticket from the box office—built into a column complete with mosaic—is an experience in itself. The arches, columns and stained-glass windows have a dominant theme of Catalan culture and nationalism, and suggest even more incredible things inside the building. In the auditorium, the stained-glass windows let in an amazing amount of natural light, while the glass ceiling, which looks like both a hanging bowl and a chandelier, adds to the magical effect. The busts of famous musicians, horses, and muses complete the somewhat chaotic but unique atmosphere of the Palau.

PALAU DE LA VIRREINA **29** J4 Ⓜ Liceu 🚊 Rambla
La Rambla 99; tel. 301-77-75. Book in advance.
The Palau de La Virreina was completed in 1778 for the Viceroy of Peru, Manuel Amat. On its ground floor is an office of the city's cultural

department, where information about concerts, museums and other events can be obtained. As the viceroy died soon after moving in, the Palau was named after his widow. It was bought by the city authorities in 1944, and renovated during the 1980s to serve as an information office and site for various cultural exhibitions.

PALAU
DE LLOCTINENT   **29** K4

Ⓜ Jaume I
🚊 Via Laietana

Comtes 2; tel. 315-02-11. Book in advance.
A former wing of the Palau Reial, rebuilt in 1557 to house the Lieutenant, the king's representative in the city. These days, the royal archives of the kings of Aragon are kept in the building. It is entered by leaving the palace square and turning right on to Carrer dels Comtes; from the patio, walk up the impressive staircase making sure to note the remarkable **17** carved wooden ceiling.

PALAU GÜELL   **28** J3

Ⓜ Liceu 🚊 Rambla

Nou de la Rambla 3; tel. 317-39-79. Monday to Saturday 11 a.m.–2 p.m. and 5–8 p.m.
One of the first major works to be completed by the famous modernist architect, Antoni Gaudí. The Palau Güell shows many of the dominant themes to emerge in Gaudí's later work. Like so many of his designs, it was commissioned by the leading industrialist, Eusebi Güell, who was to prove so supportive of the architect throughout his life. Gaudí designed the building to connect with the main house owned by the family on the Rambla. Built between 1885 and 1889, the structure is said to encompass many ideas taken from the architecture of the Far East and of Victorian Britain. Particularly impressive is the interior hall (which rises to the sixth floor of the palace) and the 127 columns in the interior, some of which are functional and others purely decorative. The palace now houses the Museu de les Arts de l'Espactacle, the theatrical museum (see Museums).

PALAU MARCH   **29** J3

Ⓜ Liceu 🚊 Rambla

Rbla. Santa Mónica 8; tel. 318-50-04.
One of the first buildings constructed on the Rambla after the 1775 dismantling of the wall which reached the royal shipyards at the Drassanes. In around 1780, a Catalan businessman, Francesc March, ordered it built, it is believed, by the same architect as designed the Llotja (see p.14), Joan Soler. It was redecorated in 1791, and some of the paintings from that period remain in the palace in the rooms around the central patio. The patio itself was covered over at the end of the 19th

century, and a floor was added, when the building was taken over by the Bank of Spain. The Generalitat acquired the building in 1982, and the regional government's cultural department has been installed.

PALAU NACIONAL **19** E4

Ⓜ Espanya

🚃 Av. Reina Maria Cristina

Mirador del Palau 6; tel. 280-19-64.
This large and (by dint of its position a little up Montjuïc) dominating palace was the Spanish national pavilion built for the 1929 International Exhibition. It now houses one of the world's finest collections of Romanesque art (see Museums) and a museum of ceramics. The Palau was originally planned by the modernist architect, Puig, whose designs were altered because of political changes. The result was to keep the original, monumental design planned by Puig, but to add more of the so-called illustrative art of the period—art and design from the rest of the world. The parts of the palace to be used for the 1929 exhibition of art and archaeology were also tacked on. In addition, a throne room was added to the blueprint, as well as other royal chambers for the use of the Spanish monarchs during their visit to the Exhibition. The museum of art was opened in 1934, though the exhibits were moved at the beginning of the Civil War to escape the bombardments from Franco's forces.

18

PALAU REIAL DE PEDRALBES **11** D9

Ⓜ Palau Reial

🚃 Av. Diagonal

Av. Diagonal 686; tel. 280-19-64. Book in advance.
On land belonging originally to the industrialist and patron of architect Gaudí, Eusebi Güell, this royal palace was designed for King Alfonso XIII. Although work started in 1919, and went on until 1929, the king did manage to stay here in 1926, while changes to the original plan were put into effect. The design is similar to Italian Renaissance palaces, but is not especially inspiring, although the interior fixtures and fittings, complete with ceramics, paintings and tapestries, are worth a look. The gardens are the more interesting aspect of the palace (see Walks), while the museum of carriages (see Museums) occupies what were intended to be the stables attached to the palace.

PARC DE L'ESCORXADOR (See Walks & Tours: Leafy Retreats)
The famous Miró sculpture that resembles a totem pole dominates this city park. The Escorxador, named after a slaughterhouse that once stood on the site, now makes for a pleasant break from the city's main exhibition centre.

PAVELLO MIES Ⓜ Espanya
VAN DER ROHE **19** D/E5 🚌 Av. Reina Maria Cristina
Av. Marqués de Comillas s/n. Daily 9 a.m.–6 p.m.
The Bauhaus architect, Ludwig Mies Van der Rohe, designed a building named the German Pavilion on this site for the 1929 International Exhibition—but it was demolished after the show. The glass and marble edifice was carefully reconstructed during the 1970s, and renamed the Barcelona Pavilion. Today, it houses a design foundation.

POBLE Ⓜ Espanya
ESPANYOL **19** E 4/5 🚌 Av. Marqués de Comillas
Av. Marqués de Comillas 25; tel. 325-78-66. Monday 9 a.m.–8 p.m., Tuesday until 2 a.m., Wednesday and Thursday until 3 a.m., Friday and Saturday until 6 a.m., Sunday until 2 a.m.
This complex of buildings constructed for the 1929 International Exhibition was intended to reproduce styles of urban and rural architecture from all over Spain. It contains 115 different edifices, as well as streets and squares. The buildings had been allowed to fall into disrepair until 1988 when the complex was relaunched. It now boasts modern attractions for families (bars, restaurants, discos, cinemas, artisans at work, and other expensive features) and is worth a visit, if only to get a hint of what the rest of Spain is like. (See also Walks and Tours.)

REIALS DRASSANES **28** H/J3 Ⓜ Drassanes 🚌 Rambla
Portal de la Pau 1; tel. 318-32-45. Tuesday to Saturday 10 a.m.–2 p.m. and 4–7 p.m., Sunday and public holidays until 2 p.m.
The royal shipyards were started in the middle of the 13th century, and gradually expanded as work increased, until the 18th century. In these shipyards, the vessels of war used by the kings of Aragon and later the rest of Spain were constructed and repaired, though after the Americas were discovered, the work shifted to the Atlantic coast. The fortified exterior dates from the end of the 17th century. It wasn't until the 1930s that the establishment became the city's Military Museum.

SAGRADA Ⓜ Sagrada Família
FAMÍLIA **22** M6 🚌 Padilla
Provença 450; tel. 236-69-33. Daily 10 a.m.–6 p.m.
The twisty spires of the "Temple Expiatori de la Sagrada Família" dominate a city skyline more distinctive these days for its few very modern tower blocks. The so far unfinished work of architect Antoni Gaudí—he was run over by a tram before he could complete his major project—stands out in more ways than one from its surroundings. The architect

19

spent 43 years working on the church, and in recent years, the debate over how he would have carried on (which includes computer predictions) has caused considerable controversy among modern architects. The church of the 20th century which Gaudí wanted to create was to feature a total of 20 spires, four on each side, to honour the Apostles. What has been built is an astonishing sight, and a lift (or stairs if you have the energy) takes you aloft to splendid examples of the architect's work, as well as an incomparable view.

SALÓ DEL TINELL
REIAL MAJOR **29** K4

Ⓜ Jaume I
🚋 Via Laietana

Pl. Rei 9; tel. 315-11-11. Tuesday to Saturday 9 a.m.–8 p.m., public holidays until 1.30 p.m.

Christopher Columbus is supposed to have reported back to Ferdinand and Isabella here in 1493, after his trip to the Americas, rather than on the steps to the palace as paintings would have us believe. The Saló del Tinell was built in 1359 to host royal audiences; it also provided the chamber for occasional meetings of the Catalan Corts—the parliament.

TEATRE GREC (See Nightlife: Theatre)
Another of the results of the 1929 International Exhibition, this outdoor theatre on Montjuïc recalls a Greek amphitheatre, and these days is the centre of a major arts festival held every summer in the city.

CHURCHES

All churches in Barcelona are open daily from 8 a.m. to 8.30 p.m.

CATEDRAL
DE BARCELONA **29** K4

Ⓜ Jaume I
🚋 Via Laietana

Pla de la Seu.

It took six centuries to complete the city's cathedral, a dominant feature of the Barri Gòtic. Built on the site of several earlier churches, the cathedral was started at the very end of the 13th century, with the part that features the Sant Iu gate on Calle Comtes de Barcelona. It was this section of the cathedral which gained infamy in later years as the local headquarters for the Inquisition. The beautiful shady cloisters, completed in the 15th century, enclose trees, plants and a flock of geese, who plod around oblivious to the visitors admiring the surrounding chapels. Much of the rest of the cathedral, though apparently Gothic, is actually much more modern—the façade was not finished until 1892, for example, paid for by the city banker and sometime mayor, Manuel Girona. Other features of the cathedral worth special mention are the tomb of Santa Eulàlia (one of Barcelona's two patron saints) and the twisted figure of Christ, the Cristo de Lepanto. On principal saints' days or religious holidays, a queue to light a candle stretches right around the cathedral.

ESGLÉSIA
CAPILLA DEL PALAU   29 J3

Ⓜ Liceu
🚌 Rambla

Ataülf 2.

The only remaining building from a medieval palace that hit its height of fame in the second half of the 14th century. During the reign of Peter IV (Pere el Cerimoniós), the palace and its grounds featured the city's first zoo, and citizens flocked there to see the royal lions. Although the palace itself was demolished in the 19th century to make way for new buildings, the chapel remains. It was restored in the 16th century and was maintained by the Jesuits, who used it as a residence.

ESGLÉSIA CASTRENSE
PARC DE LA CIUTADELLA   29 L3

Ⓜ Ciutadella
🚌 Zoo

Pg. Picasso 15.

Built in the 18th century by the French architect Alexandre de Retz, and among the first buildings in the city to employ the French classic style, this simple church—with virtually no sculptural adornment inside or out—is pleasing to the eye. The church now serves as a place of worship for the armed services.

ESGLÉSIA MARE DE DÉU
DE BETLEM   21 J4

Ⓜ Liceu
🚌 Rambla

Xúcla 2.

One of the two churches on the Rambla and known usually just as the Betlem. Designed at the end of the 17th century by Josep Juli, the interior of the church was badly damaged at the beginning of the Civil War.

ESGLÉSIA MARE DE DÉU
DE LA MERCÉ   29 J3

Ⓜ Drassanes
🚌 Rambla

Pl. Mercé 1.

Dedicated to one of Barcelona's two patron saints (the other, Santa Eulàlia, has her tomb in the cathedral), this 13th-century church used to form part of the Mercé Convent, which was renovated in the second half of the 18th century. Much of the convent building was taken over by the area's naval command in 1846, but the church remains and sits in a pretty square. Traditionally, the city's leading sports teams visit the church to dedicate their trophies to the saint.

ESGLÉSIA
SANT AGUSTÍ   **28** J4

Ⓜ Liceu
🚌 Rambla

Pl. Sant Agustí 2.
This 18th-century church, designed by Pere Bertran, has an unfinished look to it. Overlooking a picturesque square, the building was the site, in 1971, for the constitution of the Catalan Assembly. The lower half of the façade was renovated a few years ago.

22

ESGLÉSIA
SANT FELIP NERI   **29** J4

Ⓜ Liceu
🚌 Rambla

Pl. Sant Felip Neri 5.
A baroque church (built in 1752) with a sorry history to it. Twenty children died here during a bombardment of the city in January, 1938. The façade of the church still bears the scars of battle from the Civil War. The altar is a notable feature.

ESGLÉSIA
SANT JAUME   **29** J3

Ⓜ Jaume I
🚌 Via Laietana

Ferrán 28.
Originally a synagogue, the building changed faiths and became a place of worship for Jews converted to Christianity, at the end of the 14th century. Physical changes came about in the following century and in the 17th, while the latest renovations, mainly to the interior of the church, were carried out in the second half of the 19th century.

ESGLÉSIA SANT JOSEP
I SANTA MONICA   **29** J3

Ⓜ Liceu
🚌 Rambla

La Rambla 7.
Said to be the only building over 300 years old still standing on the Rambla, the church is all that remains of the Augustinian convent started in 1626 and finished 10 years later. It became a parish church in the 19th century. The latest renovation has provided the former convent with an art gallery.

ESGLÉSIA
SANT MIQUEL DEL PORT   **29** J3   Ⓜ Liceu
🚌 Rambla
Sant Miquel 39.
In spite of its Romanesque appearance, the church was built in 1755 and was intended to form the centre of the new barrio of Barceloneta that was rising up around it. It has survived many changes since then, including the latest remodelling of the area, which has opened the city up to the sea once again.

ESGLÉSIA
SANT PAU DEL CAMP   **28** H3   Ⓜ Liceu
🚌 Rambla
Sant Pau 101.

23

Starting life during the 9th century as a Benedictine monastery standing in the country (camp), this small and attractive church contains the remains of Guifré (Wilfred) II, who died in 912. Sant Pau's is a fine example of Romanesque architecture; and in addition, its 13th-century triple-arched cloister is particularly beautiful. Used for many years as a hospital and barracks, and even abandoned completely for some time, the church was rescued only at the beginning of this century.

ESGLÉSIA
SANT PERE DE PUEL-LES   **21/22** L4   Ⓜ Arc de Triomf
🚌 Pg. Lluís Companys
Lluís El Piadós 1.
The church is one of the few remaining parts of a Benedictine monastery that stood here until 1879. Several fires and botched reforms have since destroyed much of the original, though several Romanesque columns and part of a chapel dedicated to the victory over the Moors in 801 can still be seen.

ESGLÉSIA
SANT SEVER   **29** J4   Ⓜ Jaume I
🚌 Via Laietana
Sant Sever 9.
One of the few well-preserved examples of baroque architecture still standing in the city. Built into a niche above the door on the simple façade of the church is an image of Sant Sever. The profusely decorated interior is also worth a look. Building took place between 1698 and 1705.

ESGLÉSIA
SANTA ANA   **21** J4   Ⓜ Jaume I   🚊 Via Laietana
Rivadeneyra 3; tel. 301-35-76.
The date of this Gothic church's foundation is not known exactly, but part of the Romanesque origins remain from what was a much bigger monastery. An interesting feature is the 15th-century cloister.

ESGLÉSIA
SANTA MARIA DE MONTALEGRE   **20** J4/5   Ⓜ Liceu   🚊 Rambla
Montalegre 5.
This church, tucked away in a side street off the Rambla, forms part of the complex of buildings established by the Opus Dei order.

24 ESGLÉSIA
SANTA MARIA DEL MAR   **29** K3   Ⓜ Jaume I   🚊 Via Laietana
Pl. Santa Maria.
Said to be a perfect example of Catalan Gothic architecture, this large church overlooks an attractive inner-city square. Building started in 1329, and the church was added to significantly during the following century. The interior's relatively bare look is due to a fire that destroyed nearly all of it in 1936 at the outbreak of the Civil War. Try to visit it for one of the regular concerts; the acoustics are near-perfect.

ESGLÉSIA
SANTA MARIA DEL PÍ   **29** J4   Ⓜ Liceu   🚊 Rambla
Pl. Pí.
An octagonal bell tower over 50-metres (164-feet) high dominates this attractive church, completed in 1453. The other outstanding feature is the large rose window in the façade. The pretty square in front, the Plaça del Pí (pine), and the adjoining square were formed during the early 19th century when the local cemetery was closed for public health reasons.

ESGLÉSIA
SANTS JUST I PASTOR   **29** J3   Ⓜ Jaume I   🚊 Via Laietana
Rera Sant Just 1.
One of the oldest churches in Barcelona. The latest of several renovations gave it a Gothic style (a further reconstruction is under way). The church is famous as the place where you can swear a will without using a notary (in front of the altar dedicated to Saint Felix), which is recognized by the courts.

SAGRADA FAMILIA (See p. 19)

TOWN HOUSES

Many of these town houses are open to the public, but you must book a visit in advance. Ask at an information office (See Practical Information).

CASA
AMATLLER   **21** J6   Ⓜ Pg. de Gràcia
Pg. de Gràcia 41.   🚌 Pg. de Gràcia

The middle of three modernist town houses (the others are the Batlló and the Lleó Morera, see below) built at the turn of the century on Passeig de Gràcia. The three houses, designed by supposedly deadly rivals Gaudí, Puig and Domènech, form what is known popularly as the Mançana de la Discordia—either the block, or the apple of discord, since the Catalan word is the same for both. The Amatller house, designed by Josep Puig i Cadafalch (1867–1957), was completed in 1900 and features a cubical design on its façade, and an apparently Flemish-inspired glazed-tile roof.

25

CASA
BATLLO   **21** J6   Ⓜ Pg. de Gràcia
Pg. de Gràcia 43.   🚌 Pg. de Gràcia

The house designed by Antoni Gaudí for Enric Batlló, a noted textile industrialist, in 1905, is actually a re-design of a building already owned by the family on this spot. The famous architect added a new floor on to the house, with separate access for the family; moved the staircase and the inside courtyard; and covered over the patio with white and blue glazed tiles which become lighter or darker according to how much natural light reaches them. The façade of the house and the tiled roof are the most distinctively Gaudíesque features, with fragments of coloured glass imbedded in the wall and the mask-like parapets of the balconies. The tower and cross rising from the roof are said to have been added in order to compensate for the difference in height with the Amatller house next door (see above).

CASA
BELLESGUARD   **5** H11   Ⓜ Pg. Bonanova
Bellesguard 16–20.   *Main line train:* Peu Funicular

Gaudí designed this building for the Figueras family, and put it up on the ruins of a royal hunting lodge, originally constructed in 1408. Working on it between 1900 and 1909, the architect decided to give the building a neo-Gothic look to commemorate its former existence. The square house, open on all sides and with a view over the city, is topped by a tall spire, complete with Catalan flag, a royal crown, a four-armed cross and an arrow. Grey and green brick and slate are the predominant materials used in the façade of the house, and there is an interesting three-dimensional rose window.

CASA CALVET   21/22 K5

Ⓜ Catalunya
🚌 Pg. de Gràcia

Caspe 48.

This was the first house designed by Gaudí in the Eixample area of Barcelona, and the architect received a prize for his work from the municipal authorities when it was finished in 1900—the only one he received during his lifetime. Commissioned as a town house with offices and a shop, the building itself is fairly standard for this business area, and stands out from the crowd only because of the Gaudí details on the façade.

26

CASA DE LES PUNXES   21/22 K6

Ⓜ Diagonal
🚌 Pl. Mn. J. Verdaguer

Av. Diagonal 416.

Also known as the Casa Terrades, this house was designed by Puig and built between 1903 and 1905. Standing at a crossroads, the house stands out in more ways than one, as its tall towers and spires contrast strongly with the architecture of the surrounding buildings. It is said to have been inspired by the Gothic architecture of Scandinavian cities, and looks rather like a medieval castle.

CASA FUSTER   21 K7

Ⓜ Pg. de Gràcia
🚌 Pg. de Gràcia

Pg. de Gràcia 132.

Right at the top of Passeig de Gràcia, this house designed by Domènech—one of his last projects—dominates the avenue with its height and its white and pink marble façade covered with windows. Several influences seem to have been combined by the architect in this house, finished in 1912.

CASA LLEO MORERA   21 J5/6

Ⓜ Pg. de Gràcia
🚌 Pg. de Gràcia

Pg. de Gràcia 35.

The third of the "Manzana de la Discordia" houses (see Casa Amattler above). This was designed by Lluís Domènech i Montaner (1850–1923) in 1905 and stands on a corner of Passeig de Gràcia and Carrer de Consell de Cent. Although the bottom two floors were gutted to make commercial premises, the remaining façade, with its combination of Gothic and Moorish styles is a beautiful reminder of the original building. Columns and balconies, dragons and flowers adorn the front of the house. A casual visit to the city's tourist department, now housed here, will at least provide a quick view of the magnificent interior, which in many rooms is decorated with scenes from mythology.

CASA MILÀ (LA PEDRERA)   21 K6
Ⓜ Pg. de Gràcia
🚃 Pg. de Gràcia
Pg. de Gràcia 92.

While Antoni Gaudí was working on the Casa Batlló (see p. 25) in 1905, he was commissioned by a businessman, Pere Milà, and his wife, Roser Segimon, to draw up plans for a building on the corner of Passeig de Gràcia and Carrer de Provença, covering a 1,000-square-metre (1,196-square-yard) plot of land. What emerged was Gaudí's largest civil project, which the architect worked on from 1906 to 1910.

27

It's an impressive sight, which leaves both devotees of his work and agnostics bemused. The apartment block's five storeys and two half-storeys (the latter at street level) resemble a giant cake or loaf of bread sinking into the ground; the naturalistic style of the building distinguishes it completely from the surrounding buildings. Although the building is relatively modern, the use of stone gives it an older, more established appearance. The undulating façade, broken by wrought iron balconies and railings, looks like a rockface suffering constant erosion. The combination of this effect and the two large interior patios, led to the building gaining its nickname of "La Pedrera"—the stone quarry. Rising well above the roof are the building's chimneys, fantastic twisting turrets topped with sculptures that look like helmeted warriors.

CASA VIÇENS   21 K8
Ⓜ Fontana 🚃 Gran de Gràcia
Carolines 18–24.

The appearance of this town house, one of the first designed by Gaudí, owes much to Moslem influences and perhaps to the business of the man who commissioned the work, the ceramics manufacturer, Manuel Vicens. It was built between 1883 and 1888, although Gaudí is said to have carried on with detail work for some time after that. The first signs of the modernist style are clear in the decoration. Green and white tiling and bare red brick are the dominant features of the angular façade, while the building is topped with structures resembling prayer towers.

CITY SQUARES

PLA DE LA BOQUERIA   **29** J4   Ⓜ Liceu 🚌 Rambla

Perhaps not recognizably a square in the traditional sense, but at least an open space and intersection in the centre of the Rambla. The Pla—plain or square—is a little further down the Rambla de Sant Josep from the entrance to the Boqueria Market (see p. 14), which gives it its name. Across the road lies the access to the heart of the Ciutat Vella. In this slightly wider section of the Rambla, the trees that flank the rest of the boulevard give way to an area where people stand, stroll or rush by as the mood or need takes them. Right at the centre of the Pla is a mosaic designed in 1976 by Joan Miró which has become a symbol for the Rambla.

28

**PLAÇA
DE BERENGUER EL GRAN**   **29** K4   Ⓜ Jaume I 🚌 Via Laietana

When you walk down the very busy Via Laetana, in the heart of the business district, it comes as a relief to reach this quieter, if small, square. It is dominated by the statue of the Aragonese count, Ramon Berenguer III or El Gran—the Great—straddling his horse. Behind the statue are benches and remains of the city's Roman wall, and behind them the Royal Palace and the Capella de Santa Àgata.

**PLAÇA
DE CATALUNYA**   **21** J5   Ⓜ Catalunya 🚌 Pl. Catalunya

When the city was remodelled at the end of the 19th century, this large square was intended to be the centre of Barcelona. Since then, the square has seen many changes, the latest of which was completed in 1992. The result is intended to allow the Rambla to join up with the Rambla de Catalunya with the minimum interference to pedestrians from road traffic. Whether the remodelling will change the character of this large city square remains to be seen, but in spite of trees, pigeons and people, it is not really a place to spend much time. Dominating the square are large banks and official buildings, and the main branch of the Corte Inglés department store. The remaining adornments are the impressive statues and fountains, and wide steps which descend towards the Portal de l'Àrgel and the busy shopping district in the Ciutat Vella. Beware of slipping if the surface of the square is wet, and remember that if you want to sit on one of the many chairs scattered around the square, sooner or later someone will ask you to pay.

PLAÇA
DE ESPANYA   **19** F5

Ⓜ Espanya
🚇 Pl. Espanya

A busy square that is situated at the southern entrance to the city. At the very centre of the roundabout in the middle of the square is a magnificent fountain—just renovated—created as a decoration to the entrance of the 1929 International Exhibition fairground, the Fira. These days, many busy roads converge on the square, but a large area in front of the impressive Fira buildings is quiet enough, when there are no throngs visiting one of the many international exhibitions held nearby. It's a real pleasure to stand there and look up the avenue towards the mountain and the Palau Nacional, just as visitors did in 1929. Opposite the Fira, stands the now disued Les Arenes bullring, while one of the main city police stations occupies another section of the square.

PLAÇA
DE SANT FELIP NERI   **29** J4

Ⓜ Jaume I
🚇 Via Laietana

No traffic is allowed into this square. It is surrounded by churches and former guild houses, and dominated by the baroque church of the same name (see p. 22). Children play around the column in the centre, which is now missing the statue that once adorned it. The two guild houses, moved here as reconstruction went on around the cathedral, are the Calderers (cauldron-makers) and the Sabaters (shoemakers); the latter housing the guild's Museu Historia del Calçat (see Museums).

PLAÇA
DE SANT JUST   **29** J/K3

Ⓜ Jaume I
🚇 Via Laietana

Taking the narrow Carrer d'Hércules from Plaça Sant Jaume, beside the Ajuntament, you come almost immediately on to a little square overlooked by the church of Sants Just and Pastor. In front of the church is Barcelona's oldest fountain, installed in 1367 and restored during the 18th century. The fountain still works, off and on. Other interesting features around the square are a second-hand bookshop, an 18th-century palace (the Moixó) and a pleasant bar.

PLAÇA
DEL DOCTOR FLEMING   **29** J4

Ⓜ Liceu
🚇 Rambla

Behind the Boqueria Market's car park, and flanking the academy of medicine, can be found a small square containing a bust dedicated to Sir Alexander Fleming, the famous British doctor and discoverer of penicillin. A couple of shacks standing in the square house a host of scribes who will compose letters for you—even declarations of love. More mundanely, they also help fill in declarations to the tax authorities.

PLAÇA DEL PORTAL DE LA PAU

PLAÇA
DEL PORTAL DE LA PAU   **28/29** J3   Ⓜ Drassanes   🚊 Rambla

Marking the end of the Rambla, and the opening to the sea, this square is dominated by the monument to Christopher Columbus (see p. 15). By this point, the Rambla has widened considerably. To the right as you look out to sea are the royal shipyards, the Drassanes, and the maritime museum. To the left is the imposing building that houses the city's military governor.

PLAÇA
NOVA   **29** J4   Ⓜ Liceu/ Jaume I   🚊 Rambla/ Via Laietana

This small and busy square gives on to the large space in front of the cathedral and two of the towers remaining from the Roman walls of the city. The "new" square was, in fact, created in 1356. Following an extensive redevelopment of the area (including the building of an underground car park, during which traces of former cities were discovered), the square should be able to return to its former glory. Most importantly, the traditional market held here in December, selling Christmas decorations, will be able to operate more comfortably. Antiques dealers also set up stall every Thursday, except in August.

PLAÇA REIAL   **29** J3   Ⓜ Liceu   🚊 Rambla

When a Capuchin convent was demolished in the mid-19th century, this beautiful square was created on the spot, and it has retained much of its charm. The square is surrounded by arched walkways, shade is provided by several tall palm trees, and relief is provided by a fountain—depicting the Three Graces—in the centre. Firm efforts have been made recently to move-on the collection of unsavoury characters who had made it their home (and often their business place), but in spite of a heavy police presence, it may not be the best spot for a late-night wander. On Sundays, the square is taken over by scores of coin and stamp dealers.

PLAÇA SANT JAUME   **29** J4   Ⓜ Jaume I   🚊 Via Laietana

A cobbled square that has been the scene of much of Barcelona's history. And it still forms the focal point for popular manifestations of all kinds, from political or social demonstrations, to celebrations by winning city sports teams and their supporters. Stand in the centre of the square (avoiding the traffic that drives through) and you'll be positioned between the two symbols of Catalan power, the Generalitat and the Ajuntament. As has so often been the case, they are currently at political odds. The square is always busy with people crossing from one part of the Barri Gòtic to the other, or just stopping to look.

THE OLYMPICS

When Barcelona was awarded the 25th Olympic Games in 1986, it led to what one local politician described as 20 years of infrastructure improvements compressed into three. Difficult though it has been for the inhabitants of the city to cope with what seemed to have been a permanent building site over those three years, both they and the visitor to Barcelona will be left with a modern system, blessed at last with sufficient hotel rooms, roads and—probably—telephone lines. In addition to the sports installations that existed before the award of the Games (many of which have been improved), completely new arenas have been constructed, and the Barcelona of 1993 should provide sports facilities to suit all tastes.

It should be remembered that Olympic Games are always awarded **31** to a city, and the 25th such occasion was given to Barcelona, not Catalunya and not Spain, although of course everyone shares in some of the pride and honour. The award has put the city on the map once again—the opening ceremony, for example, commands a worldwide television audience estimated at 3,500 million people, and has been described as the biggest advertisement ever.

It was decided that in Barcelona, the Games should be given a Spanish flavour, and Pelota is among the exhibition sports to be played, along with Roller Hockey and Taekwondo. Pelota, a sport played predominantly but not exclusively in the Spanish and French Basque Country, is fast, furious and very exciting for the spectator, involving a small hard ball, a wicker "bat" attached to the arm, and a wall.

The following is a list of venues hosting the main events of the 1992 Olympic Games.

Archery

**CAMP DE TIR AMB ARC
DE LA VALL D'HEBRON**   **6** M11   Ⓜ Pg. Vall d'Hebrón
Between Pg. Vall d'Hebon and Pare Mariana.

Athletics

ESTADI OLÍMPIC   Ⓜ Espanya
DE MONTJUÏC   **27** E3   🚊 Av. de l'Estadi
Av. de l'Estadi 54; tel. 426-40-19.

Badminton

PAVELLÓ DEL PARC ESPORTIU DE LA MAR BELLA   **24/31** P3
Bach de Roda—Prim.

Baseball

E.M. BEISBOL L'HOSPITALET, ESTADI MUNICIPAL DE BEISBOL DE L'HOSPITALET   **26** B2   Ⓜ L'Hospitalet
Feixa Llarga s/n (Residencia Princeps d'Espanya); L'Hospitalet.

32 **E.M. BEISBOL VILADECANS, ESTADI MUNICIPAL DE BEISBOL DE VILADECANS**   *Train:* R.E.N.F.E.
Av. del Molí s/n (Parc Torre Roja); Viladecans (14 km – 9 miles – from Barcelona on the C246).

Basketball

P.M.E. DE BADALONA, PALAU MUNICIPAL D'ESPORTS DE BADALONA   Ⓜ Badalona   *Train:* R.E.N.F.E.
Alfonso XIII–Ponent, Badalona (11 km – 7 miles – from Barcelona on the A19).

Boxing

P.B. JOVENTUD BADALONA, PAVELLÓ DEL CLUB DE BÀSQUET JOVENTUD DE BADALONA   Ⓜ Badalona   *Train:* R.E.N.F.E.
Ausias March 61–77, Badalona (11km – 7miles – from Barcelona on the A19); tel. 387-10-77.

Canoeing

PARC ESPORTIU DEL SEGRE   *Main line train:* R.E.N.F.E.
Pl. del Oms 1, La Seu d'Urgell; tel. 973-35-00-10.

Cycling

VELÒDROM MUNICIPAL　　　　　　　Ⓜ Montbau
D'HORTA　　7 O12　　　　　🚌 Pg. Vall d'Hebrón
Pg. Vall d'Hebrón s/n; tel. 427-92-42.

Fencing

PALAU　　　　　　　　　　　　　Ⓜ Espanya
DE LA METALURGIA　　19 F5　🚌 Av. Reina Maria Cristina
Av. Reina Maria Cristina 1–13.

33

Football

E.M. LA ROMAREDA, ESTADIO MUNICIPAL DE FÚTBOL
LA ROMAREDA　　　　　　*Main line train:* R.E.N.F.E.
Luis Bermejo 1–3, Zaragoza (296 km – 185 miles – from Barcelona on the A7 and A2); tel. 976-56-77-77.

E.M. NOVA CREU ALTA, ESTADI DE LA NOVA CREU
ALTA DE SABADELL　　　　*Main line train:* R.E.N.F.E.
Pl. Olimpia s/n, Sabadell (26 km – 16 miles – from Barcelona on the A18); tel. 716-75-91.

ESTADI DE FÚTBOL　　　　　　　Ⓜ Collblanc
CLUB BARCELONA　　10 C8　🚌 Aristides Maillol
Aristides Maillol 12–18; tel. 330-94-11.

ESTADI DE LUIS CASANOVA　　*Main line train:* R.E.N.F.E.
Artes Gráficas 46, Valencia (347 km – 217 miles – from Barcelona on the A7); tel. 96-360-05-50.

ESTADI DE SARRIÀ DEL REIAL CLUB
DEPORTIU ESPANYOL　　12 F9　　🚌 Av. Sarrià
Ricardo Villa 2–4; tel. 203-48-00.

Gymnastics

PALAU D'ESPORTS SANT JORDI   **27** E4   Ⓜ Av. de l'Estadi
Pg. Minici Natal 5; tel. 426-20-89.

PALAU MUNICIPAL   Ⓜ Poble Sec
D'ESPORTS DE BARCELONA   **19/20** F4   🚍 Av. Paral-lel
Lleida 4; tel. 424-27-76.

Handball

34   **P.M. ESPORTS GRANOLLERS, PALAU MUNICIPAL D'ESPORTS**
DE GRANOLLERS   **12** F9   *Main line train:* R.E.N.F.E.
Prat de la Riba 84, Granollers (32 km – 20 miles – from Barcelona on the A7 or A17); tel. 870-02-92.

PALAU   Ⓜ Espanya
D'ESPORTS SANT JORDI   **27** E4   🚍 Av. de l'Estadi
Pg. Minici Natal 5; tel. 426-20-89.

Hockey

Z.E. L'ABAT MARCET DE TERRASSA, ZONA ESPORTIVA DE
L'ABAT MARCET DE TERRASSA   *Main line train:* Terrassa
Av. l'Abat Marcet s/n, Terrassa.

Ice Hockey

P. CLUB PATÍ DE VIC, PAVELLÓ
DEL CLUB PATÍ DE VIC   *Main line train:* R.E.N.F.E.
Av. Olimpia s/n, Vic (70 km – 44 miles – from Barcelona on the A7 and N152); tel. 885-24-00.

P.M. SANT SADURNÍ, PAVELLÓ MUNICIPAL AGRÍCOLA DE
SANT SADURNÍ   *Main line train:* R.E.N.F.E.
José Rovira 14 , Sant Sadurní (39 km – 24 miles – from Barcelona on the A7); tel. 891-03-42.

**P.O.M. DE REUS, PAVELLÓ MUNICIPAL
D'ESPORTS DE REUS**　　　　*Main line train:* R.E.N.F.E.
*Milà i Fontanals s/n, Reus (110 km – 69 miles – from Barcelona on the
A7 and A2).*

PALAU BLAU GRANA　　**11** D8　　　　🚌 Aristides Maillol
Aristides Maillol 12–18; tel. 330-94-11.

Ice Rinks

FUTBOL CLUB　　**11** D8　　　　Ⓜ Collblanc
BARCELONA　　　　　🚌 Aristides Maillol
Aristides Maillol 12–18; tel. 330-94-11.

SKATING　　**21/22** L5/6　　Ⓜ Verdaguer　🚌 Pg. de Sant Joan
Roger de Flor 168; tel. 245-28-00.

Judo

PALAU BLAU GRANA　　**11** D8　　　　🚌 Aristides Maillol
Aristides Maillol 12–18; tel. 330-94-11.

Modern Pentathlon

**C. DE TIR DE MOLLET, CAMP DE TIR OLÍMPIC DE MOLLET DEL
VALLÉS**　　　　*Main line train:* R.E.N.F.E.
*Escola de Policia de Catalunya, Mollet del Vallés (20 km – 13 miles – from
Barcelona on the CN 152); tel. 593-75-62.*

**ESTADI EQÜESTRE (MINIESTADI DEL FUTBOL CLUB
BARCELONA)**　　**10** C8　　　🚌 Aristides Maillol
Aristides Maillol s/n; tel. 330-94-11.

PALAU　　　　　Ⓜ Espanya
DE LA METALURGIA　　**19** F5　　🚌 Av. Reina Maria Cristina
Av. Reina Maria Cristina 1–13.

PISCINES BERNAT PICORNELL　　**19/27** E4　　Ⓜ Av. de l'Estadi
Av. de l'Estadi 30–40; tel. 325-92-81.

Olympic Shooting

**C. DE TIR DE MOLLET, CAMP DE TIR OLÍMPIC
DE MOLLET DEL VALLÉS** *Main line train:* R.E.N.F.E
*Escola de Policía de Catalunya, Mollet del Vallés (20 km – 13 miles – from
Barcelona on the CN 152); tel. 593-75-62.*

Pelota

**CENTRE MUNICIPAL DE PILOTA
DE LA VALL D'HEBRÓN** **6/7** M11/12 Ⓜ Pg. Vall d'Hebrón
Between Vall d'Hebrón and Pare Mariana.

36

FRONTÓ COLOM **28** J3 Ⓜ Liceu 🚌 Rambla
Rbla. Santa Mónica 42.

Rowing

ESTANY DE BANYOLES *Main line train:* R.E.N.F.E.
*Pge. del Lago s/n, Banyoles (123 km –77 miles – from Barcelona on the
A7 or A17); tel. 570-859.*

Showjumping

CIRCUIT D'HÍPICA DEL MONTANYÀ Ⓜ Av. Montseny
*Av. del Montseny s/n, El Montanyà (50 km – 31 miles – from Barcelona
on the A7, N152 and the B5303); tel. 884-04-84.*

**ESTADI EQÜESTRE (MINIESTADI DEL FÚTBOL CLUB
DE BARCELONA)** **10** C8 Ⓜ Collblanc 🚌 Aristides Maillol
Aristides Maillol s/n; tel. 330-94-11.

Squash

SQUASH 2000 **22** L7 Ⓜ Camp de l'Arpa 🚌 Camp de l'Arpa
Sant Antoni Maria Claret 84–86; tel. 258-22-02.

SQUASH BARCELONA　　　　　　Ⓜ Doctor Marañón
Tel. 334-02-58.

SQUASH　　　　　　　　　　　Ⓜ Verdaguer
DIAGONAL　　**21/22** L6　　🚌 Pg. de Sant Joan
Roger de Flor 193; tel. 258-34-09.

Swimming Pools

COMPLEX ESPORTIU
CAN CARELLEU　**10** F11/12　　Ⓜ Major de Can Carelleu
Esports 2–8; tel. 203-78-74.

PISCINA MUNICIPAL DE MONTJUÏC　**28** F/G3　　Ⓜ Av. Miramar
Av. Miramar 31; tel. 441-34-04.

PISCINA MARITIM　　**30** M2　　Ⓜ Pg. Marítim
Pg. Marítim 35; tel. 309-34-12.

PISCINA PARC DE LA　　　　　　Ⓜ Vallcarca
CREUETA DEL COLL　　**13/14** L10　🚌 Av. de la República
Pg. Mare de Déu del Coll 87; tel. 210-44-01.

PISCINES BERNAT PICORNELL　**19/27** E4　　Ⓜ Av. de l'Estadi
Av. de l'Estadi 30–40; tel. 325-92-81.

Table Tennis

POLIESPORTIU MUNICIPAL　　　　Ⓜ Marina
DE L'ESTACIÓ DEL NORD　**23** L4　🚌 Av. Meridiana
Napols 20–60.

Taekwondo

PALAU　　　　　　　　　　　Ⓜ Collblanc
BLAU GRANA　　**11** D8　　🚌 Aristides Maillol
Aristides Maillol 12–18; tel. 330-94-11.

Tennis

CAN MELIC
Av. 11 de Septiembre s/n, Sant Just Desvern; tel. 372-82-11.

**CENTRE MUNICIPAL DE TENNIS
DE LA VALL D'HEBRÓN**   **6/7** M11/12   Ⓜ Pg. Vall d'Hebrón
Between Pg. Vall d'Hebrón and Pare Mariana.

CAN CARALLEU   **4** F11/12   Ⓜ Major de Can Caralleu
Esports 2–8; tel. 203-78-74.

38 **REIAL SOCIETAT
DE TENNIS POMPEIA**   **19** E4/5   Ⓜ Av. Marqués de Comillas
Pg. Simón Bolívar s/n; tel. 423-97-47.

Volleyball

CR. CASTELLDEFELS, CANAL DE REGATES   Ⓜ Castelldefels
DE CASTELLDEFELS   *Main line train:* R.E.N.F.E
Castelldefels *(19 km – 12 miles – from Barcelona on the C246).*

PALAU D'ESPORTS   Ⓜ Espanya
SANT JORDI   **27** E4   ▭ Av. de l'Estadi
Pg. Minici Natal 5; tel. 426-20-89.

Water Polo

PISCINA MUNICIPAL   Ⓜ Espanya
DE MONTJUÏC   **28** F3   ▭ Av. de l'Estadi
Av. Miramar 31; tel. 441-34-04.

PISCINES   Ⓜ Espanya
BERNAT PICORNELL   **19/27** E4   ▭ Av. de l'Estadi
Av. de l'Estadi 30–40; tel. 325-92-81.

Weightlifting

**PAVELLÓ MUNICIPAL
DE L'ESPANYA INDÚSTRIAL**   **19** F5
Bejar.

Ⓜ Tarragona
🚌 Tarragona

Wrestling

**INSTITUT NACIONAL D'EDUCACIÓ FÍSICA
DE CATALUNYA**   **16** R8
Sant Mateu s/n, Esplugues de Llobregat; tel. 371-90-11.

Ⓜ Esplugues
🚌 Esplugues

39

Yachting

PORT OLÍMPIC DE BARCELONA
Paseo Carlos I, Av. Litoral.

THE CULTURAL OLYMPICS

A wide spectrum of cultural events has been planned to take place around the time of the Olympic Games, in addition to scheduled events that are normally programmed during the summer months. Most are to take place in July and August, though others start earlier or finish later.

The following is a selection of the events that are expected to be staged during this period. A fuller programme, as well as details of location, times etc., should be obtained from information offices belonging to either the Ajuntament (city) or the Generalitat (region). (See Practical Information.)

BORN MARKET

The former Born Market is to host "Menjar i Beure a Espanya", an exhibition of food and drink from around Spain. In July and August 1992, the Market is also to be the venue for an exhibition of photographs that plot the development of sport throughout Spain.

CASA MILÀ (LA PEDRERA) (See p. 27)

An art exhibition featuring the Catalan avant-garde (1906–1939) is to be held in Gaudí's Casa Milà from July to September 1992.

GREC '92

This annual city festival of theatre, dance and music takes on a special role in 1992 because of the Games. Among the performers will be B.B. King, Joan Manuel Serrat, and a programme of "An Evening With...", featuring Vittorio Gassman, Peter O' Toole, and Max von Sydow.

40 GUIDED TOURS OF THE CITY

A series of 12 guided tours on historical themes have been organized. Subjects include the city guilds, the Civil War, and the royal visits. These are run in addition to arranged visits to specific areas, and around particular themes.

LA CAIXA'S SCIENCE MUSEUM

"Evolution's Record-Breakers", an interactive exhibition that attempts to link the Olympic search for records with the science of measurement, human evolution and cultural influences, is to be held here from June to December 1992.

MUSEU D'ART DE CATALUNYA (See Museums)

The Museum of Catalan Art is due to re-open in July 1992 after extensive renovation, and the inaugural exhibition will feature art from the Romantics to the 20th century.

MUSIC

A varied assortment of classical concerts to be held, featuring some of the best orchestras from Spain and abroad. Many are to be staged in the Liceu Opera House, or the Palau de la Mùsica Catalunya. In addition, a series of concerts by jazz and blues performers has been scheduled. Megastars such as Quincy Jones, Liza Minelli and Frank Sinatra are on the bill.

OPEN-AIR AND BAR PERFORMANCES

Open-air performances are set to take place in the areas around the Moll de la Fusta; the Colombus Monument by the port; and along the Rambla. They are to be set around the themes of music hall, cabaret (featuring Inspector Tuppence and the Sexy Firemen, and Jango Edwards and his friends).

SERT PAVILION

The Sert Pavilion (reconstructed to resemble the 1930s' original) is to hold a "Barcelona of the Future" exhibition, featuring models, plans and photographs of the radical changes made or being made to the city.

41

SPORT FROM ANCIENT GREECE

An exhibition of art from the period in which the Olympic Games originated, held from May to July 1992. Venue to be decided (check with the tourist office).

THEATRE

Productions in Catalan, Spanish and other languages, some produced especially for the Olympics, are to be staged all over the city during the summer of 1992. Performances range from a German production of *Macbeth*, to a show, in English, by the Stuffed Puppet Theatre of Holland. Check with the tourist office for details of venues.

B arcelona has surprisingly few museums for a city of its size and importance, but there are some outstanding artefacts and art displayed in them. The best of Gaudí is there, while Picasso and Miró, the other famous artists associated with the city, each have a museum devoted to their work. These three collections should form part of any visit to the city, especially as they are well set out and fun to visit.

Otherwise, the main exhibition of art and sculpture is contained in the Palau Nacional at the foot of Montjuïc, which is to be the sight of the new Modern Art Museum, and the remodelled Catalan Art Museum.

An assortment of museums based on unusual themes—perfume, amusement arcade marionettes, holographs, bullfighting and Barcelona soccer club—complete the picture, along with the more traditional museums of natural history, science, and geology. During the lead-up to the Olympics, the city authorities decided to spruce up and refurbish many of their museums, and some collections have been moved to newer buildings. Therefore, check with the tourist office to make sure that opening hours, etc. remain the same.

43

ART AND HISTORY MUSEUMS

CASA-MUSEU GAUDÍ   **13/14** L9   Ⓜ Lesseps   🚌 Crta. Carmel
Crta. Carmel s/n; tel. 317-52-21. Daily except Saturday 10 a.m.–2 p.m. and 4–7 p.m. Closed December and February.
Set within the Park Güell (see Walks and Tours), this is the house in which the famous architect lived between 1906 until just before he died. In 1960, the house was converted into a museum showing Gaudí's creations, and each part of it contains a different aspect of his work, along with many of his personal belongings. As well as the fruits of Gaudí's own exertions (especially pieces of furniture), there are also fine examples of work carried out by his closest associates, such as Berenguer, Martorell and Jujol.

Brighten up your day with a trip to the Fundació Joan Miró.

FUNDACIÓ
ANTONI TÀPIES   **20** J6   Ⓜ Pg. de Gràcia
                                   🚋 Pg. de Gràcia
Aragó 255; tel. 487-03-15. Tuesday to Sunday 11 a.m.–8 p.m.
A semi-permanent exhibition of over 300 pictures and sculptures produced by the well-known Antoni Tàpies (born 1923), is usually on display here. However, the Foundation which bears his name also acts as
a gallery for lesser-known and aspiring young artists. Before entering
the building, stand on the other side of this busy road and admire the
wire sculpture, *Núvol i cadira* (cloud and chair), which graces the roof
and caused a stir when installed.

FUNDACIÓ
JOAN MIRÓ   **27** F3   Ⓜ Espanya
                               🚋 Av. de l'Estadi
*Pl. Neptú s/n; tel. 329-19-08. Tuesday, Wednesday, Friday and Saturday
11 a.m.–7 p.m., Thursday until 9.30 p.m., Sunday and public holidays
10.30 a.m.–2.30 p.m.*
Opened in 1975, the building dedicated to the work of Joan Miró looks
from the outside like a bland and relatively uninteresting example of
the architecture of the time. But a visit to Montjuïc really should include
at least a dip into the beautifully planned interior, the natural design of
which guides you through rooms of sculpture and other art, never bring-
ing you back over old ground. In keeping with the artist's desire to establish the Foundation as a centre for 20th-century modern art, there are
also exhibitions of young creators' work; and lectures, films and con-
ferences are held on all aspects of art. Its small theatre also stages regular performances for children. In addition, the Foundation's library contains a fine collection of literature on contemporary art, as well as
documentation on the life of Miró himself.

GABINET POSTAL   **11** D9   Ⓜ Palau Reial 🚋 Palau Reial
Av. Diagonal 686; tél. 280-18-74.
A large collection of stamps, seals and the like are displayed here, together with an exhibition which traces the long history and variety of the
postal service in Spain, including the domestic equivalent of the Pony
Express. The philatelic collection has been built up around a 65,000-
stamp donation which stretches from 1840, the year in which the modern postal service began, to 1940. This fascinating collection is expected
to re-open in its new home at the Pedralbes Palace towards the end of
1992.

MUSEU
ARQUEÒLOGIC   27 F4

Ⓜ Espanya
🚌 Av. Paral.lel

Pg. Santa Madrona s/n; tel. 423-21-49. Tuesday to Saturday 9.30 a.m.–
1 p.m. and 4–7 p.m., Sunday 10 a.m.–2 p.m.

With an accent on the archaeological origins of Catalunya, including
the Balearics, this fine collection of exhibits is housed in one of the
buildings constructed for the 1929 International Exhibition. In addition,
a restoration centre on the site carries out important work in re-
constructing archaeological remains, while the specialized anthropo-
logical unit is devoted to the study of human and animal life from pre-
history.

MUSEU CLARÀ   12 G10   Ⓜ Tres Torres 🚌 Via Augusta

Calatrava 27; tel. 203-40-58. Daily except Monday 9 a.m.–2 p.m.

Created in 1969, the museum is situated in the house that belonged to
the well-known sculptor, Josep Clarà, who died in 1958. As well as
a good selection of his modernist sculptures, especially from his period
in Paris, the museum also shows a collection of sketches and paintings,
including the self-portrait executed when Clarà was 11 years old. Around
the house are the artist's personal belongings, and his studio has been
re-created to appear as it was in the days when he worked there.

45

MUSEU D'ART
DE CATALUNYA   19 4E

Ⓜ Espanya
🚌 Av. Reina Maria Cristina

Mirador del Palau 6; tel. 423-18-24.

One of the finest collections of Romanesque art in the world can be found
in this museum, currently being renovated to welcome the Museum of
Modern Art (see below). Housed in the Palau Nacional on Montjuïc and
opened in 1934, the collection owes much to the "boom" in Romanesque
churches built between the 9th and 13th centuries, although examples
of later art, especially Gothic-style from the 14th and 15th centuries, are
also held here. Sections of the museum, including the key Romanesque
and Gothic collections, are scheduled to re-open in May 1992. Check
with the tourist office or the museum itself whether the works are complete before making the visit.

MUSEU D'ART MODERN   29 L3 Ⓜ Ciutadella 🚌 Pg. Picasso

Pl. d'Armes s/n; tel. 319-57-28. Tuesday to Saturday 9 a.m.–7 p.m.,
Sunday and public holidays until 3 p.m., Monday 3–7 p.m.

Expected to complete its move to the Palau Nacional on Montjuïc during 1993, the modern art museum is a collection which traces the work

of Catalan artists from as far back as the beginning of the 19th century. Although the earlier work is interesting (see, for example, Fortuny's massive La Batalla de Tetuán) as testimony to the development of artistic styles in Catalunya, most visitors will want to see the impressionist works—by Ramon Casas or Santiago Rusiñol for example—or the more recent pieces by Salvador Dalí, Josep-Maria Sert or Antoni Tàpies. Check with the tourist office for the exact date of opening.

MUSEU D'ARTS DECORATIVES   11 D9

Ⓜ Palau Reial
🚊 Palau Reial

Av. Diagonal 686; tel. 280-50-24. Weekdays 10 a.m.–1 p.m. Book in advance.

Furniture, glassware, gold and silverware, porcelain, clocks, enamel-work and other decorative art from the 16th to the 20th century all form part of the collection to be housed at the palace. Check with the tourist office on the expected opening date, although visits can be arranged in the meantime by prior notification.

46

MUSEU D'HISTÒRIA DE LA CIUTAT   29 K4

Ⓜ Jaume I
🚊 Via Laietana

Pl. del Rei s/n; tel. 315-11-11. Tuesday to Saturday 9 a.m.–8.30 p.m., Sunday and public holidays until 1.30 p.m., Monday 3.30–8 p.m.

The 15th-century house which has become the city's museum was actually knocked down and rebuilt on its present site during one of Barcelona's earlier construction projects. Roman and medieval archaeological remains excavated from within the city are on show underground and towards the cathedral. The Arab and Jewish influences on Barcelona's past are also examined, while a principal theme is the changes in urban life which have taken place since the 14th century, including official seals and other paraphernalia.

MUSEU D'HISTÒRIA DE LA MEDICINA DE CATALUNYA   21 J6

Ⓜ Diagonal
🚊 Rbla. Catalunya

Ptge. Mercader 11; tel. 216-05-00. Thursday 10 a.m.–1 p.m.

Mainly a collection of medical instruments used over the 18th and 19th centuries, tracing how treatment evolved during that period and into the 20th century. The personal belongings of several Catalan doctors of note are exhibited, including those of Josep Trueta, who gained fame during and after World War II in Britain.

MUSEU D'HISTÒRIA
DEL CALÇAT 29 J4

Ⓜ Jaume I
🚌 Via Laietana

Pl. Sant Felip Neri s/n; tel. 302-26-80. Daily except Monday 11 a.m.–2 p.m.

If you tire of walking around the city, stop here and imagine how uncomfortable people must have been wearing certain of the antique shoes, of impossibly narrow size, on show in this museum. As well as the range of footwear from the 18th century onwards, cobblers' tools from a much earlier period are exhibited.

MUSEU
DE CERÀMICA 11 D9

Ⓜ Palau Reial
🚌 Palau Reial

Av. Diagonal 686; tel. 280-16-21. Tuesday to Sunday 9 a.m.–2 p.m. Closed Monday and public holidays.

Recently moved to its new permanent home, this extensive collection of china and ceramics traces the history of Spain from the 12th century, during the Arab occupation, to the 20th century, including work by Picasso and Miró. The beauty of the museum is that it combines purely decorative ceramics with pieces used every day, and simply demonstrates the evolution both of design and technique over the centuries.

47

MUSEU
DE LA CATEDRAL 29 K4

Ⓜ Jaume I
🚌 Via Laietana

Pla de la Seu s/n; tel. 315-35-55. Daily 11 a.m.–1 p.m.

Within the main city cathedral (see Sights) is a collection of paintings from the 14th to the 18th centuries, as well as sculpture from much the same period. The rest of the museum is devoted to religious artefacts from the 17th to the 19th centuries.

MUSEU
DE LA MÚSICA 21 K6

Ⓜ Diagonal
🚌 Rbla. Catalunya

Av. Diagonal 373; tel. 217-11-57. Daily except Monday 9 a.m.–2 p.m.

The music museum is situated in a period town house or palace dating from the beginning of the century. It contains a collection of musical instruments from over the centuries. As well as the more recognizable keyboard, wind, string and percussion instruments from Spain and the rest of Western Europe, the museum also houses an assortment of instruments from countries and cultures farther afield.

MUSEU
DE LES ARTS GRÀFIQUES   19 E4

Ⓜ Espanya
🚃 Av. Marqués de Comillas

Poble Espanyol, Av. Marqués de Comillas; tel. 426-19-99. Weekdays. Book in advance.

A museum of printing through the ages, containing a workshop in which you can witness the process from written word to printed work, and also experiment with some of the material. All methods from artisan printing to industrial processing are covered, including an exhibition of printing blocks and other elements of the graphical art from the past.

MUSEU
DEL TEMPLE EXPIATORI   23 M6

Ⓜ Sagrada Família
🚃 Padilla

Mallorca 401; tel. 255-02-47. September to March: daily 9 a.m.–7 p.m.; April to June: daily 9 a.m.–8 p.m.; July to August: daily 9 a.m.–9 p.m.

48 Situated in the crypt of the unfinished cathedral, this museum shows graphically the painful and lengthy process that has gone into the building's construction so far. Gaudí's original plans are on view, showing how he created a much more ambitious project than that originally conceived by the first designer, Francisco de P. Villar. Photographs of the construction process over the years, together with several models created by Gaudí, make for a fascinating exhibition.

MUSEU ETNOLÒGIC   27 F4   Ⓜ Poble Sec   🚃 Av. Paral.lel

Pg. Santa Madrona s/n; tel. 424-64-02. Tuesday to Saturday 9 a.m.–8.30 p.m., Sunday and public holidays until 2 p.m., Monday 2–8.30 p.m.

The theme of this museum is the study of human life, both biological and social. It uses material gathered from expeditions to various parts of the world. Notable among the exhibits are examples of cultures from Central and Latin America (concentrating on matter relating to their Hispanic origins), and the results of recent work in the west of Africa.

MUSEU
FREDERIC MARÈS   29 K4

Ⓜ Jaume I
🚃 Via Laietana

Pl. Sant Lu; tel. 310-58-00. Tuesday to Saturday 9 a.m.–2 p.m. and 4–7 p.m., Sunday and public holidays until 2 p.m.

The sculptor Frederic Marès (born 1893) gathered together a vast collection of miscellaneous objects during his frequent visits around Spain and the rest of Europe. The best of them are exhibited here, including a collection of female adornments through the ages, smokers' requisites, photographic equipment and religious artefacts. Definitely worth a visit.

MUSEU GALERIA DE CATALANS IL.LUSTRES   **29** K3

ⓜ Jaume I
🚎 Via Laietana

Bisbe Caçador 3; tel. 315-00-10. Book in advance.
A museum dedicated to famous Catalan personalities from the past thousand years. Almost 50 portraits, together with a biography, are on display. The worlds of the arts, industry, science, the military and religion are all represented in this fascinating portrayal of Catalunya's history.

MUSEU MARÍTIM   **28** J3

ⓜ Drassanes   🚎 Rambla

49

Portal de la Pau 1; tel. 318-32-45. Tuesday to Saturday 10 a.m.–2 p.m. and 4–7 p.m., Sunday and public holidays until 2 p.m.
Divided into thematic sections, the Maritime Museum traces the rich naval history of Barcelona and Catalunya. Sections are devoted to navigation, shipbuilding, stevedoring and fishing, along with others portraying ships' figureheads, maritime art and models of sailing and steamships.

MUSEU MILITAR   **27** F2

ⓜ Espanya   🚎 Av. Miramar

Castell de Montjuïc s/n; tel. 329-86-13. Tuesday to Saturday 10 a.m.– 2 p.m. and 3.30–8 p.m., Sunday and public holidays 10 a.m.–7 p.m.
Within the castle on top of Montjuïc (see Monuments), the military museum contains a collection of arms and armour through the centuries. Exhibits also include a marvellous set (23,000-strong) of model soldiers, models of some of the castles around Catalunya, and paintings depicting military themes.

MUSEU MONESTIR DE PEDRALBES   **4** E11

ⓜ Reina Elisenda
🚎 Pedralbes

Bda. Monestir 9; tel. 203-92-82. Daily except Monday 9.30 a.m.–2 p.m.
The 14th-century Pedralbes monastery contains a museum displaying monastic effects donated by the brethren. A fascinating view of daily life can be seen in the kitchens, where the utensils used over the years to prepare meals are on show.

MUSEU PALAU REIAL DE PEDRALBES　**11** D9

Ⓜ Palau Reial
🚋 Palau Reial

Av. Diagonal 686; tel. 203-75-01.

In the former royal palace, opened to the public in 1960, several museums compete for the visitor's attention. The contents of the palace itself form one of the museums, and exhibits include carpets and tapestries, paintings and furniture from the 18th and 19th centuries, plus a fine collection of porcelain from the 17th to the 20th centuries. The museum is due to re-open in 1992: check with the tourist office for details.

MUSEU PICASSO　**29** K3

Ⓜ Jaume I　🚋 Via Laietana

Montcada 15; tel. 319-63-10. Tuesday to Saturday 10 a.m.-8 p.m.; Sunday until 3 p.m.

50

Although it isn't the best or biggest exhibition of Picasso's work—that is in Paris—this collection is among the most attractive and representative. Following the artist's progress from childhood to his death in 1973, the museum contains examples of paintings, sketches, lithographs and ceramics donated by the artist himself and by friends and family. Even if you don't like his later abstract work, there is a wealth of more accessible material from the earlier periods. Ever since the museum opened in 1963, it has gradually been expanded to house the large collection. It now occupies three adjoining palaces on Calle Montcada, the Palaus Berenguer d'Aguilar, del Baró de Castellet and Meca, built between the 13th and 15th centuries. The problem with using these beautiful buildings rather than a purpose-built construction is that space can be a bit cramped, and the visitor is constantly going up and down stairs, along narrow passages and in and out of smallish rooms, so it isn't really a place for wheelchairs or prams.

MUSEU TÈXTIL I DE LA INDUMENTÀRIA　**29** K3

Ⓜ Jaume I
🚋 Via Laietana

Montcada 12–14; tel. 310-45-16. Tuesday to Saturday 9 a.m.–2 p.m. and 4.30–7 p.m., Sunday and public holidays 9 a.m.–2 p.m.

Clothing and textiles over the past 16 centuries are the subject matter of this museum—the Barcelona tailors of the 4th century were probably considered to be as much in the vanguard of design as their modern day equivalents. As well as showing examples of the materials and techniques used in Spain, the museum also contains examples of clothing from other parts of the world. Sections cover seven centuries of religious garb, tapestries, accessories, jewellery, mannequins and other material relating to the industry.

MUSEU VERDAGUER
Ⓜ Peu Funicular

Crta. de les Planes; tel. 204-78-05. Daily except Monday 9 a.m.–2 p.m.
The well-known poet, Jacint Verdaguer, died in this country house in 1902, following a period of convalescence from an illness. The museum created there to commemorate his life contains personal effects, books and documents, and the interior has been conserved, to look as it was almost a century ago.

SCIENTIFIC AND THEMATIC MUSEUMS

CARRUATGES   **11** D9   Ⓜ Palau Reial   🚇 Zona Universitaria
Av. Diagonal 686; tel. 280-19-64.
Housed in the stables of the Pedralbes royal palace, the museum contains a collection of horse-drawn carriages used by the rich, as well as those used by lesser folk and for mundane deliveries. Check with the tourist office for opening times.

51

INSTITUT BOTÀNIC
Ⓜ Espanya
DE BARCELONA   **19** E4
🚇 Av. Reina Maria Cristina
Av. Montanyans s/n; tel. 325-80-50. Open April to September: Monday to Saturday 3–7 p.m.; October to March: Monday to Saturday 3–5 p.m., Sunday and public holidays all year 9 a.m–2 p.m.
The Botanical Institute is accessible only to students and specialists, but anyone can visit its gardens on Montjuïc, where many examples of flora from Catalunya, the Pyrenees and the rest of Spain are grown. It's a pleasure to walk around in the peace and calm of the gardens, where microclimates create the natural habitats of flora from around the world. Replanting works are expected to be finished in the spring of 1992.

MUSEU D'AUTÒMATES
Ⓜ Funicular Tibidabo
DEL TIBIDABO   **5** J13
Parc d'Atraccions del Tibidabo; tel. 211-79-42. Open April to September: daily 11 a.m.–8 p.m.; October to March: weekends and public holidays 11 a.m.–8 p.m.
An unusual collection, contained within the Tibidabo complex, of coin-operated marionettes of the kind that used to be a feature of amusement arcades and travelling fairs. It includes a fascinating array of figures, as well as mechanical dolls and toys that still manage to keep the children amused, at least for a while.

MUSEU DE CARRUATGES
FÚNEBRES   22 M4
Ⓜ Marina
🚃 Pg. Carles I

Sancho de Avila 2; tel. 300-50-61. Weekdays 9 a.m.–1 p.m. and 3–6 p.m., Saturday until 1 p.m. Closed Sunday and public holidays.

Something different: a museum containing funeral hearses from the 19th and 20th centuries, together with the formal dress worn by the attendants. As well as the horse-drawn carriages, you'll also find more recent motorized hearses used to make a stylish exit from this world.

MUSEU DE CERA
DE BARCELONA   29 J3
Ⓜ Drassanes
🚃 Rambla

Ptge. de la Banca 7; tel. 317-26-49. Weekdays 10 a.m.–1.30 p.m. and 4–7.30 p.m., weekends and public holidays until 8 p.m.

52   There are some horribly realistic waxworks among the 300 or so on show here: the accent is on getting the detail absolutely right. Famous characters from history, politics, the arts and the world of entertainment are represented.

MUSEU DE GEOLOGIA
(MUSEU MARTORELL)   29 L3
Ⓜ Arc de Triomf
🚃 Pg. Picasso

Parc de la Ciutadella; tel. 319-68-95. Daily except Monday 9 a.m.–2 p.m.

One of the first buildings purpose-built by the city authorities to house a museum. The geological composition of, in particular, Catalunya, is explained in depth, but there are also sections devoted to fossils, space travel, the formation of planets and the origins of the Earth.

MUSEU DE LA CIENCIA   5 J11
Ⓜ Av. Tibidabo   🚃 Balmes

Teodor Roviralta 55; tel. 212-60-50. Daily except Monday 10 a.m.–8 p.m.

Both children and adults can enjoy a visit to the Science Museum, where there is an accent on interactive exhibits. A wide interpretation is given here to science, and exhibits include phenomena from the natural world, space and the stars, as well as more conventional scientific displays. Visitors can also participate in gathering data from the weather station in the gardens. There are multilingual presentations, and special sessions for young children, while regular film shows concentrate on scientific themes.

MUSEU DE LA HOLOGRAFIA 29 K3

Ⓜ Jaume I
🚌 Via Laietana

Jaume I 1; tel. 315-34-77. Tuesday to Saturday 11 a.m.–1.30 p.m. and 5.30–8.30 p.m.

A small but impressive collection of about 30 holograms is held in this relatively new museum, the only such one in Spain, and situated right in the middle of the Barri Gòtic. As well as the purely artistic displays held in the museum upstairs, the shop on the ground floor has holograms for sale, in the form of medallions or framed pictures. Leaflets offer explanations as to how holograms are produced, and describe the history of this recent art form.

MUSEU DE LA ZOOLOGIA 29 L4

Ⓜ Arc de Triomf
🚌 Pg. Picasso

Pg. Picasso s/n; tel. 319-69-12. Daily except Monday 9 a.m.–2 p.m.

The modernist building housing the zoological museum was originally planned to be a restaurant for the 1888 Universal Exposition, but wasn't finished in time. With an accent on the wildlife of Catalunya, but with exhibits from other parts of the world, the museum contains a captivating display of the insect world, including live bees and ants at work.

53

MUSEU DE LES ARTS D'ESPECTÀCLE 29 J3

Ⓜ Liceu
🚌 Rambla

Nou de la Rambla 3–5; tel. 317-39-74. Monday to Saturday 11 a.m.–2 p.m. and 5–8 p.m. Closed Sunday and public holidays.

Set within the Gaudí-designed Palau Güell (see Sights), the museum gathers together a fascinating assortment of material from the world of the spectacle—dance and opera, theatre and cinema. In the theatre section, for example, is a collection of models, costumes and documents, including original scripts, from the stage, and similar exhibits from the ballet world. The museum also has a vast library and a collection of video recordings telling the story of stage and screen.

MUSEU DEL FÚTBOL CLUB BARCELONA 11 D8

Ⓜ Aristides Maillol
🚌 Collblanc

Aristides Maillol s/n; tel. 330-94-11. October to March: weekdays 9 a.m.–1 p.m. and 4–6 p.m., weekends and public holidays 10 a.m.–1 p.m.; April to September: Monday to Saturday 10 a.m.–1 p.m. and 4–7 p.m., public holidays 10 a.m.–1 p.m.

Like other famous and successful football clubs around the world, "Barça" had to set up a museum to house its collection of national and international trophies won over the years since it was founded in 1899. But there is also a vast collection of photographs illustrating the history of the club, and a spectrum of souvenirs and other paraphernalia from the soccer world. And since the club also operates successfully in the basketball, handball and roller-hockey fields, trophies from these sports too share the shelf space.

MUSEU   Ⓜ Pg. de Gràcia
DEL PERFUM   **21** J 5/6   🚃 Pg. de Gràcia
Pg. de Gràcia 39; tel. 215-72-38. Weekdays 10 a.m.–1.30 p.m. and 4–7.30 p.m. Closed weekends and public holidays.

54 Started almost as an afterthought by a commercial perfumier at the beginning of the 1960s, this unusual museum gathers together a vast array of perfume bottles and containers from past centuries and various civilizations. Roman, Greek and Egyptian scent bottles are among the highlights, together with raw materials and instruments of the industry.

MUSEU ETNOGRÀFIC   Ⓜ Maria Cristina
ANDINO-AMAZÒNIC   **11** E10   🚃 Pl. Maria Cristina
Cardenal Vives i Tutó 2–16; tel. 204-34-58. First Sunday of every month from noon to 2 p.m.

An interesting collection of artefacts from the Andes and the Amazon region (as well as other far-flung lands) has been gathered by Capuchin missionaries over the years, and the best are displayed here. Alongside the objects are explanations of their origin and background. Although normal opening hours are very restricted, special visits can be made by prior arrangement with the Order.

MUSEU I LABORATORI DE GEOLOGIA   Ⓜ Universitat
DEL SEMINARI   **21** J5   🚃 Pl. Universitat
Diputació 231; tel. 245-16-00. Weekdays 11 a.m.–1 p.m. and 5–7 p.m. Closed weekends and public holidays.

A perfectly catalogued and classified collection of over 40,000 fossils, including traces of mammoths, provides a fascinating insight into this down-to-earth subject.

MUSEU MENTORA ALSINA **5** J13 Ⓜ Funicular Tibidabo
Crta. de Vallvidrera 56; tel. 417-57-34. Book in advance.
Scientific instruments from the 19th and 20th centuries, relating mainly to physics. Electricity, magnetism and sound are among the areas covered. It's just like school, but much more fun.

MUSEU TAURÍ **22** M5 Ⓜ Glòries 🚏 Pl. Glòries
Gran Via de les Corts Catalanes 749; tel. 245-58-03. April to September: daily 10 a.m.–1 p.m. and 3.30–7 p.m.
On days when no fights are being held in the modernist Monumental bullring, visitors can see inside without having to witness the killing of a bull. A visit to the museum should give some insight into bullfighting. Exhibits include beautiful "suits of lights", posters, photographs and even the mounted heads of the more "valiant" animals—some without ears.

55

MUSEU Y CENTRE D'ESTUDIS Ⓜ Hospital Clínic
DE L'ESPORT "DR. MELCIOR COLET" **12** H7 🚏 Buenos Aires
Buenos Aires 56–58; tel. 439-89-07. Weekdays 10 a.m.–2 p.m. and 4–8 p.m. Closed weekends and public holidays.
A potted history of sport in Catalunya during the 20th century, featuring the medals, emblems and clothes won and worn by sportsmen and women.

PLANETARI Ⓜ Sarrià
BARCELONA **12** G10 🚏 Major de Sarrià
Escoles Pies 103; tel. 211-64-16. Sessions: Monday to Saturday 9.30 a.m., 10.30 a.m., 11.30 a.m., 3 p.m., 4 p.m. and 5 p.m.; Sunday and public holidays noon, 2 p.m. and 6.30 p.m.
The accent is on active study at the city's main astronomical centre: there are all kinds of instruments and displays to experiment with. It was closed for refurbishment at the beginning of 1992; check with the tourist office on the scheduled re-opening.

C learly, art and design play a very important part in the everyday life of Barcelona. Frequent exhibitions are held in the museums, but the private galleries and the several public cultural centres are also places to see a wide range of work, both old and new.

A whole string of galleries can be found in the area around Rambla de Catalunya and Consell de Cent in the Eixample district, off Passeig de Gràcia. Be warned that, like other businesses in the city, most of the private galleries close down during August for the annual holiday. The bigger exhibitions, of course, are mounted in the more extensive cultural complexes, some of which stay open during the summer months.

Not to be missed are the works of Rusiñol and Casas, Catalan artists from the turn of the 20th century. Their paintings are to be found in museums and major art collections, as well as occasionally in exhibitions mounted by private art galleries. The base they built for Catalan art was an inspiration for Picasso and Isidre Nonell, as well as Joaquim Mir. Later, Joan Miró, Salvador Dalí and Antoni Tàpies formed the vanguard of Catalan art, while the latest generation could be said to be led by Miquel Barceló.

The following is a list of the main galleries and cultural centres regularly mounting exhibitions. Best either to wander around the areas with the main concentration of galleries, or to check the weekly listings magazines (such as the one accompanying El País on a Friday) and choose what takes your fancy.

57

COMMERCIAL ART GALLERIES

GALERIA D'ART
AMBIT   21 J5

ⓜ Pg. de Gràcia
🚌 Pg. de Gràcia

Consell de Cent 282; tel. 301-70-40. Tuesday to Friday 10 a.m.–2 p.m. and 4.30–9 p.m., Saturday 10.30 a.m.–2 p.m. and 5–9 p.m.

As well as running a gallery exhibiting contemporary art, the Ambit company also publishs art books.

Style and sophistication in a Barcelona gallery.

GALERIA D'ART ARTUR RAMON Ⓜ Liceu 🚇 Rambla
Palla 23–25; tel. 302-59-70. Tuesday to Saturday 10 a.m.–1.30 p.m. and 5–8 p.m.
A prestigious antiques shop that includes a gallery specializing in Catalan painters from the 19th century to the present day (see Shopping: Antiques and Collectors' Items).

GALERIA D'ART 🚇 Calvet
BARBIÉ   12 G8 Main line train: Muntaner
Johann Sebastian Bach 14; tel. 201-08-88. Weekdays 9.30 a.m.–2 p.m. and 5–9 p.m., Saturday 10 a.m.–2 p.m. and 5–9 p.m.
As well as a fine selection of antique furniture, this gallery (established in 1971) shows an eclectic range of paintings, but specializes in Spanish artists from the turn of the century.

58

GALERIA D'ART Ⓜ Pg. de Gràcia
CARLES TACHÉ   21 J5 🚇 Pg. de Gràcia
Consell de Cent 290; tel. 318-18-87. Tuesday to Saturday 10 a.m.–2 p.m. and 4–8.30 p.m.
Probably best known for its association with Antoni Tàpies. Regular exhibitions of relatively well-established artists are held.

GALERIA D'ART Ⓜ Pg. de Gràcia
CIENTO   21/22 K/L6 🚇 Pg. de Gràcia
Consell de Cent 347; tel. 215-63-65. Tuesday to Saturday 11 a.m.–1.30 p.m. and 5–8.30 p.m.
Formerly one of the galleries best known for promoting young artists. Others have recently jumped on the bandwagon, and Ciento now concentrates on more established modern artists.

GALERIA D'ART Ⓜ Pg. de Gràcia
COMAS   21 K7 🚇 Pg. de Gràcia
Pg. de Gràcia 114; tel. 415-32-99. Weekdays 10 a.m.–1.30 p.m. and 4.30–8 p.m., Saturday 10 a.m.–1.30 p.m. and 5–8 p.m.
Top-notch exhibitions of Catalan artists' works are mounted in this gallery, which is slightly off the beaten track from the main concentration of showrooms on Passeig de Gràcia.

**GALERIA D'ART
DAU AL SET   21/22** K6

Ⓜ Pg. de Gràcia
🚍 Pg. de Gràcia

*Consell de Cent 333; tel. 301-12-36. Monday to Saturday 10 a.m.–
1.30 p.m. and 4–8.30 p.m.*

Named after a group of Catalan painters, whose work is exhibited regularly. Other local artists, as well as avant-garde art from the rest of Spain and abroad, are also represented.

**GALERIA D'ART
FERNANDO ALCOLEA   12** G8

🚍 Calvet
Main line train: Muntaner

*Pl. St. Gregori Taumaturg 7; tel. 209-27-79. Monday to Saturday
10.30 a.m.–2 p.m. and 5–9 p.m.*

Thanks to its branch in New York, this gallery is becoming known for introducing to Spain artists who are little known here.

**GALERIA D'ART
IGNACIO DE LASSALETA   21** J5

Ⓜ Pg. de Gràcia
🚍 Pg. de Gràcia **59**

*Rbla. Catalunya 47; tel. 301-05-90. Tuesday to Saturday 10 a.m.–
1.30 p.m. and 5–8.30 p.m.*

Top-level exhibitions of contemporary artists, leaning heavily on the less obscure currents in modern art.

**GALERIA D'ART
JOAN PRATS   21** J5

Ⓜ Pg. de Gràcia
🚍 Pg. de Gràcia

*Rbla. Catalunya 54; tel. 216-02-84. Tuesday to Saturday 10.30 a.m.–
1.30 p.m. and 5–8.30 p.m.*

Regular exhibitions of international contemporary artists are held here. The gallery has won a good and solid reputation for prestigious shows.

**GALERIA D'ART
KREISLER   21** J6

Ⓜ Pg. de Gràcia
🚍 Pg. de Gràcia

*València 262; tel. 215-74-05. Tuesday to Saturday 11 a.m.–1.30 p.m. and
5–9 p.m.*

Situated near the main concentration of galleries off Passeig de Gràcia, Kreisler usually features the works of Catalan and Spanish modern painters.

GALERIA D'ART
LA PINACOTECA   **21** K5   Ⓜ Pg. de Gràcia
        🚊 Pg. de Gràcia
Pg. de Gràcia 34; tel. 318-17-43. Weekdays 10 a.m.–1.30 p.m. and 4–8 p.m., Saturday 10 a.m.–1.30 p.m. and 5–8 p.m.
The emphasis at La Pinacoteca is mostly on modern Catalan art.

GALERIA D'ART
MAEGHT   **29** K3   Ⓜ Jaume I
        🚊 Via Laietana
Montcada 25; tel. 310-42-45. Tuesday to Saturday 9.30 a.m.–2 p.m. and 3–8 p.m.
Housed in a 16th-century palace, this distinguished gallery is placed fittingly near the Picasso Museum to mark its long association with modern art. Both home-grown talent and the best from abroad is on show.

60 **GALERIA D'ART**
MANEL MAYORAL   **20** K5   Ⓜ Pg. de Gràcia
        🚊 Pg. de Gràcia
Consell de Cent 286; tel. 302-75-30. Tuesday to Saturday 10 a.m.–2 p.m. and 4.30–8.30 p.m.
High-quality exhibitions, retrospectives and thematic collections.

GALERIA D'ART
RENÉ METRAS   **21/22** K6   Ⓜ Pg. de Gràcia
        🚊 Pg. de Gràcia
Consell de Cent 331; tel. 302-05-39. Tuesday to Saturday 11 a.m.–1.30 p.m. and 5–8.30 p.m.
Exhibitions of Catalan and Spanish artists are regularly featured at the René Matras, which is among the more established galleries on Consell de Cent.

GALERIA D'ART
SALA DALMAU   **21/22** K/L6   Ⓜ Pg. de Gràcia
        🚊 Pg. de Gràcia
Consell de Cent 349; tel. 215-45-92.
Long associated with modern Catalan artists such as Miró, the Sala Dalmau mounts regular exhibitions which have recently included work by the Paris School.

GALERIA D'ART
SALA GASPAR   **21/22** K6   Ⓜ Pg. de Gràcia
                                             🚌 Pg. de Gràcia
Consell de Cent 323; tel. 318-87-36. Tuesday to Saturday 11.30 a.m.–1.30 p.m. and 5.30–8 p.m.
A long-established gallery which still provides visitors with a view of current trends in Spanish art, often through simultaneous exhibitions.

GALERIA D'ART
SALA GAUDÍ   **21/22** K6   Ⓜ Pg. de Gràcia
                                             🚌 Pg. de Gràcia
Consell de Cent 337; tel. 318-41-76. Tuesday to Saturday 10.30 a.m.–1.30 p.m. and 5–8.30 p.m.
The work of younger, lesser-known Catalan and Spanish artists and sculptors is displayed here. Exhibitions are changed regularly.

GALERIA D'ART
SALA NONELL   **12** G8   🚌 Calvet
                            Main line train: Muntaner
Johann Sebastian Bach 16; tel. 201-69-11. Daily except Sunday 10 a.m.–2 p.m. and 5–8.30 p.m.
Named after the Catalan painter, this gallery usually manages to stage high-quality exhibitions. Recent treats have included the "Masters of the 19th Century", as well as the work of collectives of Catalan and Spanish artists.

GALERIA D'ART
SALA PARÉS   **29** J4   Ⓜ Liceu
                                          🚌 Rambla
Petrixol 5; tel. 318-70-20. Daily except Sunday 10 a.m.–1.30 p.m. and 4–8 p.m.
The oldest-established gallery in Barcelona features a yearly exhibition of the well-known collective, Pintors de Fama.

GALERIA D'ART
SALA VAYREDA   **21** K6   Ⓜ Pg. de Gràcia
                                             🚌 Pg. de Gràcia
Rbla. Catalunya 116; tel. 218-29-60. Weekdays 10 a.m.–1.30 p.m. and 4–8 p.m., Saturday 10 a.m.–1.30 p.m. and 5–8 p.m.
Regular exhibitions of work of an eclectic nature, including "Art on Paper" or "Paintings from the 19th and 20th Centuries".

ART GALLERIES

GALERIA D'ART   Mallorca
THEO   **4** G12   *Main line train:* Provença
Enric Granados 27; tel. 323-08-48. Tuesday to Saturday 10.30 a.m.–
1.30 p.m. and 4.30–8.30 p.m.
The Barcelona offshoot of the popular gallery in Madrid.

EXHIBITION HALLS

ANTIC HOSPITAL   Ⓜ Liceu
DE LA SANTA CREU   **28** H4   Rambla
Hospital 56; tel. 242-71-71. Tuesday to Saturday 10 a.m.–2 p.m. and
4–8 p.m., Sunday 10 a.m.–2 p.m.
Several of the bigger, semi-permanent exhibitions are mounted in the
buildings surrounding the church, just off the Rambla.

62

ANTIC MERCAT   Ⓜ Barceloneta
DEL BORN   **29** K3   Pla del Palau
Pl. Comercial 12; tel. 319-60-30. Flexible opening hours.
A multicultural centre, converted from a market, that regularly stages art,
theatre and music events. It is well known for its exhibitions of young and
avant-garde artists.

CENTRE CÍVIC   Ⓜ Pg. de Gràcia
CASA ELIZALDE   **21/22** K6   Pg. de Gràcia
València 302; tel. 215-97-80. Flexible opening hours.
A municipal cultural centre that often houses theatre and art exhibitions.
Visitors can wander through the recently restored patio to see the gar-
dens behind the town house.

CENTRE CULTURAL FUNDACIÓ CAIXA   Ⓜ Girona
DE PENSIONS DE BARCELONA   **21/22** L6   Pg. Sant Joan
Pg. Sant Joan 108; tel. 258-89-07. Tuesday to Saturday 11 a.m.–2 p.m.
and 4–8 p.m., Sunday 11 a.m.–2 p.m.
The biggest financial institution in Catalunya, "La Caixa", sponsors cultural exhibitions of all kinds here and in the Montcada centre listed
below.

HIVERNACLE   **29/30** L3   Ⓜ Ciutadella 🚌 Zoo
Parc Ciutadella s/n; tel. 310-22-91. Flexible opening hours.
This iron and glass structure stands in the Ciutadella Park, which was built for the 1888 Universal Exposition. It is now used as a cultural centre, and occasional exhibitions, especially of sculpture, are held in it.

PALAU DE LA VIRREINA   **29** J4   Ⓜ Liceu 🚌 Rambla
La Rambla 99; tel. 301-77-75. Tuesday to Saturday 10 a.m.–2 p.m. and 4.30–8.30 p.m., Sunday 10 a.m.–2 p.m.
As well as providing a home for the municipal Department of Culture, this 18th-century palace holds regular, top-quality exhibitions from Spain and abroad.

REIALS DRASSANES   **28** H3   Ⓜ Drassanes 🚌 Rambla
Pg. Josep Carner 26 bis; tel. 301-88-85. Flexible opening hours.
The city's maritime museum is set in land occupied by the royal shipyards. Regular exhibitions are mounted in it.

63

SALA D'EXPOSICIONS MONTCADA   Ⓜ Jaume I
CAIXA DE PENSIONS DE BARCELONA   **29** K3 🚌 Via Laietana
Montcada 14; tel. 310-06-99. Tuesday to Saturday 11 a.m.–2 p.m. and 4–8 p.m., Sunday 11 a.m.–2 p.m.
The Caixa exhibition centre tends to feature the work of young artists who aren't yet commercial enough to win an exhibition in a private gallery.

SALÓ DEL TINELL   **29** K4   Ⓜ Jaume I 🚌 Via Laietana
Pl. del Rei 9; tel. 315-11-11. Flexible opening hours.
This large 14th-century chamber, originally used for royal audiences, now serves as a magnificent exhibition area for art of all kinds.

Barcelona is best known for being a centre of design and fashion, both for clothes and accessories, and this is amply reflected in the wealth of shops and boutiques brimming with goods to suit virtually all tastes.

The other main characteristic of the city, which is perhaps surprising for a place of its size, is that there are only two department stores, each with two branches. One of the few things the Catalans have in common with the rest of Spain is an obstinate preference for shopping in individual shops for particular things, although this is gradually changing.

The two chains, El Corte Inglés and Galerías Preciados, are well known in Spain, and their Barcelona stores are big enough to carry the full range of goods in their stock. The four stores differ considerably, according to the area and type of clientele they serve.

While department-store shopping is the quickest and most convenient way of discovering a range of goods under one roof, the best way of finding just the right shop is to wander around one of the main shopping districts. The greatest concentration can be found in the corridor of Passeig de Gràcia/Rambla de Catalunya, which stretches between Av. Diagonal and Gran Via. The leading international boutiques as well as a variety of up-market shops and shopping boulevards are all in this district.

A large number of boutiques, specialist stores and "interesting" shops are to be found in the narrow twisting streets in the heart of the Ciudad Vella, to the east of the Rambla towards the Cathedral.

65

The top-of-the-range boutiques and shops are on Av. Diagonal, between Plaza Juan Carlos I and Av. Carlos III, as are other shopping boulevards. This area, which includes branches of El Corte Inglés and Galerías, is much more geared towards the tourist shopper.

Most establishments in Barcelona, except the department stores and a growing number of smaller shops, follow the Mediterranean habit of closing at lunch time, usually at 1.30 or 2 p.m., and re-opening three hours later. The advantage of this sometimes annoying habit is that the shops then stay open until 7.30, 8 p.m. or sometimes even later, allowing for cooler shopping.

If you can stand the crowds, there are regular sales, including during the summer, when bargains can be picked up almost everywhere in Barcelona. Just look for the "Rebajas" and "Rebaixes" signs plastered all over the shop windows.

Barcelona's stylish shops cater for all tastes.

Finally, shopping can easily become a frustration if the visitor is used to immediate service, or objects to being overtaken in a queue. In some shops, it may seem that the "barge-in" method works best, and some patience is required to deal with an assistant who breaks off to answer another customer. Above all, remember that small shops appear to have survived the longest in Spain because they provide the best opportunity for lengthy conversations between the shopkeeper and customer. Don't wait politely for the conversation to finish, but break in with a "disculpe" if and when there is a pause, and put your question.

DEPARTMENT STORES AND SHOPPING MALLS

LA AVENIDA 21 J6/7 Rbla. Catalunya *Main line train*: Provença *Rbla. Catalunya 121; tel. 317-13-98. Monday to Saturday 10.30 a.m.– 2 p.m. and 4.30–8.30 p.m.*
A mall of boutiques similar to the Bulevard Rosa, with the addition of more non-clothes shops.

66

BULEVARD ROSA 21 J6 Ⓜ Pg. de Gràcia Pg. de Gràcia *Pg. de Gràcia 55, tel. 309-06-50. Monday to Saturday 10.30 a.m–8.30 p.m. Also at Av. Diagonal 609–615, tel. 419-12-80 (102 shops); Av. Diagonal 474, tel. 309-06-50 (39 shops).*
Shopping malls containing a collection of boutiques, mostly clothes and mainly for women, although there are also shops selling children's clothes, toys and shoes. Bars and restaurants are on hand to refresh weary shoppers.

EL CORTE INGLÉS 21 J5 Ⓜ Catalunya Pl. Catalunya *Pl. Catalunya 14, tel. 322-00-12. Monday to Saturday 10 a.m.–9 p.m. Also at Av. Diagonal 617–619, tel. 302-12-12.*
The Place Catalunya store is the bigger of the two branches, and scheduled for expansion. Its floors contain most things a visitor might want all under one roof. It caters for foreign shoppers as well, especially during the summer: there are multilingual floor directories and an internal phone information service in several languages. Designer boutiques are alongside El Corte's own-brand fashion goods. Beware of pickpockets and card-sharks on the street outside. The Av. Diagonal branch is smaller and posher, aimed at the up-market tourist as well as the year-round client.

GALERÍAS PRECIADOS   **21** J4   Ⓜ Catalunya

Av. Portal de l'Angel 19–20, tel. 317-00-00. Monday to Saturday 10 a.m.–9 p.m. Also at Av. Diagonal 471–473, tel. 322-30-11.

This British-owned chain has recovered from near-bankruptcy, thanks to a mixture of better-quality goods and clever marketing. It is generally cheaper than El Corte Inglés, but has a smaller range of merchandise. The Av. Diagonal store has several franchised sections—Marks and Spencer without the food but with much higher prices, MotherCare, etc. It often seems there are more staff than customers, which makes shopping relaxed.

GALERIES MALDÀ   **21** J4   Ⓜ Liceu   🚌 Rambla

Portaferrissa 22; tel. 318-89-40. Monday to Saturday 10.30 a.m.–2 p.m. and 4–8.30 p.m.

A shopping mall housed on the ground floor of a 17th-century palace in the Barri Gòtic. Although there is a sprinkling of other establishments, most of the 75 shops sell fashionable clothes.

VIA WAGNER   **12** G8   🚌 Pl. Francesc Macià

Bori i Fontestà 17; tel. 200-16-46. Monday to Saturday 10.30 a.m.–2 p.m. and 4.30–9 p.m.

Just north of the main shopping district on Diagonal, this mall houses a hundred or so stores, most of which sell fashions.

67

FASHION

The establishments listed in this section are inevitably a subjective choice. Although some designers—Toni Miró, David Valls and Purification Gàrcia—remain ever popular, the speed with which some drop from the scene or appear as new lights means that the section is not exhaustive. In addition, the blurring of age groups in current fashion has led to the use of "young", "younger" or "classical", none of which is intended to portray exclusivity, and nor does it, if you look around at the fashions worn by the people of Barcelona.

ADOLFO DOMINGUEZ   **21** J6   Ⓜ Pg. de Gràcia   🚌 Pg. de Gràcia

Pg. de Gràcia 89; tel. 215-13-39.

The Barcelona branch of one of Spain's leading designers. This two-floor establishment, designed by Dominguez, features clothes for both men and women.

ALAIN
MANOUKIAN　　**11** F8　　　　Ⓜ Maria Cristina
　　　　　　　　　　　　　　🚊 Pl. Maria Cristina
Bulevard Rosa Pedralbes, Av. Diagonal 609.
International designer with a chain of shops selling clothes intended primarily for younger women.

ALFREDO　　　　　　　　　　🚊 Rbla. Catalunya
VILLALBA　　**21** J6　　　*Main line train:* Provença
Rbla. Catalunya 88; tel. 215-05-42.
Clothes sold at this boutique are produced by a fashionable designer and are intended mainly for younger women.

D'ALMA　　**12** G8　　　🚊 Pl. Francesc Macià
St. Fé de Nuevo Méjico 5–7; tel. 200-37-88.
Designs on show in this boutique include among others, Christian Lecroix, and Valentino.

ARAMIS　　**21** J6　　🚊 Rbla. Catalunya　*Main line train:* Provença
Rbla. Catalunya 103; tel. 215-16-69.
One of the most exclusive shops in Barcelona, selling a range of clothes for men and women.

68

ARCE　　**12** H9　　　　　　🚊 Muntaner
Muntaner 519; tel. 418-88-90.
A men's fashion boutique, catering for young businessmen. It carries a range of international labels.

BENETTON　　**12** H7　　　🚊 Pl. Francesc Macià
Av. Diagonal 588, tel. 209-55-49. Also at Ganduxer 30, tel. 201-74-69;
Via Augusta 128, tel. 200-87-24; Fontanella 3, tel. 301-19-69.
This well-known chain sells children's clothes as well as the full range of women's wear, especially woollens.

CAMPER　　**12** H7/8　　　🚊 Av. Diagonal
Muntaner 248, tel. 201-31-88. Also at València 249, tel. 215-63-90;
Av. Pau Casals 5, tel. 209-58-46.
Very fashionable Spanish-made shoes, particularly popular with the younger generation.

CARMEN RUBIO 11 F8 ⓜ Maria Cristina 🚌 Pl. Maria Cristina
Bulevard Rosa Pedralbes, Av. Diagonal 609; tel. 419-03-21.
A boutique selling clothes from, among others, Margarita Nuez and Roser
Marcé, the current fashionable Barcelona designers.

CHARO 12 H8 🚌 Pl. Francesc Macià
Ferran Agulló 18; tel. 209-13-47.
Women's clothes from designers including Valentino, Gianni Versace,
Les Copains and many more.

CHEMISSE 21 J6 🚌 Rbla. Catalunya *Main line train:* Provença
Rbla. Catalunya 117 bis; tel. 237-67-34.
Fashion with a touch of class, for young men and women.

CHOSES 21 J6 ⓜ Pg. de Gràcia 🚌 Pg. de Gràcia
Pg. de Gràcia 97, tel. 215-07-46. Also at Ferrán Agulló 3, tel. 209-07-62.
Very elegant women's fashions, including designs by Chloe and Claude
Barthelemy.

CHRISTIAN DIOR MONSIEUR 12 G/H8 🚌 Pl. Francesc Macià **69**
Av. Pau Casals 7; tel. 201-68-80.
Little introduction is needed for this Barcelona branch of the famous
chain. It is packed with the French designer's clothes for men, a little dark
and sombre but nevertheless classic.

CONTI 12 G8 ⓜ Diagonal 🚌 Av. Diagonal
Av. Diagonal 512, tel. 416-12-11. Also at Av. Pau Casals 7, tel. 201-19-33; Rbla. Catalunya 78, tel. 215-32-32.
Men's fashion, including a tailoring service.

CRAVANE 12 G8 🚌 Pl. Francesc Macià
Sta. Fé de Nuevo Méjico 1–3; tel. 201-71-61.
International women's fashion, including designs from Thierry Mugler,
Blumarine and others.

DIEZ 21 J7 🚌 Rbla. Catalunya *Main line train:* Provença
Rbla. Catalunya 124; tel. 213-04-10.
Women's fashions, especially designs from Moschino's Cheap & Chic
collection as well as pieces from Hechter.

DONALDSON   **11** F8   Ⓜ Maria Cristina   🚊 Pl. Maria Cristina
Bulevard Rosa, Av. Diagonal 609; tel. 419-17-00.
Clothes for the young, including shirts with all the Disney characters.

DON   🚊 Rbla. Catalunya
ALGODON   **21** J6   *Main line train:* Provença
Rbla. Catalunya 102; tel. 215-67-34. Monday to Saturday 10 a.m.–
1.30 p.m. and 4.30–8 p.m.
The place to buy reasonably priced cotton clothes, particularly if you be-
long to the younger set.

DON   🚊 Rbla. Catalunya
CARLOS   **21** J6   *Main line train:* Provença
Mallorca 236; tel. 216-04-07.
International women's fashions of the more elegant kind.

EFECTOS   Ⓜ Pg. de Gràcia
ESPECIALES   **21** J6   🚊 Pg. de Gràcia
Bulevard Rosa, Pg. de Gràcia 55.
High-fashion designs from Claire Deve, Gaultier, Reminiscence
70 and others.

EMPORIO ARMANI   **21** J7   Ⓜ Diagonal   🚊 Via Augusta
Via Augusta 10; tel. 218-76-79.
The clothing on sale here, by well-known Italian designer, Giorgio Armani,
is well presented in elegant surroundings. It is aimed mostly at younger
men.

FANCY MEN   **12** H7   Ⓜ Diagonal   🚊 Av. Diagonal
Av. Diagonal 463; tel. 430-64-20.
Suppliers of men's clothes from Spain and elsewhere. But can you bear
to be seen with a carrier bag showing the shop's name?

FANTASY SHOP   **21** J4   Ⓜ Liceu   🚊 Rambla
Portaferrissa 25; tel. 447-01-17.
Fashion for young men and women, including shoes from Free-Lance
and Junior Gaultier, and a selection of hats from Britain.

FARRERAS   **21** J6   Ⓜ Pg. de Gràcia Pg. de Gràcia
Pg. de Gràcia 79, tel. 215-01-07. Also at Av. Diagonal 586, tel. 200-10-62; Doctor Ferrán 2, tel. 205-10-62.
One of the most established clothes shops in the city, with men's and women's wear to match.

FIORUCCI–NAF NAF   **21** J6   Ⓜ Pg. de Gràcia Pg. de Gràcia
Bulevard Rosa, Pg. de Gràcia 55, tel. 215-22-89. Also at Bulevard Rosa, Av. Diagonal 474, tel. 237-13-92.
"Happy" fashion for young people at low prices.

FUREST   **12** G8   Pl. Francesc Macià
Av. Pau Casals 3, tel. 201-25-99. Also at Pg. de Gràcia 12–14, tel. 301-20-00; Av. Diagonal 468, tel. 218-26-65.
Another of the classical clothes shops of Barcelona, with traditional menswear by the yard. In addition to off-the-peg clothes—from Cerrutti and others—a tailoring service is available.

GALES   **21** K5   Ⓜ Pg. de Gràcia Pg. de Gràcia
Pg. de Gràcia 32, tel. 318-20-04. Also at Av. Diagonal 490 tel. 217-67-16; Av. Diagonal 596, tel.200-47-16.
High-quality classical clothes for men, women and children, together with accessories to match. Tailored men's suits also available.

71

GIORGIO ARMANI   **12** G8   Pl. Francesc Macià
Av. Diagonal 624; tel. 200-99-01.
International design for men and women by the famous Italian modiste, at Barcelona prices. The shop, on two floors, has been recently re-designed and is in the swish shopping district.

GONZALO COMELLA   **21** J7   Ⓜ Diagonal Via Augusta
Via Augusta 2, tel. 416-15-16. Also at Pg. de Gràcia 6, tel. 217-33-34; Capitán Arenas 5, tel. 218-33-58.
Clothes for men, women and children are sold in this traditional shop that has been serving the gentry of Barcelona for generations.

GROC   **21** J6   🚇 Rbla. Catalunya   *Main line train:* Provença
*Rbla. Catalunya 100 bis; tel. 215-01-80. Monday 11 a.m.–noon and
5–8 p.m., Tuesday to Saturday 10 a.m.–2 p.m. and 4.30–8 p.m.*
Dependable and constantly innovative—at least for the past 20 years—
fashions for men and women by the well-known Catalan designer Antonio
Miró.

GUCCI   **21** J7   Ⓜ Diagonal 🚇 Av. Diagonal
Av. Diagonal 415; tel. 416-06-20.
Pretty much the same in Barcelona as in other cities around the world—
elegant, exclusive and very expensive.

HÉROES   **12** H8   🚇 Santaló
*Laforja 103, tel. 201-32-90. Also at Bulevard Rosa, Av. Diagonal 474;
Bulevard Rosa, Av. Diagonal 609.*
Reasonably priced, elegant men's fashion, mainly for young blades.

JEAN PIERRE BUA   **12** H7   🚇 Pl. Francesc Macià
*Av. Diagonal 469; tel. 439-71-00. Monday to Saturday 10.30 a.m.–
2.30 p.m. and 3.30–8.30 p.m.*
Women's fashion from national and international designers (Vittorio and
Lucchino, Gaultier and Hamnett). Definitely the in-place for the die-hard
fashion-conscious.

72

JEAN PIERRE VICTIM'S   **12** H7   Ⓜ Diagonal 🚇 Av. Diagonal
Bulevard Rosa, Av. Diagonal 474; tel. 237-03-34.
Alternative fashion for the young is displayed in this small shop.

KAYFI   **12** G8   🚇 Pl. Francesc Macià
Maestro Nicolau 7; tel. 201-82-95.
International fashion for women, at modest prices.

LOEWE   **21** J5/6   Ⓜ Pg. de Gràcia 🚇 Pg. de Gràcia
*Pg. de Gràcia 35, tel. 216-04-00. Also at Av. Diagonal 570, tel. 200-09-
20; Johann Sebastian Bach 8, tel. 202-31-50.*
A full range of beautiful leather goods, from handbags to briefcases, is
sold alongside elegant clothes at the three branches of Loewe. The
Passeig de Gràcia shop is particularly smart.

LA MANUAL
ALPARGATERA **29** J3   Ⓜ Jaume I
🚏 Via Laietana
Avinyó 7; tel. 301-01-72.
Handmade rope-soled and canvas sandals, espadrille-style, for all the
family. Select a style, colour and adornment and see your shoes being
made for you by the staff of women shoemakers.

MARIA PILAR **12** H8   🚏 Pl. Francesc Macià
Calvet 11–13; tel. 200-37-80.
Women's fashion, including lines from Burberry's.

MASIMO   🚏 Gala Placidia
DUTTI **13** J8   *Main line train:* Gràcia
*Via Augusta 33, tel. 217-73-06. Also at Av. Diagonal 602, tel. 200-98-15;
Rbla. Catalunya 60, tel. 215-64-21.*
Reasonably priced men's fashion, especially shirts, in original designs.
Particularly good during sale time.

MATRICULA **12** H8   🚏 Pl. Francesc Macià **73**
Av. Pau Casals 24; tel. 201-23-08.
Acutely fashionable clothes—Gaultier, Ozbek and the like—for men and
women.

MG **21** J7   Ⓜ Diagonal 🚏 Via Augusta
Pl. Narcís Oller 3–5; tel. 238-16-55.
International lines, especially from Britain and the Netherlands, are the
mainstay of MG's stylish stock. Both men and women are catered for.

MOIRÉE **12** G8/9   🚏 Pl. Francesc Macià
Dr. Flemming s/n; tel. 201-84-50.
Women's fashion of the sophisticated type. Designs are by Ungaro, Sonia
Rykiel and many others.

PEDRO MORAGO **12** J7   Ⓜ Diagonal 🚏 Av. Diagonal
Av. Diagonal 520; tel. 201-60-50.
A current rave in the Spanish fashion world.

LA PERLA GRIS   21 J6   Ⓜ Pg. de Gràcia   🚋 Pg. de Gràcia
Rosselló 220, tel. 215-29-91. Also at Consell de Cent 300, tel. 301-16-83; Rbla. Catalunya 94, tel. 215-04-84; Balmes 285, tel. 217-82-30.
Classical lingerie in classical surroundings.

PERUOMO   12 H8   🚋 Pl. Francesc Macià
Calvet 51, tel. 201-37-69. Also at Mallorca 251, tel. 487-00-14.
Men's fashion based on classical clothes made modish.

POLO   21 J6   Ⓜ Pg. de Gràcia   🚋 Pg. de Gràcia
Bulevard Rosa, Pg. de Gràcia 55; tel. 215-74-47.
Original, though classical, men's fashion at reasonable prices.

POLO DE RALPH LAURENT   12 H7   🚋 Pl. Francesc Macià
Av. Diagonal 463 bis (inside Cortefiel); tel. 322-82-92.
The famous designer's clothes for men can be found in this boutique contained within the Cortefiel chain store.

SALVATORE FERRAGAMO   21 J7   Ⓜ Diagonal   🚋 Av. Diagonal
Av. Diagonal 415; tel. 200-99-01.
The Barcelona base for this well-known Italian designer is set in cool and comfortable surroundings.

SANTA EULALIA   21 K6   Ⓜ Pg. de Gràcia   🚋 Pg. de Gràcia
Pg. de Gràcia 60, tel. 215-42-16. Also at Pg. de Gràcia 93, tel. 215-06-74; Av. Pau Casals 8, tel. 201-70-51.
Very classy clothes for men and women. Considered one of the best shops in Barcelona.

SANTACANA   21 J6   🚋 Rbla. Catalunya
Main line train: Provença
Rbla. Catalunya 90, tel. 215-04-13. Also at Rbla. Catalunya 94, tel. 215-04-84; Via Augusta 180, tel. 209-00-00.
Stylish lingerie and swim wear for women.

SPAGHETTI   21 J6   🚋 Rbla. Catalunya   *Main line train:* Provença
Rbla. Catalunya 104, tel. 487-17-27. Also at Via Augusta 35, tel. 415-01-99.
Young fashion at very keen prices.

SPLEEN 21 J6/7   Rbla. Catalunya
Main line train: Provença
*La Avenida, Rbla. Catalunya 121, tel. 217-78-81. Also at Bulevard Rosa,
Pg. de Gràcia 55, tel. 215-90-31.*
Large selection of modern imitation jewellery.

TODO PARA   Rbla. Catalunya
LA MUJER 21 J6   *Main line train:* Provença
Rbla. Catalunya 56; tel. 216-02-53.
Fashionable clothes and accessories for women.

TÖN 21 J6   Ⓜ Provença   Rbla. Catalunya
Provença 290; tel. 215-67-48.
Women's fashions from Jesus del Pozo, Roser Marcé and many more.

TORRENS 21 J5   Ⓜ Pg. de Gràcia
    Gran Via de les Corts Catalanes
*Gran Via de les Corts Catalanes 630, tel. 301-09-08. Also at Av. Diagonal
576; tel. 209-44-22.*
One of the highly reputed shops of Barcelona, with clothes for men,
women and children.

75

TRAU 11 F8   Ⓜ Maria Cristina   Pl. Maria Cristina
Bulevard Rosa, Av. Diagonal 609; tel. 419-51-11.
Considered to be one of the most elegant boutiques in the city. Women's
fashions make up the stock.

TRECCE 12 G8/9   Pl. Francesc Macià
Escuelas Pias 2; tel. 209-07-34.
Exclusive fashions for women, mainly by Italian designers.

URBE 29 J4   Ⓜ Liceu   Rambla
Boters 8, tel. 301-81-92. Also at Portaferrissa 21, tel. 302-26-85.
Jeans and shirts are among the reasonably priced clothes for young
people.

ZARA 21 J5   Ⓜ Catalunya
Pelayo 58, tel. 301-09-78. Also at Rbla. Catalunya 67, tel. 215-86-41.
Fashion for the young at reasonable prices.

DISCOUNT AND SECOND-HAND CLOTHES

BURRADAS   **23** O/P6   Ⓜ Clot   🚍 Mallorca
València 662-664; tel. 231-22-61.
Discount clothes, especially from Burberry's, with small imperfections.

CONTRIBUCIONES   **21** J7   Ⓜ Diagonal   🚍 Av. Diagonal
Riera San Miguel 30; tel. 238-18-88.
Old stock, including international labels, is sold at a discount.

INTERCAMBIO   **13/14** K8   Ⓜ Fontana   🚍 Gran de Gràcia
Gran de Gràcia 262, princ. 1a; tel. 237-46-19.
A mass of second-hand clothes, including international labels, together
with evening wear, shoes, handbags and much more.

NOU I VELL   **21/22** K5
Roger de Llúria 43; tel. 301-50-44.
"New and Old" sells antique clothes, second-hand and new, "at
incredible prices".

TAXI   🚍 Balmes
MODA   **13** J10   *Main line train:* Putxet
Balmes 438; tel. 418-58-94.
Designer collections from past seasons, often at a quarter the original
price. Les Copains, Gianni Versace, Gianfranco Ferre, and Giorgio
Armani are but a few of the famous labels to be found.

THIERRY ASHE   **12** G8   🚍 Av. Diagonal
Ganduxer 8; tel. 209-98-93.
International collections from past seasons are sold at an average 50
per cent discount.

TONTADAS   **12** J10   🚍 Balmes   *Main line train:* Av. Tibidabo
Teodora Lamadrid 52-60; tel. 417-52-92.
The place to go for designer jeans and children's clothes at a discount.

ANTIQUES AND COLLECTORS' ITEMS

The following is a list of good antique shops in the city. In addition to these, a major concentration of establishments can be found in the Bulevard dels Antiquaris (Passeig de Gràcia 55).

ANA ROS 21 J6 Ⓜ Pg. de Gràcia 🚃 Pg. de Gràcia
Pg. de Gràcia 55; tel. 215-80-15. Monday to Saturday 10.30 a.m.–2 p.m. and 4.30–8.30 p.m.
Mainly art deco furniture, mirrors and clocks.

L'ANCIEN BIJOU 21 J6 Ⓜ Pg. de Gràcia 🚃 Pg. de Gràcia
Pg. de Gràcia 55; tel. 215-85-19. Monday to Saturday 10.30 a.m.–2 p.m. and 4.30–8.30 p.m.
Jewellery from the turn of the century is a speciality here, as well as lamps and other objets d'art from the same period.

ANTIGA 20 H7 🚃 Av. Diagonal
Pje. Lluís Pellicer; tel. 419-10-25. Weekdays 10.30 a.m.–1.30 p.m. and 5–8 p.m., Saturday 10.30 a.m.–1.30 p.m.
Furniture from the second half of the 19th century.

77

ANTIGÜEDADES Ⓜ Jaume I
NOIRJEAN 29 J4 🚃 Via Laietana
Sant Sever 9; tel. 302-69-42. Weekdays 10 a.m.–2 p.m. and 5–8 p.m., Saturday 10 a.m.–2 p.m.
In addition to furniture, this shop stocks religious artefacts, as befits its situation near the cathedral.

ARKUPE 29 K3 Ⓜ Jaume I 🚃 Via Laietana
Placeta de Montcada 1–3; tel. 319-15-72. Monday to Saturday 11 a.m.–2 p.m. and 4–8 p.m.
Furniture and porcelain of all kinds are the order of the day at Arkupe.

ARTUR RAMON 29 J4 Ⓜ Liceu 🚃 Rambla
Palla 25; tel. 302-59-70. Monday to Saturday 10 a.m.–1.30 p.m. and 5–8 p.m.
Furniture mostly from the 18th century, but also earlier, as well as ceramics, silver, and paintings (see Art Galleries).

ATLAN   **12** H8   🚊 Pl. Francesc Macià
*Amigó 42; tel. 209-61-67. Weekdays 10.30 a.m.–2 p.m. and 5–8 p.m.,
Saturday 10.30 a.m.–2 p.m.*
Art deco furniture and ornaments, including a wide selection of lamps,
from the 1940s and '50s.

CAMILLA   🚊 Aribau
HAMM   **20** H7   *Main line train: Provença*
*Rosselló 197; tel. 218-22-11. Weekdays 10.30 a.m.–2 p.m. and 4.30–
8 p.m., Saturday 10.30 a.m.–2 p.m.*
Hamm designed this antique shop-cum-gallery which has a regular
turnover of stock, especially furniture. The art deco style and the 1940s
and '50s are well represented.

ELS   Ⓜ Glòries
ENCANTS   **23** N5   🚊 Gran Via de les Corts Catalanes
*Pl. de les Glòries; tel. 246-30-30. Monday, Wednesday, Friday and
Saturday 8 a.m.–7 p.m.*
More a flea market than an antiques market, but a place where bargains
can be found.

78

GALUCHAT   **29** K3   Ⓜ Pla del Palau   🚊 Pla del Palau
*Calders 4; tel. 319-30-25. Weekdays 10.30 a.m.–1.30 p.m. and 5.30–
8.30 p.m., Saturday 10.30 a.m.–1.30 p.m. Closed Saturday in July and
August.*
Furniture of all kinds from the 1950s, as well as a fascinating collection
of fashionable—then and now—objets d'art from the period are crammed
into a rather small space.

LES LILES   **29** K3   Ⓜ Jaume I   🚊 Via Laietana
*Princesa 40; tel. 315-16-09. Monday to Saturday 10.30 a.m.–2 p.m. and
5–8 p.m.*
Lamps, china and furniture from the 1920s to the 1940s.

LUCCA   **20/21** J7   🚊 Balmes *Main line train: Provença*
*Enric Granados 151; tel. 414-32-89. Weekdays 11 a.m–2 p.m. and
4.30–8.30 p.m., Saturday 11 a.m.–2 p.m.*
Specializes in Catalan and French furniture.

MERCAT GÒTIC   Ⓜ Liceu
D'ANTIGUITATS   **29** J4   🚊 Rambla
Pl. del Pí/ Pl. de Sant Josep Oriol; tel. 317-19-96. Wednesday 9 a.m.–8 p.m. Closed in August.
A market held in and around one of the main concentrations of antique shops. Reasonably priced smaller antiques are sold here, along with a whole range of other bric-a-brac.

NOVECENTO   **21** J6   Ⓜ Pg. de Gràcia 🚊 Pg. de Gràcia
Pg. de Gràcia 75; tel. 215-11-83. Monday to Saturday 10 a.m–2 p.m. and 4.30–8 p.m.
The place to go for antique jewellery.

EL TINELL   **21/22** K6   Ⓜ Diagonal 🚊 Av. Diagonal
Pau Claris 190; tel. 215-52-48. Monday to Saturday 10 a.m.–2 p.m. and 4.30–8 p.m.
Furniture and household goods from the second half of the 19th century, as well as lamps, porcelain and bronze ornaments.

79

The following is a selection of the many bookshops in Barcelona, including several which specialize in particular subjects. Paperback books in English are available in a few bookshops, such as the one inside the Corte Inglés department store, but most of the newspaper kiosks along Passeig de Gràcia and the Rambla have a stand selling them, at least during the summer months.

ALCORA I DELFÍN   **12** H7   Ⓜ Diagonal 🚊 Av. Diagonal
Av. Diagonal 564; tel. 200-07-46. Monday to Saturday 9.30 a.m–1.45 p.m. and 4.15–8 p.m.
Set in a 1950s time warp, Alcora y Delfín specializes in art, design and photography.

ALTAIR FORÇA   **21** J6   Ⓜ Pg. de Gràcia 🚍 Balmes
*Balmes 69; tel. 451-13-38. Monday to Saturday 10 a.m–1.30 p.m. and
4–8 p.m.*
The Altair part of this bookshop specializes in travel literature of all kinds,
while Força 6 (Force 6) stocks the kind of material that sailors, dry-land
or practising, will revel in.

ANTIFAZ COMIC   **13/14** K8   Ⓜ Fontana 🚍 Gran de Gràcia
*Gran de Gràcia 205; tel. 237-81-19. Tuesday to Saturday 10.30 a.m–
2 p.m. and 5–8.30 p.m.*
As the name suggests, this shop specializes in comics of all kinds.

BALAGUÉ   **20/21** J6/7   Ⓜ Diagonal 🚍 Balmes
*Enric Granados 80; tel. 415-89-53. Monday to Saturday 10 a.m.–
1.30 p.m. and 4–7.45 p.m.*
Antiquarian books form the bulk of the stock here.

BOSCH   **21** J5   Ⓜ Universitat 🚍 Ronda Universitat
*Ronda Universitat 11; tel. 317-53-08. Monday to Saturday 9.30 a.m –
1.30 p.m. and 4–7.30 p.m.*
A general bookshop with a good selection of textbooks, including
Spanish for foreigners, to suit its site near the university.

CASA ALMIRALL   **29** K3   Ⓜ Jaume I 🚍 Via Laietana
*Princesa 16; tel. 319-80-06. Weekdays 9.30 a.m.–1.30 p.m. and
4–7.30 p.m., Saturday 9.30 a.m.–1.30 p.m.*
Religious texts and art books.

CASTELLS   **21** J/K5   Ⓜ Universitat 🚍 Ronda Universitat
*Ronda Universitat 13; tel. 317-06-46. Monday to Friday 9.30 a.m.–
1.30 p.m. and 4–7.30 p.m., Saturday 9.30 a.m.–1.30 p.m.*
A general bookshop with a good collection of academic textbooks and
language courses for foreign students.

CINC D'OROS   **21** J7   Ⓜ Diagonal 🚍 Av. Diagonal
*Av. Diagonal 462; tel. 416-19-33. Weekdays 10 a.m.–2 p.m. and
4–8.30 p.m., Saturday 10 a.m.–2 p.m. and 5–8.30 p.m.*
The social sciences are particularly well represented at this general
bookshop.

CINELANDIA **20** G5 Ⓜ Urgell 🚌 Gran Via
*Diputatió 115; tel. 323-20-33. Weekdays 10 a.m.–2 p.m. and 5–8 p.m.,
Saturday 10 a.m.–2 p.m.*
Film buffs come here to browse through books and paraphernalia from
the world of cinema.

CRÒNICA **12** H9 🚌 Muntaner *Main line train:* Muntaner
*Muntaner 421; tel. 414-27-20. Monday to Saturday 9 a.m.–2 p.m. and
4.30–8 p.m.*
A shop much favoured by professionals from the worlds of architecture,
fashion and design, who come in search of texts on their subjects. It also
has a good children's section.

CRISOL **21** J6 Ⓜ Pg. de Gràcia 🚌 Rbla. Catalunya
*Rbla. Catalunya 81; tel. 215-27-20. Monday to Saturday 10 a.m.–10 p.m.,
Sunday 11 a.m.–3 p.m. and 5–9 p.m.*
A late-night bookshop with a range of literature, records, art volumes and
an excellent selection of children's books.

DOCUMENTA **29** J4 Ⓜ Liceu 🚌 Rambla
*Cardenal Casañas 4; tel. 317-25-27. Monday to Saturday 9.30 a.m.–
8.30 p.m.*
A general bookshop, but with a particularly good selection of humani-
ties texts.

81

EDELSA **20** F7 Ⓜ Entença 🚌 Rocafort
Rosselló 55; tel. 439-99-08. Weekdays 9 a.m.–1.30 p.m. and 3.30–7 p.m.
Language texts, videos and other teaching tools share space with a good
selection of classics in various languages.

THE ENGLISH BOOKSHOP **12** H8
Calaf 52.
A wide selection of works in English, from dictionaries to science fiction
and children's books, as well as a section of video and audio tapes, especially with teaching in mind.

HAPPY BOOKS **21** J5 Ⓜ Universitat 🚌 Ronda Universitat
*Pelai 20, tel. 317-07-68. Weekdays 9.30 a.m.–2.30 p.m. and 4–9 p.m.,
Saturday 9.30 a.m.–9 p.m. Also at Pg. de Gràcia 77, tel. 310-79-24.*
Remaindered books are sold at very low prices in the two branches of
this establishment. The Passeig de Gràcia shop is particularly good for
bargains.

HERDER **21** J5 Ⓜ Catalunya 🚊 Balmes
Balmes 26; tel. 317-05-78. Monday to Saturday 9 a.m.–1.30 p.m. and 4–7.30 p.m.
Scientific books are the forte, but there is also a good selection of books in German.

HOGAR Ⓜ Catalunya
DEL LIBRO **21** J5 🚊 Ronda Universitat
Bergara 3. Monday to Saturday 9 a.m.–1.30 p.m. and 4–7.30 p.m.
Religion, philosophy and theatre studies are the star subjects among a good range of books.

LAIE **21** K5 Ⓜ Urquinaona 🚊 Pau Clarís
Pau Clarís 85; tel. 318-17-39. Monday to Saturday 10 a.m.–8 p.m.
Art, cinema, travel guides and children's books all share shelf-space here. Eat or drink in the attached café-cum-restaurant while you read the latest best seller.

82

LIBRERÍA DE LA EMPRESA **20/21** K6 Ⓜ Verdaguer 🚊 Bruc
Bruc 134; tel. 258-44-53. Weekdays 10 a.m.–2 p.m. and 4–8 p.m., Saturday 10 a.m.–2 p.m.
All the books and manuals covering the world of business, finance, law, etc. that the successful or aspiring businessman or woman might want.

LIBRERÍA FRANCESA **21** J6 Ⓜ Diagonal 🚊 Pg. de Gràcia
Pg. de Gràcia 91; tel. 215-14-17. Weekdays 9.30 a.m.–1.30 p.m. and 4–7.30 p.m., Saturday 9.30 a.m.–1.30 p.m. and 5–8 p.m.
A general bookshop with an emphasis on French texts.

LLIBRERIA 🚊 Balmes
ANGLESA **20** H6 *Main line train: Provença*
Provença 203; tel. 453-12-04.
A small bookshop specializing in English titles, but with the Spanish reader in mind. So don't expect the latest Deighton.

LOOK   21 J7   🚃 Balmes *Main line train:* Provença
Balmes 155–157; tel. 415-17-45. Weekdays 10 a.m.–9 p.m., Saturday
10 a.m.–2 p.m. and 5–9 p.m.
Among a general selection of books in this large establishment are sections on tourism, art, computers and design.

MILLA   28 H3   Ⓜ Liceu 🚃 Rambla
Sant Pau 21; tel. 318-62-36. Monday to Saturday 9 a.m.–1.30 p.m. and
5–8 p.m.
Books on the theatre a speciality.

MOTS   13/14 K7   🚃 Gran de Gràcia
Travessera de Gràcia 157; tel. 218-89-86. Monday to Saturday
10 a.m.–1.30 p.m. and 5–8 p.m.
A good selection of literature on parapsychology, astrology and alternative living.

NORMA   Ⓜ Arc de Triomf **83**
COMICS   21/22 L4/5   🚃 Pg. Sant Joan
Pg. de Sant Joan 9; tel. 245-45-26. Weekdays 10 a.m.–1.30 p.m. and
4.30–8 p.m., Saturday 10 a.m.–2 p.m. and 5–8 p.m.
A rainy-day haven, with hordes of comic books for children and adults, in several languages.

NOVECIENTOS   21 J/K4   Ⓜ Jaume I 🚃 Via Laietana
Llibretaria 10–12; tel. 315-39-04. Weekdays 9 a.m.–2 p.m. and 4–8 p.m.,
Saturday 9 a.m.–2 p.m.
Second-hand books at reasonable prices.

TOCS   21 J6   Ⓜ Pg. de Gràcia 🚃 Pg. de Gràcia
Consell de Cent 341; tel. 215-31-21. Monday to Saturday 10 a.m.–9 p.m.
Books, records, and videos are among the goods on sale in this superstore. There are good sections on art and travel, as well as many Spanish and foreign magazines.

JEWELLERY

ALICE
RAMON   12 G8

🚌 Av. Diagonal
Main line train: Muntaner

Bori i Fontestà 14; tel. 201-35-22. Monday to Saturday 10 a.m.–1.30 p.m. and 4.30–8 p.m.
Exclusively designed jewellery for younger women sold at affordable prices.

BAGUÉS   21 J5/6

Ⓜ Pg. de Gràcia   🚌 Pg. de Gràcia

Pg. de Gràcia 41; tel. 216-01-73. Tuesday to Friday 9.30 a.m. –1.30 p.m. and 4.30–8 p.m., Monday and Saturday 10 a.m.–1.30 p.m. and 4.30–8 p.m.
Ever since it first opened shop 100 years ago in the Casa Amettler (see Sights: Town Houses), this celebrated establishment has been providing classic jewellery for Barcelona's rich and famous.

CARTIER   12 G8

🚌 Av. Diagonal

Av. Diagonal 622; tel. 200-48-99. Weekdays 10 a.m.–2 p.m. and 4.30–8 p.m., Saturday 10 a.m.–1 p.m.
The renowned French jewellers sell their full range of exclusive goods in the Barcelona branch, which occasionally holds art shows as well.

84

DIAMANTISSIMO   12 H8

🚌 Muntaner   *Main line train:* Muntaner

Muntaner 337; tel. 209-21-25. Weekdays 10 a.m.–1.30 p.m. and 4.30–8 p.m., Saturday 10 a.m.–1.30 p.m. and 5–8 p.m.
Beautifully designed fashion jewellery, mainly for younger or more extrovert women.

ENRIC
MAJORAL   13 J8

🚌 Balmes
Main line train: Gràcia

Laforja 19; tel. 238-07-52. Weekdays 9.30 a.m.–1.30 p.m. and 4.30–8.30 p.m., Saturday 10.30 a.m.–1.30 p.m.
Exclusive designer jewellery, using various precious and non-precious metals (especially silver) and sometimes even plastic.

JOAQUÍN BERAO   13 J/K 6/7

Ⓜ Diagonal   🚌 Pg. de Gràcia

Rosselló 277; tel. 218-61-87. Weekdays 10.30 a.m.–2 p.m. and 4.30–8 p.m., Saturday 10.30 a.m.–2 p.m.
This magnificently designed, if rather cramped shop displays an interesting collection of original, rather unconventional designer jewellery.

ORIOL   12 G8   🚃 Av. Diagonal   *Main line train:* Muntaner
*Bori i Fontestà 11; tel. 201-03-77. Weekdays 10 a.m.–1.30 p.m. and
4.30–8 p.m., Saturday 10 a.m.–1.30 p.m.*
Tasteful, almost classical jewellery, is sold alongside a range of silverware that is in similar, well-chosen taste.

PUIG DORIA   12 G8   🚃 Av. Diagonal
*Av. Diagonal 612; tel. 201-29-11. Weekdays 10 a.m.–1.30 p.m. and
4–8 p.m., Saturday 10 a.m.–1.15 p.m.*
A high-class jeweller's offering some beautiful and original pieces.

ROCA   21 K5   Ⓜ Pg. de Gràcia   🚃 Pg. de Gràcia
*Pg. de Gràcia 18; tel. 318-32-66. Monday to Saturday 9.30 a.m.–1.30
p.m. and 4–8 p.m.*
The shop itself, designed in 1933 by Josep Lluís Sert, is as much a pleasure to behold as its collection of expensive gemstones.

SENDON   20/21 J7   Ⓜ Diagonal   🚃 Av. Diagonal
*Av. Diagonal 423–425; tel. 209-14-00. Weekdays 9.30 a.m.–1.30 p.m.
and 4.30–8 p.m., Saturday 9.30 a.m.–1.30 p.m.*
Attractive designer jewellery at unattractively high prices.

85

SOLER   🚃 Av. Diagonal
CABOT   12 G8   *Main line train:* Bonanova
*Pl. Sant Gregori Taumaturg 7; tel. 201-96-66. Monday to Saturday
9.30 a.m.–2 p.m. and 4.30–8 p.m.*
Classic jewellery designs with a touch of modernism are sold by this old
firm. Soler Cabot also has an enviable reputation for its original silverware.

THE WATCH GALLERY   12 G8   🚃 Av. Diagonal
*Av. Diagonal 626; tel. 414-37-11. Weekdays 10 a.m.–2 p.m. and 4.30–
8 p.m., Saturday 10.30 a.m.–2 p.m. and 5–8 p.m.*
A vast range of watches, from the relatively cheap to the extremely expensive, is displayed in this large shop.

UNION SUIZA   21 J7   Ⓜ Diagonal   🚃 Av. Diagonal
*Av. Diagonal 482; tel. 416-11-21. Weekdays 9.30 a.m.–1.30 p.m. and
4.30–8.30 p.m., Saturday 10 a.m.–1.30 p.m. and 4.30–8.30 p.m.*
The best of Switzerland's famous time-telling exports can be found here.

ZAPATA   **12** H10   🚌 Mandri   *Main line train:* Putxet
Mandri 20; tel. 418-18-74. Weekdays 9.30 a.m.–2 p.m. and 4.30–8 p.m.,
Saturday 9.30 a.m.–2 p.m.
A dazzling shop, filled with jewellery, clocks and *objets* in classical
designs.

PERFUME AND COSMETICS

L'ARTISAN   🚌 Calvet
PERFUMERIER   **12** H8   *Main line train:* Muntaner
Calvet 66; tel. 414-54-13. Monday to Saturday 10 a.m.–1.30 p.m. and
4.30–8 p.m.
This establishment invents and produces its own interesting essences,
and sells them in various preparations packed in beautiful containers.

THE BODY   Ⓜ Diagonal 🚌 Rbla. Catalunya
SHOP   **20/21** J6   *Main line train:* Provença
Provença 245; tel. 215-22-44. Weekdays 10 a.m.–1.45 p.m. and
4.30–8.30 p.m., Saturday 10.30 a.m.–1.45 p.m. and 5–8 p.m.
The complete range of balms and lotions from the well-known British
chain is on sale in its Barcelona branch.

CELIA COSMETIC   Ⓜ Diagonal 🚌 Rbla. Catalunya
CENTER   **21** J6   *Main line train:* Provença
Provença 251; tel. 215-13-00. Weekdays 10 a.m.–8 p.m., Saturday
10 a.m.–2.30 p.m. and 4.30–8 p.m.
Everything you need to pamper, care for and anoint your body can be
found in this beauty supermarket.

EL CORTE INGLÉS (See Department Stores and Shopping Malls)
Perfumes and cosmetics are sold in both branches of this department
store, with more personal attention for those buying the more expensive
lines.

GALERÍAS PRECIADOS (See Department Stores and Shopping Malls)
A reasonable range of cosmetics and perfumes is stocked—better in
the store on Diagonal.

KRISTEL   **21/22** K7   Ⓜ Diagonal   ▭ Pg. de Gràcia
Còrsega 341; tel. 218-99-91. Weekdays 9.30 a.m.–2 p.m. and 4.30–8 p.m., Saturday 9.30 a.m.–2 p.m.
The most prestigious brands in the world of perfume and cosmetics find shelf-space here, along with a selection of adornments and costume jewellery to complete the image.

PRIMAVERA   **21** J6   Ⓜ Diagonal   ▭ Rbla. Catalunya
Rbla. Catalunya 108; tel. 215-09-30. Weekdays 10 a.m.–1.45 p.m. and 4.30–8 p.m., Saturday 10 a.m.–1.45 p.m. and 5–8 p.m.
Perfumes and cosmetics from the more prestigious international companies.

REGIA   **21** J5/6   Ⓜ Pg. de Gràcia   ▭ Pg. de Gràcia
Pg. de Gràcia 39; tel. 216-01-21. Weekdays 10 a.m.–1.30 p.m. and 4–8 p.m., Saturday 10 a.m.–1.30 p.m. and 5–8 p.m.
As well as perfume and cosmetics from Spain and abroad, this branch of Barcelona's largest chain of perfumeries features a fascinating little perfume museum.

87

MUSIC

ALGUERO   **13** J7   ▭ Balmes
Balmes 199; tel. 217-46-26. Monday to Saturday 10 a.m.–1.30 p.m. and 4–8 p.m.
A record shop in the traditional style. It offers the latest in pop and rock, the best in classical music, a good compact-disc selection and the now rare opportunity to hear the tunes before you buy.

CASTELLO   **28/29** J3   Ⓜ Liceu   ▭ Rambla
Nou de la Rambla 15, tel. 302-42-36. Monday to Saturday 10 a.m.–2 p.m. and 4.30–8 p.m. Also at Tallers 3, tel. 318-20-41. Monday to Saturday 10 a.m.–2 p.m. and 4.15–8.15 p.m.
Music to suit virtually all tastes, from African tribal to AC/DC, with a sprinkling of rarities. The Tallers shop specializes in classical music.

JAZZ
COLLECTORS   **13** J10

🚋 Balmes   *Main line train: Av. Tibidabo*
Ptge. Forasté 4; tel. 212-74-78. Weekdays 10.30 a.m.–2 p.m. and 4.40–8.30 p.m., Saturday noon–2 p.m.
An emporium of enjoyment for the jazz lover and collector, this shop is famous beyond Spain's frontiers for its wide selection of jazz of all kinds, including some genuine rarities.

NOU DISC   **28** J4

Ⓜ Liceu   🚋 Rambla
Hospital 46; tel. 318-76-00. Monday to Saturday 10 a.m.–1.30 p.m. and 4.30–8.30 p.m.
Rock forms the bulk of the music sold here, although the shop also stocks a selection of opera to exploit its position near the Liceu.

PELAYO 14   **20/21** J5

Ⓜ Universitat   🚋 Rda. Universitat
Pelai 14; tel. 318-77-76. Monday to Saturday 10 a.m.–2 p.m. and 4.30–8.30 p.m.
Little-known and up-and-coming performers are well represented here, making the shop a favourite with the local student population. Otherwise, there's a good selection of music of all types.

SONY MITO   **13** J9

🚋 Balmes   *Main line train: Padua*
Balmes 365; tel. 211-20-54. Tuesday to Saturday 9.30 a.m.–1.30 p.m. and 4.30–8.30 p.m., Monday 4.30–8.30 p.m.
In addition to acting as a showroom for the Japanese electronics manufacturer, this shop holds a vast collection—allegedly some 10,000 titles—of compact discs, more than half of them classical.

DESIGN

ATRI   **13** J10

🚋 Balmes   *Main line train: Av. Tibidabo*
Balmes 427; tel. 211-30-66. Weekdays 9.30 a.m.–1.30 p.m. and 4–8 p.m., Saturday 9.30 a.m.–1.30 p.m.
Furniture for the home and office, mainly of Italian design.

B.D. EDICIONES
DE DISEÑO   21/22 K6
Ⓜ Pg. de Gràcia
🚌 Pg. de Gràcia
Mallorca 291–293; tel. 258-69-09. Monday to Saturday 10 a.m.–1.30 p.m. and 4–8 p.m.
Some of the best classic design pieces, mostly furniture, created by Gaudí, Mies van der Rohe, and the like, are displayed at the Domènech-designed Casa Thomas (built in 1895). The work of many fine, more contemporary designers (Bofill, Tusquets) is also represented.

DAE   20 H7
🚌 Av. Diagonal
Londres 99; tel. 410-99-89. Monday to Saturday 9 a.m.–1.30 p.m. and 4.30–8 p.m.
This recent addition to the design scene contains everything from lights and lamps, to spiral staircases and chimney pieces.

EN LINEA BARCELONA   12 H9
🚌 Santaló
Copèrnic 48–50; tel. 200-25-33. Weekdays 9.30 a.m.–1.30 p.m. and 4.30–8 p.m., Saturday 10 a.m.–1.30 p.m.
Ultramodern as well as classical furniture is sold here. The work is mainly Italian, but there's plenty of pieces by other foreign and Spanish designers.

89

GRES   12 G8
🚌 Calvet
Johann Sebastian Bach 7; tel. 201-29-99. Monday to Saturday 9.30 a.m.–2 p.m. and 4–8 p.m.
Both modern and traditional furniture designs are sold in this shop, which itself resembles somebody's home.

HABITAT   12/13 J7
🚌 Av. Diagonal
Av. Diagonal/Tuset; tel. 209-31-22. Monday to Saturday 10.30 a.m.–8.30 p.m.
One of the originals, struggling to keep abreast of a city bent on design. It still sells an extensive collection of furniture, fixtures and fittings mainly for the home.

IDEA MUEBLE   12 H8   🚌 Muntaner   *Main line train:* Muntaner
Via Augusta 185; tel. 209-31-22. Monday to Saturday 9.30 a.m.–1.30 p.m. and 4.30–8 p.m.
Furniture of Catalan and Italian design is on display here, in a two-floor showroom which is almost an art gallery.

INSÒLIT   **21/22** K6   Ⓜ Verdaguer   🚌 Av. Diagonal
*Av. Diagonal 353; tel. 207-49-19. Monday to Saturday 10 a.m.–2 p.m.
and 4.30–8 p.m.*
Very unusual furniture—things that aren't what they seem—can be found
here.

MODO   **20** H6   Ⓜ Urgell   🚌 Gran Via
*Consell de Cent 207; tel. 254-47-03. Monday to Saturday 9.30 a.m.–
1 p.m. and 4–8 p.m.*
A range of furniture, and other ornaments for the home, mostly "Made
in Spain", in styles to suit most tastes.

PILMA   **21** J7   Ⓜ Diagonal   🚌 Av. Diagonal
*Av. Diagonal 403; tel. 416-13-99. Monday to Saturday 10 a.m.–2 p.m.
and 4.30–8.30 p.m.*
Domestic and imported modern design for the home, in a large store
which needs to be explored.

ROCHE BOBOIS   **12** H8   🚌 Av. Diagonal
*Muntaner 266–268; tel. 209-39-44. Weekdays 10 a.m.–1.30 p.m. and
4–8 p.m., Saturday 10.30 a.m.–1.30 p.m. and 5–8 p.m. Also at Josep
Tarradellas 116 bis.*
While the Bobois establishment on Muntaner specializes in contemporary
furniture design, the newer shop features solid, country-style furniture
for less adventurous tastes.

TECMO   **13** J10   🚌 Balmes   *Main line train:* Av. Tibidabo
*Balmes 468; tel. 417-48-05. Monday to Saturday 10 a.m.–1.30 p.m. and
4–8 p.m.*
Contemporary design furniture by modern Catalans—Mariscal,
Tusquets, etc.— is sold alongside classic pieces.

VINÇON   **21** K6   Ⓜ Diagonal   🚌 Pg. de Gràcia
*Pg. de Gràcia 96; tel. 215-60-50. Monday to Saturday 10 a.m.–2 p.m.
and 4.30–8 p.m.*
A large establishment full to the brim with designer goods, from lighting to beds to toys for all ages. Prices range from being a little over-the-
top, to positively ridiculous. Treat it as an exhibition of style.

GOURMET SHOPS

In a city known throughout Spain for its magnificent cuisine, it's no wonder that Barcelona is chock-a-block with excellent delicatessens, groceries, patisseries and gourmet shops. Instead of buying a gaudy souvenir, why not buy a Catalan delicacy for your friends and family to enjoy?

AIRO   **12** H10   🚌 Mandri
Mandri 29–31; tel. 417-64-73. Monday to Saturday 9 a.m.–2.30 p.m. and 5–9 p.m., Sunday 9 a.m.–9 p.m.
A well-established shop, renowned for its confectionery, pastries and meat.

ALIWORD   **13** J8   🚌 Via Augusta   *Main line train:* Pl. Molina
Via Augusta 90; tel. 238-14-39. Weekdays 10 a.m.–1.30 p.m. and 5–8 p.m.
A fascinating collection of fine wines and spirits, as well as an assortment of coffees.

91

L'ANEC   **12** F10   🚌 Major de Sarrià
Main line train: Reina Elisenda
Major de Sarrià 72; tel. 205-49-59. Daily 10 a.m.–midnight.
Spanish and imported *charcuterie*, at a price, to eat in or take away.

AUGUSTA   **21** J7   Ⓜ Diagonal   🚌 Av. Diagonal
Via Augusta 8; tel. 237-65-18. Weekdays 9.30 a.m.–2 p.m. and 4.30–8 p.m.
Wines and spirits are the order of the day at Augusta. There's an especially good selection of champagne and cava.

BAIXAS   **12** H8   🚌 Muntaner   *Main line train:* Muntaner
Muntaner 331; tel. 209-25-42. Monday to Saturday 8 a.m.–2.30 p.m. and 4.30–8.30 p.m., Sunday 8 a.m.–3 p.m.
Pastries of superior quality, as well as sweets and a large *charcuterie* section. A catering service is provided and there's a café on site so that you can sample the fare.

LA BARCELONINA DE VINS I ESPIRITS   **21/22** K6

Ⓜ Pg. de Gràcia
🚏 València

València 304; tel. 215-70-83. Daily 7 p.m.–2 a.m.
Wines and reams of specialist literature to accompany them. Experts are on hand to offer advice.

BOPAN   **12** H10

🚏 Muntaner

Muntaner 532; tel. 211-45-41. Monday to Saturday 7.30 a.m.–9 p.m., Sunday 9 a.m.–3 p.m. and 5–9 p.m. Also at Rbla. Catalunya 119.
A range of bread and pastries are sold in the two branches of Bopan, together with delectable chocolates. Definitely a place to avoid if you're on a diet.

BRUSI. TIN I MONTSE   **13** J8/9

🚏 Balmes
Main line train: Sant Gervasi

St. Elies 11–19; tel. 209-77-49. Tuesday to Saturday 10 a.m.–3 p.m. and 5.30–9 p.m., Sunday 10 a.m.–3 p.m.
Charcuterie and prepared meat dishes are the strengths of this high-quality establishment.

92

CAMARASA   **12** H10

🚏 Gral Mitre

Torras i Pujalt 48–50; tel. 211-23-42. Monday to Saturday 8 a.m.–2.30 p.m. and 5–8.30 p.m.
Exotic fruits, conserves, oils and aromatic herbs.

CASA DEL BACALAO   **21** J4

Ⓜ Urquinaona 🚏 Via Laietana

Comtal 8; tel. 301-65-39. Weekdays 9.30 a.m.–2 p.m. and 5–8 p.m., Saturday 9.30 a.m.–1.30 p.m.
Imported cod—the "bacalao" in the name—appears in all sorts of guises.

CASA PEPE   **13** J9

🚏 Balmes
Main line train: Putxet

Balmes 337; tel. 417-11-76. Tuesday to Saturday 10 a.m.–3 p.m. and 6–10 p.m., Sunday 10 a.m.–3 p.m.
Jabugo hams, cheese, *charcuterie* and shellfish from Galicia.

CASALS   **29** K3

Ⓜ Jaume I 🚏 Via Laietana

Sta. Maria 6; tel. 319-91-87. Monday to Thursday 7.30 a.m.–4 p.m., Friday and Saturday 7.30 a.m.–5 p.m.
Specialists in fresh fruit and vegetables.

CELLER
DE GELIDA   **11** E7   Ⓜ Pl. del Centre   🚌 Pl. del Centre
Vallespir 65; tel. 339-26-41. Monday to Saturday 9 a.m.–2.30 p.m. and 5–9 p.m.
Wines and spirits of the highest quality are offered in this emporium dedicated to the grape. Friendly advice from a real expert is also supplied.

CHARCUTERÍA   🚌 Balmes
MOLINA   **13** J8   Main line train: Sant Gervasi
Pl. Molina 1; tel. 200-57-69. Tuesday to Saturday 8 a.m.–9 p.m., Sunday 8 a.m.–2 p.m.
Cheeses, *charcuterie* and prepared dishes are the forte of this establishment. Wash down the food at Molina's own bar.

COLMADO MURRIÁ   **21/22** K6   Ⓜ Pg. de Gràcia   🚌 Llúria
Roger de Llúria 85; tel. 215-57-89. Monday to Saturday 9 a.m.–2 p.m. and 5–9 p.m.
This old-established shop is stocked with quality foods such as cheese, pastries and chocolates. Look for the antique advertisements in the shop window.

CONFIT   **12** G8   🚌 Av. Diagonal   Main line train: Bonanova **93**
Ganduxer 44; tel. 201-17-00. Tuesday to Saturday 9.30 a.m.–2.30 p.m. and 5–9 p.m., Sunday 9.30 a.m.–2.30 p.m.
Purveyors of prepared provisions.

CROISSANT   **21** J6   Ⓜ Pg. de Gràcia   🚌 Rbla. Catalunya
Rbla. Catalunya 65; tel. 215-68-10. Monday to Saturday 9 a.m.–11 p.m.
As you might expect, croissants, plain or packed with all kinds of delicious fillings, are the speciality here, along with a range of salads and sandwiches.

DA GIORGIO   **12** G8   🚌 Av. Sarrià
Av. Sarrià 67; tel. 322-86-59. Weekdays 9 a.m.–2 p.m. and 5–8 p.m., Saturday 9 a.m.–2 p.m.
Some 25 types of fresh pasta are sold in a variety of delicious sauces.

DESII   **12** H9/10   🚌 Muntaner
Muntaner 515; tel. 211-48-64. Monday to Saturday 9 a.m.–2 p.m. and 5–8 p.m., Sunday 9 a.m.–2 p.m.
Pasta, ice cream and other Italian produce.

DRUGSTORE DAVID   **13** J7   🚌 Av. Diagonal
Tuset 19–21; tel. 209-69-75. Daily 9 a.m.–3 a.m.
Late shopping for *charcuterie*, gifts, books, records, perfume and the like.

ESCRIBÁ PASTISSERIES   **20** H5   Ⓜ Urgell   🚌 Gran Via
Gran Via de les Corts Catalanes 546, tel. 454-75-35. Tuesday to Saturday 9 a.m. –2.30 p.m. and 5–8.30 p.m., Sunday 9 a.m.–3 p.m. and 5–8.30 p.m. Also at Rbla. Sant Josep 83, tel. 301-60-27.
Cakes, pastries and ice creams are served alongside prepared dishes in this shop with a lovely modernist frontage.

LA FARGA   **21** J7   Ⓜ Diagonal   🚌 Av. Diagonal
Av. Diagonal 391; tel. 416-02-25. Monday to Saturday 9 a.m.–midnight, Sunday 9 a.m.–3.30 p.m.
Home-made pastries, ice creams and prepared foods are what draw the customers to this establishment. Farga also features a swish tea room and restaurant.

94

FLECA BALMES   **21** J7   Ⓜ Diagonal   🚌 Balmes
Balmes 156; tel. 218-07-10. Weekdays 7 a.m.–3.30 p.m. and 5–8.30 p.m., Saturday 7 a.m.–3 p.m.
Freshly-baked and imported bread of all shapes and sizes.

FORN   🚌 Gral. Mitre
DE PA BARRIL   **13** J9   *Main line train: Putxet*
Bertrán 4; tel. 211-55-72. Monday to Saturday 7 a.m.–2 p.m.
Worth visiting just to take in the delicious aroma of bread being baked in a wood-burning stove.

FOIX   🚌 Major de Sarrià
DE SARRIÀ   **12** F10   *Main line train: Reina Elisenda*
Pl. de Sarrià 9; tel. 203-04-73. Daily 8 a.m.–9 p.m.
Pastries, sweets and cakes all beautifully crafted in traditional ways to match the original modernist design dating from 1886.

GODIVA   **21** J7   🚇 Balmes *Main line train:* Provença
Balmes 147; tel. 237-40-59. Monday to Saturday 10 a.m.–8 p.m., Sunday 10 a.m.–2 p.m.
The Barcelona branch of this famous Belgian chocolate maker is currently winning over the Catalans.

EL GRAN   Ⓜ Pg. de Gràcia
COLMADO   **21** J6   🚇 Pg. de Gràcia
Consell de Cent 318; tel. 302-26-26. Monday to Saturday 10 a.m.– 12.30 a.m.
An up-market, almost designer grocer's that sells imported produce as well as a wide variety of fresh cheeses, seafood and meats. Its restaurant attracts the smart set, who can afford the high prices. A catering service is also provided.

HERBORISTERÍA GUARRO   **21** J4   Ⓜ Catalunya 🚇 Rambla
Xuclà 23; tel. 301-14-44. Weekdays 9 a.m.–2 p.m. and 4–8 p.m., Saturday 9 a.m.–2 p.m.
Herbs and spices of all kinds, including medicinal preparations.

HORNO DE MONTSERRAT   **13/14** K9   Ⓜ Lesseps 🚇 Bolívar
Av. República Argentina 28; tel. 212-11-74. Monday to Saturday 7 a.m.–2.30 p.m. and 4–8 p.m., Sunday 8 a.m.–3 p.m. and 6–9 p.m.
Charcuterie, pastries and bread.

LA FUENTE   **12** G/H8   🚇 Pl. Francesc Macià
Pl. Francesc Macià 5, tel. 209-99-75. Weekdays 9 a.m.–2 p.m. and 5–8.30 p.m., Saturday 9 a.m.–2 p.m. Also at Johann Sebastian Bach 20, tel. 201-15-13.
Both branches of this long-established shop are good for groceries and dairy products, as well as for a large variety of wines and spirits.

HELADOS ITALIANOS   **29** J4   Ⓜ Liceu 🚇 Rambla
La Rambla 78. Daily 9 a.m.–3 a.m.
Ice cream from Italy is sold into the night here, even though the Spanish are the lowest consumers of ice cream in Europe, behind Norway.

LASIERRA　　**20** H6　　　　　　　ⓂDiagonal　🚊 Muntaner
Rosselló 160; tel. 453-35-75. Weekdays 9.15 a.m.–2.15 p.m. and 5.30–8.30 p.m., Saturday 9.15 a.m.–2.15 p.m. and 5.30–8 p.m.
Produce from Asturias, including regional dishes based on beans and sausage.

EL MAGNÍFICO　　**29** K3　　　　ⓂJaume I　🚊 Via Laietana
Argentería 64; tel. 319-60-81. Weekdays 9.30 a.m.–1.30 p.m. and 4.30–7.30 p.m., Saturday 9 a.m.–1.30 p.m.
A wide selection of tea and coffee from around the world.

MAURI　　**21** J6　　　🚊 Rbla. Catalunya　*Main line train:* Provença
Rbla. Catalunya 102; tel. 487-29-32. Monday to Saturday 9 a.m.–9 p.m., Sunday 9 a.m.–2 p.m.
Business people have breakfast and afternoon tea at Mauri and then try to do some work—a difficult feat! Cakes and other delicacies are what lure them in.

PLANELLS DONAT　　**21** J4　　　ⓂCatalunya　🚊 Pl. Catalunya
Av. Porta de l'Angel 25; tel. 317-34-39. Daily 10 a.m.–9 p.m.
Ice cream and "turrón"—nougat—make this a haven for the sweet-toothed.

96

QUÍLEZ　　**21** J6　　　ⓂPg. de Gràcia　🚊 Rbla. Catalunya
Rbla. Catalunya 63; tel. 215-23-56. Weekdays 9 a.m.–2 p.m. and 4.30–8.30 p.m., Saturday 9 a.m.–2 p.m.
An established grocer's with plenty of canned and bottled goods, from Spain and abroad. The wine cellar is well chosen and the service is old-style.

RICHART　　**12** H9　　　　　　　　🚊 Muntaner
Muntaner 463; tel. 202-02-40. Monday to Saturday 9.30 a.m.–2 p.m. and 4–8.30 p.m.
The chocolates and other calorie bombs sold here are enticingly presented. Even if they were intended as a gift, you find yourself having a nibble.

SEMON　　**12** G8　　🚊 Pl. Francesc Macià　*Main line train:* Bonanova
Ganduxer 31; tel. 201-83-66. Monday to Saturday 10 a.m.–2 p.m. and 5–9 p.m., Sunday 10 a.m.–2.30 p.m.

Salmon, foie gras and caviar are the specialities here, in addition to other prepared foods. At a price, you can try some of the excellent dishes in the dining room.

SITJAR   **12** H8   🚇 Muntaner *Main line train:* Muntaner
Muntaner 330; tel. 209-71-10. Weekdays 8 a.m.–2 p.m. and 5–8.30 p.m., Saturday 8 a.m.–2 p.m.
Fresh fruit and vegetables, including some unusual and exotic varieties.

EL TASTOFIL   **20** H5   Ⓜ Urgell 🚇 Villaroel
Villaroel 47; tel. 323-66-25. Weekdays 9 a.m.–2 p.m. and 4.30–8 p.m., Saturday 9 a.m.–1.30 p.m.
With vinegars galore and numerous piquant sauces, El Tastofil adds a touch of spice to the city.

TIENDA REDON   **21** J6   🚇 Balmes *Main line train:* Provença
Rosselló 219; tel. 218-27-29. Weekdays 8 a.m.–2.30 p.m. and 5–8 p.m., Saturday 8 a.m.–2.30 p.m.
A general delicatessen and grocer's with some unusual meat preparations.

97

TÍVOLI   **12** H8   🚇 Muntaner *Main line train:* Muntaner
Muntaner 361, tel. 209-19-78. Tuesday to Saturday 8 a.m.–9 p.m., Sunday 8 a.m.–3 p.m. Also at Caspe 12, tel. 317-86-94. Monday to Saturday 10 a.m.–2 p.m. and 5–8 p.m.
Cheeses and prepared foods are the things to go for at Tívoli, if not a drink at the bar. Exotic fruits are the speciality of the Caspe branch.

VILAPLANA   **12** G8   🚇 Pl. Francesc Macià
Pl. Sant Gregori Taumaturg 4; tel. 201-56-66. Monday to Saturday 10 a.m.–2 p.m. and 5–9 p.m., Sunday 9 a.m.–3 p.m.
Purveyors of cakes, often very rich and elaborate, and prepared foods, together with cheese and selected meats.

MARKETS

Food Markets

ABACERÍA CENTRAL   **13/14** K7   Ⓜ Fontana   🚊 Gran de Gràcia
Travessera de Gràcia 186; tel. 213-62-86. Monday to Saturday 8 a.m.–2 p.m.
The main market for the district of Gràcia, with a large selection of food stalls. The very good reputation that many of the businesses have locally means that the market is nearly always bustling.

CONCEPCIO   **21/22** K6   Ⓜ Pg. de Gràcia   🚊 València
Aragó 317; tel. 257-09-95. Monday to Saturday 8 a.m.–2 p.m.
A beautifully designed market in the middle of the business district near Passeig de Gràcia. It features a variety of businesses selling food, flowers and plants, and the shops in the area sell quality goods at prices well below those in the posh shopping district nearby.

GALVANY   **12** H8   🚊 Santaló   *Main line train:* Muntaner
Madrazo 106–112; tel. 202-07-24. Monday to Saturday 8 a.m.–2 p.m.
A relatively small market, and quite expensive to reflect the classy district where it is situated. A big advantage, however, is the underground car park, vital in this busy *barrio*.

MERCAT DE LA BOQUERIA   **29** J4   Ⓜ Liceu   🚊 Rambla
La Rambla 91; tel. 319-24-71. Monday to Saturday 8 a.m.–8 p.m.
It's an experience just to walk around this famous market, just off the Rambla, and look at the variety of very fresh food—meat, fish, fruit and vegetables—on show, and listen to the market noises before having a meal nearby. Hold on tight to your bag or wallet.

PORVENIR (NINOT)   **20** H6   Ⓜ Hospital Clínic   🚊 Mallorca
Mallorca 133–157; tel. 253-65-12. Monday to Saturday 8 a.m.–2 p.m.
This large and well-known market, in the Eixample district, is renowned for its high-quality produce.

SANT ANTONI   **20** G/H4   🚌 Ronda Sant Antoni
Comte d'Urgell 1; tel. 423-42-87. Monday, Wednesday, Friday and Saturday 8 a.m.–8 p.m.
The fine food market here has been operating for over a century. Bigger than the Boqueria market nearby, this interesting building also features a fair sprinkling of stalls selling non-comestibles, like good second-hand and cheap new clothes. On Sundays there are other attractions (see Fleamarkets, below).

Flea Markets

ELS   Ⓜ Glòries
ENCANTS 23 N6/7   🚌 Gran Via de les Corts Catalanes
Av. Dos de Maig; tel. 246-30-30. Monday, Wednesday, Friday and Saturday 8 a.m.–7 p.m.
The biggest and best-known flea market in the city. Occasionally real finds can be made in the antiques section.

ELS ENCANTS   🚌 Ronda Sant Antoni
DE SANT ANTONI   **20** G/H4
Comte d'Urgell 1; tel. 423-42-87. Sunday.
The area around this traditional food market changes on Sundays into a magnet for collectors of second-hand books, magazines, newspapers, photographs, stamps and other printed works.

Other Markets

ESPOSICIÓ DE PINTORS   Ⓜ Sagrada Familia
DE LA SAGRADA FAMÍLIA   **22** M6   🚌 Padilla
Pl. Sagrada Família; tel. 231-73-85. Saturday, Sunday and public holidays 10 a.m.–3 p.m.
In the square around Gaudí's famous cathedral, this market sells art produced by local painters. The cathedral features strongly in the work.

FERIA DE L'ARTESANAT   **12** G/H8   🚌 Pl. Francesc Macià
Av. Pau Casals; tel. 200-61-47. First Sunday of every month 10 a.m.–
3 p.m. Closed August and September.
The place to see all kinds of individually made ceramics, glassware, met-
alwork, textiles and the like.

MERCAT DE NUMISMÀTICA   Ⓜ Liceu
I FILATELIA   **29** J3   🚌 Rambla
Pl. Reial; tel. 318-93-12. Sunday 9.30 a.m.–2.30 p.m.
Every Sunday, the coin and stamp dealers take over this famous old
square from its more regular and less interesting inhabitants to show off
a bewildering assortment of goods.

FLORISTS

100

There is a relative paucity of florists in Barcelona, and apart from the three
shops listed below, easily the best place to buy cut flowers is in one of
the many establishments on the Rambla de los Flors—actually the
Rambla de Sant Josep. The main flower market is on Calle Lleida, at the
foot of Montjuïc.

FLORES PRATS   **12** H7   Ⓜ Diagonal   🚌 Av. Diagonal
Av. Diagonal 572; tel. 200-07-41. Monday to Saturday 8 a.m.–2 p.m. and
4–8 p.m.

FORTUÑO   **21/22** K6   Ⓜ Diagonal   🚌 Roger de Llúria
Roger de Llúria 131; tel. 215-53-45. Weekdays 9 a.m.–2 p.m. and 4.30–
8 p.m., Saturday 9 a.m.–2 p.m.

VOS   🚌 Balmes
FLEURS   **13** J8   *Main line train:* Gràcia
Balmes 239; tel. 217-62-90. Weekdays 7.30 a.m.–2 p.m. and 4.30–
8.30 p.m., Saturday 7.30 a.m.–2 p.m.

GIFTS

ARPI   **29** J3   Ⓜ Liceu   🚌 Rambla
La Rambla 40; tel. 301-74-04. Monday to Saturday 9.30 a.m.–1.30 p.m. and 4.30–8 p.m.
Cameras, together with every imaginable bit of photographic material, are sold here at reasonable prices.

ASWANI PARSRAM   **29** K3   Ⓜ Liceu   🚌 Rambla
Princesa 12; tel. 319-99-53. Monday to Saturday 9.30 a.m.–1.30 p.m. and 5–8 p.m.
The world of the Orient, and especially India, is packed into this small shop—great for old hippies and others in search of unusual and often cheap gifts.

ATLAS   **21** J6   Ⓜ Pg. de Gràcia   🚌 València
València 248; tel. 215-85-21. Monday to Saturday 10.30 a.m.–2 p.m. and 4.30–8.30 p.m.
A shop for lovers of quality objects and gifts, filled to the brim with designer toys and other things to give yourself or someone else. A good selection of nostalgia gifts.

101

BEVERLY HILLS   **13** J8/9   🚌 Balmes
Main line train: Pl. Molina
Balmes 301–303; tel. 209-01-33. Weekdays 8.30 a.m.–1 p.m. and 2.30–6 p.m., Saturday 10 a.m.–2 p.m. and 4–8 p.m.
Accessories for car owners: everything from key rings to car phones.

BOSSA ART   **22** L/M7   Ⓜ Sagrada Familia
Còrsega 504; tel. 258-13-41. Weekdays 10 a.m.–2 p.m. and 4.30–8.30 p.m., Saturday 10 a.m.–2 p.m. and 5–8.30 p.m.
This is where the well-heeled go for presents and presentation gifts. There is an enormous variety of packages and packaging to wrap these treasures up in.

BOTET   **22** M5   🚌 Diputació
Diputació 433; tel. 232-64-04. Weekdays 9.30 a.m.–2 p.m. and 5–8 p.m., Saturday 9.30 a.m.–2 p.m.
An assortment of reasonably priced gifts, from pyjamas to hankies and paste jewellery.

LA CANILLA   **12** H8   🚊 Muntaner *Main line train:* Muntaner
*Muntaner 335; tel. 200-17-46. Weekdays 10 a.m.–1.30 p.m. and 4.30–
8 p.m.*
As well as selling household, bathroom and kitchen linen, and slippers,
T-shirts and blouses, staff at this shop will print just about any design
on to their goods, using a computer.

D. BARCELONA   **21/22** K6   Ⓜ Diagonal 🚊 Av. Diagonal
*Av. Diagonal 367; tel. 216-03-46. Weekdays 10.30 a.m.–2 p.m. and
4.30–9 p.m., Saturday 11 a.m.–2 p.m. and 4.30–9 p.m.*
In addition to housing a reasonable and quite popular art gallery, the
shop displays a variety of unusual gifts, many of which are reproductions of post-war household objects.

DON   **12** J7   🚊 Av. Diagonal
*Moià 20; tel. 200-27-36. Weekdays 9.30 a.m.–1.30 p.m. and 4.30–
8.30 p.m.*
A combination of tasteful designer gifts and articles for the home is sold
here. Many pieces are made from wood—from small furniture to execu-
tive toys— and there's also leather goods, attractive jewellery and small
sculptures.

102

DOS I UNA   **21** J/K7   Ⓜ Diagonal 🚊 Av. Diagonal
*Rosselló 275; tel. 217-70-32. Weekdays 10 a.m.–2 p.m. and 4.30–8 p.m.,
Saturday 10 a.m.–2 p.m. and 5–8 p.m.*
The place to go for unusual and arty design gifts, especially for
Barcelona-produced or inspired *objets* (some of which are highly
bizarre). The design of the shop, glaring pink and yellow with a metal
floor, sets the scene.

EXCLUSIVE   **21** J6   Ⓜ Pg. de Gràcia 🚊 Pg. de Gràcia
*Bulevard Rosa, Pg. de Gràcia 55; tel. 487-29-80. Monday to Saturday
10 a.m.–8.30 p.m.*
Pens and other writing implements are sold at Exclusive, some of them
at highly exclusive prices.

"GIMENO"   **21** J6   Ⓜ Diagonal 🚊 Pg. de Gràcia
*Pg. de Gràcia 101; tel. 237-20-78. Tuesday to Saturday 10 a.m.–
1.30 p.m. and 4.15–8 p.m., Monday 4.15–8 p.m.*

A refuge for the smoking minority. Stock includes a beautiful collection of pipes and a large number of lighters, from the most basic to the most expensive.

GRÀFIQUES EL TINELL   **29** K4   Ⓜ Jaume I   🚌 Via Laietana
Freneria 1; tel. 315-07-58. Weekdays 9.30 a.m.–1.30 p.m. and 3.30–7.30 p.m.
An old-style printer's shop, turning out a variety of stationery, visiting cards and the like, as well as reprints of old designs.

HOBBY ART   **12** H10   🚌 Gral. Mitre
Muntaner 516; tel. 418-06-93. Monday to Saturday 11 a.m.–2 p.m. and 4.30–9 p.m.
A shop dedicated to people with pastimes—games, puzzles, models, and comic books are all packed into a small space.

L'IMPRENTA DEL CARRER PARIS   **20** H7   🚌 Av. Diagonal
Paris 175; tel. 200-75-90. Monday to Saturday 10 a.m.–1.30 p.m. and 5–8.30 p.m.
An emporium of gifts, from the slightly tacky (though expensive) to the exquisitely tasteful.

103

INICIAL G   **13** J10   🚌 Balmes   *Main line train: Av. Tibidabo*
Balmes 458; tel. 418-56-18. Monday to Saturday 10 a.m.–2 p.m. and 4.30–8 p.m.
A large and well-stocked gift shop with hundreds of objects you might or might not need, at a spectrum of prices.

INSÒLIT   **21/22** K6   Ⓜ Verdaguer   🚌 Av. Diagonal
Av. Diagonal 353; tel. 207-49-19. Weekdays 10 a.m.–2 p.m. and 4.30–8 p.m., Saturday 11 a.m.–2 p.m. and 5–8 p.m.
As well as unusual furniture (see Shopping: Design), this very different shop features gadgets and household goods which border on the weird. Well worth a visit.

JOCS & GAMES   **20** H7   🚌 Av. Diagonal
Muntaner 193; tel. 322-09-53. Weekdays 10 a.m.–2 p.m. and 4.30–8 p.m., Saturday 10 a.m.–2 p.m. and 5–8 p.m.
An extensive collection of toys and games, many beautifully designed, plus other gifts for children and adults.

KONEMA   **21** J5   Ⓜ Pg. de Gràcia   🚎 Rbla. Catalunya
Consell de Cent 296; tel. 317-69-44. Monday to Saturday 9 a.m.–1.30 p.m. and 4.30–8 p.m.
The place to go if you are looking for practical gifts—things for the home, the kitchen, bathroom, etc. A few unusual ideas are thrown in.

PEPA PAPER   **20** H7   🚎 Av. Diagonal
Muntaner 183; tel. 419-20-82. Weekdays 10 a.m.–1.30 p.m. and 4.30–8 p.m., Saturday 10 a.m.–1.30 p.m.
An establishment devoted to all kinds of paper products, from decks of cards, through writing paper, to a vast number of paper-covered boxes.

PINUS   **12** H8   🚎 Santaló
Amigó 49; tel. 414-03-85. Weekdays 10 a.m.–2 p.m. and 4.30–8 p.m., Saturday 10 a.m.–2 p.m.
Pinus is for people who want a change from modern design. Ornaments and objects for everyday use make up the stock.

104 **SPEEDY PACHECO**   **21** J5   Ⓜ Universitat   🚎 Pl. Universitat
Ronda Universitat 3; tel. 302-12-48. Weekdays 9.45 a.m.–1.30 p.m. and 4.30–8 p.m., Saturday 9.45 a.m.–1.45 p.m. and 5–8 p.m.
A leader among hobby and toy shops, with a big selection of models, static and working, of cars, ships and planes, as well as the almost inevitable computer and electronic games.

TINTIN   **21/22** L4   Ⓜ Arc de Triomf   🚎 Pg. de Sant Joan
Pg. de Sant Joan 7; tel. 265-78-17. Monday to Saturday 10.30 a.m.–2 p.m. and 5–8.30 p.m.
The Barcelona outpost of the famous cartoon reporter, with not only his exploits recorded in various languages, including English, but also a selection of other promotional merchandise.

TOCS   **13** J5/6   Ⓜ Pg. de Gràcia   🚎 Pg. de Gràcia
Consell de Cent 341; tel. 215-31-21. Tuesday to Saturday 10 a.m.–9 p.m., Monday 4–9 p.m.
As well as being a large bookshop, this establishment stocks a range of gifts, electronic goods, photographic material and paper goods.

VIDOSA   **13** J9   🚃 Balme *Main line train:* Padua
Balmes 339–343; tel. 212-16-00. Tuesday to Saturday 10 a.m.–1.30 p.m.
and 4–8 p.m., Monday 4–8 p.m.
Household appliances, from coffee machines, through hi-fi and televisions, to fridges, are on show and on sale in this well-established shop.

VINÇON   **21** K6   Ⓜ Pg. de Gràcia   🚃 Pg. de Gràcia
Pg. de Gràcia 96; tel. 215-60-540. Monday to Saturday 10 a.m.–2 p.m.
and 4.30–8 p.m.
After admiring the designer furniture and lighting in this emporium of past and present fashion, and deciding it is very expensive, pore over the design gifts, including gadgets for household and office. Opt for something you haven't seen cheaper elsewhere.

ZABRISKIE   **20** H6   🚃 Mallorca *Main line train:* Provença
Mallorca 198; tel. 323-12-47.
Nostalgia-type gifts with many reproductions of useful objects from earlier years, such as wirelesses or lighters.

105

Barcelona welcomes hundreds of thousands of visitors every year, ranging from tourists wanting to eat cheaply, to opulent business people wanting deluxe quality. The city's restaurants manage to cater for all.

Be warned, though, that in almost all restaurants (both basic and top-priced) you're likely to be sped through the courses of your meal as rapidly as possible. The reasons behind this are varied, and nothing to do with the quality of the food or the attitude to the customer. It is assumed that, if you want to have an enjoyable and lengthy discussion, you will have it after the food has been eaten. You won't usually be pressured to leave your table, but the food part of the meal is likely to be over quickly.

If you are not in a hurry, and would prefer to finish one course before the next arrives, just ask when you order for a *pausa*, pronounced "powsa", between courses.

Menus are almost invariably produced in Spanish, as well as Catalan, and are often written in other languages too, so there should be few problems in ordering. It is worth asking for explanations of the dishes from the waiters, as most staff are amenable.

Catalan cuisine is different from that of the rest of Spain in that many dishes have been adapted from the recipes of the South of France. Meat and fish dishes are usually served with a sauce of some kind, and sometimes meat and fish are combined in a single course (see box on Catalan cuisine). As in other parts of Spain, it is rare to find a main course accompanied by vegetables of any kind—except perhaps potatoes of some description, and a fried green pepper—so it is worth asking for a salad.

107

Basic dishes, like steak, pork chops or chicken, are available in most bars and small restaurants, as is a variety of basic tapas, or snacks, and sandwiches. This is the cheapest way of eating out.

Barcelona lacks enough mid-price restaurants for a city of its size and reputation, so it is worth considering a snack lunch and a more expensive, but better quality dinner (or vice-versa) in one of the establishments listed below.

We have provided you with the approximate cost of a three-course meal and, where necessary, a sample from the à la carte menu. For most restaurants it is recommended that you reserve in advance, as eating out is one of the most popular pastimes in Barcelona—as you will discover for yourself.

A gastronomic adventure awaits the visitor to Barcelona.

Catalan cuisine

Catalan cuisine is as different from other types of cooking in Spain as Catalunya is from the rest of the country. Its roots owe much to history and geography. History reveals that parts of France and Italy were once under Catalan control, so the cooking of these two culinary giants has had a major influence; geography explains the country's position as a Mediterranean state, bordered by mountains to the north and the sea to the east. The result is a rich—sometimes too rich—mixture of styles, ingredients and presentation that, once again, mark Catalunya out as a country with a distinctive identity.

Spicy, but creamy sauces dominate Catalan cuisine: bad news for anyone on a diet. However, virtually all cooking is done using olive oil, which is healthier than most other fats. Otherwise, various combinations of olive oil, tomatoes, garlic, onions and nuts of several kinds form the bases of many Catalan dishes. As in the rest of Spain, butter and other dairy products are rarely found on tables in houses or restaurants. As an alternative to buttered bread, *pa amb tomaquet*—crispy, sometimes toasted bread, scraped with garlic, rubbed with tomato, soaked with olive oil and salted—is the usual staple to be consumed alongside a meal. It is particularly delicious with a good salted ham as a starter or tapa.

In general terms, meat—especially lamb—is served with alliolli, olive oil with crushed garlic, or samfaina, onion, tomato, courgette and aubergine fried in olive oil. Fish and meat dishes (unless ordered grilled—*parillada* in Spanish) are likely to come with a variety of sauces, some of which tend to mask the taste. This was probably the intention when quality was less consistent than today.

In spite of the city's Mediterranean location, the fish on offer in Barcelona is not as good as it ought to be. The best is brought in from other parts of the country, or from further afield. While meat is now usually reasonable, the quality is inconsistent. The solomillo (sirloin) is the best of the beef cuts, and it is often extremely good; but the lamb is generally of only acceptable quality. Try rabbit, of which Catalans are the largest consumers in the whole of Spain. And have a try of any dish described as *terra i mar*, which is a combination of fish and fowl, usually chicken and giant prawn, in a thick, creamy brown sauce.

Remember, it is very rare to be offered accompanying vegetables, apart from potatoes and fried green pepper or tomato, so ask for a green salad. Beans, lentils and other pulses are very popular in Catalunya, but are usually served as a first course. Finally, for dessert, you must not fail to sample a *crema catalana*, an eggy, sweet vanilla dish with glazed sugar on top—then visit the nearest dentist.

108

EXTRAVAGANT

The following dozen restaurants are among the best the city has to offer, but at a price that is justified only if you want a really slap-up meal in special circumstances. As well as being served superior food, you will be paying for amenities such as valet car parking, air conditioning and the most attentive service. In all cases, booking ahead, especially during the summer months, is necessary.

AZULETE   **12** G9   🚌 Via Augusta *Main line train:* Tres Torres
Via Augusta 281; tel. 203-59-43. Lunch 1.30–3.30 p.m., dinner 9–11.30 p.m. Closed Sunday, lunch on Saturday, public holidays, 1–15 August, 22 December to 7 January and Easter. Price: 7.000.-pts., sampling menu 6.800.-pts.
Definitely one of the "in" restaurants of the city, Azulete's mix of different cuisines results in a balanced menu offering some very original dishes. The main dining room, within a conservatory, is of course air conditioned during the hotter months. If you don't want to pay the price for a meal, you can watch the beautiful people from the cocktail bar attached to the restaurant.
A la carte: merluza a humada con té chino (hake smoked with Chinese tea), lasagna de crema de almejas (clam lasagna).

BOTAFUMEIRO   **13** J8   Ⓜ Fontana   🚌 Gran de Gràcia   **109**
Main line train: Gràcia
Gran de Gràcia 81; tel. 218-42-30. Service 1 p.m.–1 a.m. Closed Sunday evening, Monday, Holy Week and all of August. Price: 8.000.-pts., sampling menu 7.500.-pts.
The accent in this restaurant is on fish and shellfish dishes from Galicia, perfectly prepared and presented. It is reputedly the best of its type in Barcelona. As soon as you enter, the collection of fresh ingredients destined for the kitchen is there on show. Rumours of an accordionist passing between the tables are surely exaggerated.
A la carte: lubina a la cidra (haddock cooked with cider), assortment of seafood.

CASA ISIDRO   **28** H3/4   Ⓜ Paral.lel   🚌 Av. Paral.lel
Las Flores 12; tel. 241-11-39. Lunch 1.30–4 p.m., dinner 9–11 p.m. Closed Sunday, public holidays, Holy Week, one week during Christmas, 20 July to 20 August, 1 May to 15 June, Saturday evening and Saturdays from 15 June to 15 September. Price: 6.000.-pts., set menu 2.500.-pts.

A very well-established restaurant that is slightly cheaper than others in this category. It is especially popular at night, when a range of customers, including showbiz people, flocks to its doors. The food here changes regularly according to what is in season, but there's an accent on Catalan cuisine of the finest kind.

A la carte: foie a la crema de lentejas (liver with lentils à la crème), sesos a la manteca negra (brains cooked in black butter).

LA DAMA   **20/21** J7   Ⓜ Diagonal   🚌 Av. Diagonal
Main line train: Provença
Av. Diagonal 423–425, entlo. 2; tel. 202-06-86. Lunch 1.30–4 p.m., dinner 9 p.m.–midnight. Price: 6.000.-pts., sampling menu 5.700.-pts.
Reasonably priced for a restaurant of this category, the menu boasts a variety of Catalan and French dishes. Apart from the food, a visit here will reveal a restaurant created from a former town house, very tastefully decorated and with private dining rooms converted from the original bedrooms.

A la carte: ensalada tibia de cigalas al vinagre de naranja (warm crayfish salad with orange vinegar), patata rellena con langostinos (potatoes stuffed with crayfish).

EL DORADO   🚌 Pg. Bonanova
PETIT   **4** G11   *Main line train: Reina Elisenda*
Dolors Monseida 51; tel. 204-51-53. Lunch 1.30–4 p.m., dinner 9 p.m.–midnight. Closed Sunday and from 8–27 August. Price: 5.500.-pts., sampling menu 4.000.-pts.
It's a treat to visit this restaurant, for all sorts of reasons, but especially because of the Catalan-inspired food. The building itself exudes opulence and, weather permitting, diners can eat out on the terrace or in the garden. Considered one of the best restaurants in the city. If you are spending any time on the Costa Brava, its sister in Sant Feliu stands out from the rest in the resort.

A la carte: Gigot de conejo a la miel con cebollitas (rabbit cooked in honey with spring onions), arroz con gambas de Palamós (rice with shrimps).

FINISTERRE   **12** H7   Ⓜ Hospital Clínic   🚌 Av. Diagonal
Av. Diagonal 469; tel. 439-55-76. Lunch 1–4 p.m., dinner 9–11 p.m. Price: 5.000.-pts.
A well-established restaurant , if pricey, with food that sometimes lacks sufficient imagination to make it really special. Nevertheless, it continues to attract a regular clientele throughout the week, who

sample well-prepared food from a long menu. Dishes are inspired by cuisine from around the world. And staff don't seem to rush you through.

JAUME DE PROVENZA   20 G6

Ⓜ Entença
🚍 Calabria

Provença 88; tel. 430-00-29. Lunch 1–4 p.m., dinner 9–11.30 p.m. Closed Sunday and evenings of public holidays, Monday and August. Price: 6.000.-pts., sampling menu 4.500.-pts., gourmet menu 5.500.-pts.

Reasonably priced for its class, the Catalan cuisine on offer here is among the best available in Barcelona, and the menu changes according to seasonal availability of the ingredients. The décor is modern, but unfortunately background music accompanies your conversation. A la carte: filete de anchoas (anchovy fillets).

NEICHEL   11 E9

Ⓜ Palau Reial   🚍 Palau Reial

Av. Pedralbes 16 bis; tel. 203-84-08. Lunch 1–3.15 p.m., dinner 9–11.15 p.m. Closed Sunday, public holidays, Holy Week, Christmas week and August. Price: 10.000.-pts., sampling menu 6.500.-pts., lunch menu 4.500.-pts.

One of the best restaurants, not just in Barcelona, but in the whole of Spain, and the prices are short of being ridiculously expensive. Apart from the mainly French-inspired menu, the long list of desserts, the selection of Spanish cheeses, and the choices of tea and coffee, the building itself has won design prizes, and the service is perfect.

111

A la carte: rollitos crujientes de cigalas con jugo de vinagre de Modena (crispy pastries stuffed with crayfish in vinegar), esqueixada de atún y bogavante con compota de escalibada (marinated tuna salad and large lobster with aromatic vegetable preserves).

OROTAVA   21 J5/6

Ⓜ Pg. de Gràcia   🚍 Pg. de Gràcia

Consell de Cent 335; tel. 302-31-28. Lunch 1–4 p.m., dinner 8 p.m.– midnight. Closed Sunday. Price: 5.000.-pts., sampling menu 7.500.-pts., "Relax" menu 5.000.-pts.

The décor at Orotava allows you to step back in time, though not in price (even if this restaurant is at the lower end of the extravagant), to the 1920s. The extensive menu makes use of seasonal ingredients, though dishes are sometimes lacking in imagination. Wildfowl such as pheasant and partridge are served during the game season. Otherwise this is everything you would expect of a top-class, classical, restaurant. A la carte: nidos de patata con caviar (potato "nests" with caviar), huevos fritos con caviar (fried eggs with caviar), an assortment of game.

QUO VADIS   **21** J4

Ⓜ Liceu 🚃 Rambla
Main line train: Catalunya

Carmen 7; tel. 317-74-47. Lunch 1.15–4 p.m., dinner 8.30–11.30 p.m. Open until the end of the performance when there is an opera in the Liceu. Price: 6.500.-pts.

The superior quality Catalan cuisine available in this restaurant, at reasonable prices considering its category, comes in large portions—not for Quo Vadis the niceties of nouvelle cuisine. The customer is treated to the best and freshest meat, fish and vegetables chosen from a bewildering menu. A very well-established eating place in Barcelona, for good reason.

À la carte: potpourri de setas durante todo el año (year-round potpourri of wild mushrooms), foie fresco con ciruelas (fresh liver with plums).

RENO   **13** J7

🚃 Balmes *Main line train:* Gràcia

Túset 25; tel. 200-91-29. Lunch 1–4 p.m., dinner 9–11 p.m. Closed Saturday in July, August and September. Price: 7.000.-pts., sampling menu 6.500.-pts.

The combination of French and Catalan cuisine works perfectly in this eating place for politicians and businessmen, where the lighting and atmosphere change according to whether you are there for lunch or dinner. An excellent dessert menu completes the picture, and you can eat relatively late in the evening for a restaurant of this category.

À la carte: filetes de lenguado Reno (house speciality with fillet of sole), costillar de cabrito asado a las finas hierbas (roasted kid ribs with fine herbs).

112

VIA VENETO   **12** G8

🚃 Pl. Francesc Macià
Main line train: Bonanova

Ganduxer 10–12; tel. 200-70-24. Lunch 1.15–4.30 p.m., dinner 8.45 p.m.–midnight. Closed Saturday lunch, Sunday and 1–20 August. Price: 6.000.-pts., sampling menu priced according to availability.

The tasteful, slightly austere and quiet décor does not deter the customer from concentrating on some of the best food (Catalan but in nouvelle cuisine style) available in the city. It has won several awards. An excellent meal should be complemented by one of the wide selection of fine wines available on the extensive list, and if you are still hungry after the delicately balanced portions, finish off with something from the dessert menu, an experience in itself.

À la carte: bogavante al vapor con ramillete de ensalada (steamed lobster with green salad), medallones de filetes de buey con tuétano al Oporto (small ox fillets with marrow cooked in port).

EXCELLENT ADDRESSES

Included in the following list are restaurants where the quality of the food, especially in relation to price, can be considered excellent.

LA BALSA   **5** H11   *Main line train:* Av. Tibidabo
Infanta Isabel 4; tel. 211-50-48. Lunch 1.45–3.30 p.m., dinner 9–11.30 p.m. Closed Sunday and Monday lunch. Price: 4.500–5.000.-pts.
Although not the cheapest in this category, this restaurant provides good value for money, serving a mixture of Catalan- and Basque-inspired dishes, and all in an elegantly designed interior complete with terrace and garden.

BAZTAN   **12** H/J9   Balmes   *Main line train:* Pl. Molina
Sant Elías 68; tel. 201-67-61. Lunch 1.30–3.30 p.m., dinner 8.30–11.30 p.m. Closed Saturday lunch, Sunday, August, Holy Week and Christmas. Advance reservation recommended. Price: 3.500.-pts.
Food from the Basque Country, or more precisely Navarra, is the speciality here. It is particularly good for fish and meat dishes.
A la carte: pimientos del piquillo con cigalas y rape (peppers with crayfish and angler fish), hojaldre de puerros y gambas (a light shrimp and leek pastry), merluza koskera (typical Basque dish with hake).

113

BEL AIR   **21** J7   Ⓜ Diagonal   Av. Diagonal
Córcega 286; tel. 237-75-88. Lunch 2 p.m., dinner 9 p.m.–midnight. Closed Sunday. Advance reservation recommended. Price: 5.000.-pts.
Situated in an airy and bright, tastefully decorated town house, this restaurant has a very pleasant ambience. It's popular with luminaries of the business world, who tuck into mainly Catalan dishes inside or in the garden.
A la carte: hamburguesitas de pato (duck hamburgers), selection of rice dishes, brandada fría de rape y escórpora (cold creamed fish).

CAN TRAVI NOU   7 N11
Antic Camí de Sant Cebriá s/n; tel. 428-03-01. Lunch 1.30–4 p.m., dinner 9–11.30 p.m. Closed Sunday evening. Advance reservation recommended. Price: 4.000.-pts.
Catalan through and through, from the typical style of the building (complete with terrace and garden), to the cuisine, which varies according to the season.
A la carte: conejo con cigalas (rabbit with crayfish), albóndigas con sepia (forcemeat balls with cuttlefish).

CHICOA   20 H6   Ⓜ Hospital Clínic   🚇 Villaroel
Aribau 73; tel. 253-11-23. Lunch 1.30–3.30 p.m., dinner 8.30–11.30 p.m. Closed Saturday evening, Sunday, public holidays and August. Advance reservation recommended. Price: 4.000.-pts.
Fish dishes, especially cod, are the speciality at this currently very popular restaurant. The dessert menu is also worthy of note.
A la carte: fresolets con anchoas (black-eyed peas with anchovies), solomilla a la crema de setas (sirloin with creamy mushroom sauce), surtido de bacalaos (assortment of codfish dishes).

LA COLOMA   21/22 K5   Ⓜ Pg. de Gràcia, Girona   🚇 Girona
Diputación 301; tel. 412-40-02. Lunch 1–4 p.m., dinner 8.30 p.m.–midnight. Closed Saturday lunch and Sunday. Advance reservation recommended. Price: 4.000–10.000.-pts., daily special, according to availability, 1.000–2.000.-pts.
The speciality here is shellfish and fish, though the selection of cold meats is also worth a mention. As well as a restaurant, the Coloma doubles as a *charcuterie*. Modern but pleasant in design, with dining on different levels of the restaurant.
A la carte: bogavante de Canadá (Canadian lobster), rodaballo a la manteca negra (flounder in black-butter sauce), navajas a la plancha (grilled razor clams).

CRISTAL PARK   20 H7   Ⓜ Diagonal   🚇 Balmes
Main line train: Provença
París 192; tel. 217-06-27. Lunch 1.30–4 p.m., dinner 8.30 p.m.–midnight. Closed Sunday and public holidays. Advance reservation recommended. Price: 4.000.-pts.
Relatively pricey, but worth it just for the ambience—there's a garden and fountain—and the excellent fish dishes, prepared Catalan-style.

A la carte: tarrina de gambas y bacalao (shrimp and codfish terrine), pescados a la sal (fish baked in salt), fideos a la cazuela con gambas (noodle casserole with shrimps).

EL PESCADOR   **21/22** K6   Ⓜ Girona   🚇 Mallorca
Mallorca 314; tel. 207-10-27. Lunch 1–4 p.m., dinner 8.30 p.m.–1 a.m. Closed Sunday. Advance reservation recommended. Price: 5.000.-pts.
An excellent fish restaurant with friendly service, where shellfish specialities are served in a separate part of the establishment.
A la carte: ostras (oysters), pescados a la sal (fish baked in salt), surtido de mariscos (selection of seafood).

GORRIA   **23** L/M5   Ⓜ Monumental
🚇 Gran Via de les Corts Catalanes
Diputación 421; tel. 245-11-64. Lunch 1.30–3.30 p.m., dinner 9–11.30 p.m. Closed Sunday, August, Holy Week. Advance reservation recommended. Price: 5.000.-pts.
Gorria is a little cheaper than most in this category, and has an accent on Basque cuisine. The meat dishes, cooked in a wood-burning stove, are the speciality.
A la carte: alcachofas con almejas (artichokes with clams), rape al txacoli (angler-fish cooked in txacoli, a Basque wine), canutillos de hojaldre y crema (light, tube-shaped pastries and cream).

115

PASSADÍS DEL PEP   **29** K3   Ⓜ Barceloneta   🚇 Pla del Palau
Pla del Palau 2; tel. 310-10-21. Lunch 1.30–3.30 p.m., dinner 9.15–11.30 p.m. Closed Sunday and Monday lunch, Holy Week, Christmas and August. Price: 8.000.-pts.
A rather expensive Catalan restaurant, with an accent on fish dishes which befits its location near the port. Generous portions, together with high quality, make it very popular: it's worth reserving a table to avoid disappointment. Try not to over order.
A la carte: encebollado de cigalas (crayfish stew with onions), fideos negros (black noodles).

PEIXEROT BARCELONA   **19** F6   Ⓜ Tarragona   🚇 Tarragona
Tarragona 177 (Torre Catalunya); tel. 424-69-69. Lunch 1–4 p.m., dinner 9–11.30 p.m. Closed Sunday evening. Advance reservation recommended. Price: 5.000.-pts.

Along with its famous sister establishment in Vilanova, further down the coast, the emphasis at this restaurant is on excellently prepared fish dishes and shellfish, all consumed in an elegantly designed interior which belies its tower block location.

A la carte: arroz a la marinera (Spanish-style rice featuring a variety of seafood), zarzuela de pescados (a Spanish fish stew).

PETIT PARÍS **20** H/J6

Ⓜ Diagonal 🚆 París
Main line train: Provença

París 196; tel. 218-26-78. Lunch 1–4 p.m., dinner 8.45 p.m.–midnight. Advance reservation recommended. Price: 5.000.-pts.

If you can be squeezed on to one of the restaurant's ten tables—it's not called Petit for nothing—you'll be able to enjoy good quality Catalan cuisine, chosen from a menu that changes regularly according to seasonal availability of produce.

A la carte: solomillo con salsa de mariscos (sirloin steak with seafood sauce), lenguado relleno de vieiras y langostinos con salsa al cava (sole stuffed with scallops and crayfish in a champagne sauce).

ROIG ROBÍ **21** J7

Ⓜ Diagonal 🚆 Av. Diagonal, Via Augusta
Main line train: Gràcia

116

Séneca 20; tel. 218-92-22. Lunch 1.30–4 p.m., dinner 9–11.30 p.m. Closed Sunday and public holidays. Advance reservation recommended. Price: 5.000.-pts.

Imaginative creations based on Catalan cuisine, to be eaten at ease on the terrace or garden of this slightly posh restaurant.

A la carte: fideos con langosta (lobster and noodles), merluza Roig Robi (a house speciality featuring hake), and pollo del Prat (specially prepared chicken).

LA TARGARINA **20** H5/6

Ⓜ Urgell 🚆 Casanova

Casanova 88; tel. 323-08-35. Lunch 1–4 p.m., dinner 9 p.m.–midnight. Closed Saturday lunch, Sunday and August. Price: 5.000.-pts.

The emphasis here is on French and Catalan cuisine, especially game. The atmosphere leans towards the classical, but is very comfortable. Prices are among the highest in this category.

El TRAPÍO   **5** G10/11   *Main line train:* Reina Elisenda
Esperança 25; tel. 211-35-63. Lunch 1 p.m.–4p.m., dinner 9 p.m.–midnight. Closed Sunday. Price: 5.000.-pts.
A topnotch restaurant well removed from the city centre, but definitely worth the pilgrimage, especially in the summer when you can sit in the garden beside the pool. The menu is a mix of Catalan and French cuisine; particularly recommended are the salmon cannelloni and aubergines stuffed with wild mushrooms.

TRITON   **11** D10   Ⓜ Palau Reial   🚊 Palau Reial
Alfambra 16; tel. 203-30-85. Lunch 1–4 p.m., dinner 9 p.m.–midnight. Closed Sunday and public holidays during the month of Easter. Advance reservation recommended. Price: 3.500.-pts.
Once you recover from stepping into the innards of a sailing ship, Triton's fish dishes, based on a mixture of Catalan and Basque cuisine, will continue to distract your attention.
A la carte: ensalada de angulas con salmón (elver salad with salmon), lubina Tritón (house speciality featuring haddock), pudding de escalibada (pudding of aromatic vegetables).

VIA CLARIS   **21/22** K5   Ⓜ Pg. de Gràcia   🚊 Pau Claris
Pau Claris 116; tel. 318-36-08. Lunch 1.30–4 p.m., dinner 8.30 p.m.–midnight. Price: 4.000.-pts., sampling menu 5.000.-pts., luncheon menu 2.000.-pts.

Complete with terrace and relatively high prices, this restaurant has recently been redecorated. The mainly Catalan cuisine, though occasionally imaginative, is only of reasonable quality.
A la carte: ensalada con frutos de mar (seafood salad), jarrete de ternera con setas (veal hock with mushrooms), pescados al horno (baked fish).

XARXA   **13** J8   🚊 Pl. Molina/Balmes   *Main line train:* Pl. Molina
Pl. Molina 4; tel. 200-13-48. Lunch 1.30–4 p.m., dinner 8.30 p.m.–midnight. Closed Sunday evening, Monday and August. Price: 4.000.-pts.
Mainly fish-based dishes are served at this relatively basic though not cheap restaurant.
A la carte: lubina al horno con patatitas (haddock baked with small potatoes), rape con langostinos y "girgolas" (angler-fish with crayfish and "girgolas"), sepia estofada con guisantes (cuttlefish stuffed with peas).

ECONOMICAL

Lower down the price scale, it is still possible to get extremely good-quality meals around Barcelona, though not enough of these establishments exist in a city of this size. The following is a selection.

BILBAO   **21/22** K7   Ⓜ Diagonal
Av. Diagonal, Carrer del Torrent
Perill 33; tel. 258-94-24. Lunch 1–3.30 p.m., dinner 8.30–10.30 p.m., Saturday lunch 2–3.30 p.m., dinner 9.30 p.m.–midnight. Closed Sunday and public holidays. Price: 1.600–4.000.-pts., lunch special 750.-pts.
A popular and unpretentious place, offering mainly Catalan cuisine.
A la carte: anchoas de Cantabria (Cantabrian anchovies), gambas a la plancha (grilled prawns), espalda de Avila (shoulder of beef from Avila), calamarcitos con ajo y perejil (small squid with garlic and parsley).

CAFE DE LA ACADEMIA   **24** K3   Ⓜ Jaume I   Via Laietana
Lledó 1; tel. 315-00-26. Lunch 1–4 p.m., dinner 9–11.30 p.m. Closed weekends. Price: 2.000.-pts., lunch special 1.300.-pts.
Classical music provides the background ambience, and the food and service belie the restaurant's position in the economical category.
A la carte: arrosejat (a rice dish), pimientos del piquillo rellenos de bacalao (bell-peppers stuffed with codfish), lomo rustido con puré de patatas (roast pork with mashed potatoes).

CAN JAUME   **12** H8   Pl. Francesc Macià
Main line train: Bonanova
Pau Casals 10; tel. 200-75-12. Lunch 1–4 p.m., dinner 9–11.15 p.m. Closed weekends. Price: 1.000.-pts.
An understandably popular restaurant , with outstandingly cheap prices, and rapid and friendly service.
A la carte: arroz de montaña (mountain rice), tortilla con gambas (prawn omelette), lentejas estofadas (stewed lentils).

CAN PUNYETES   **12** H8   Sentaló
Main line train: Muntaner
Mariano Cubí 189; tel. 200-91-59. Lunch 1–4 p.m., dinner 8 p.m.–1 a.m. Price: 1.500.-pts.

118

The main business in this very busy establishment is in serving tapas. The restaurant supplements these with Catalan dishes of a high quality.

A la carte: carnes a la brasa con alioli (grilled meats with alioli, a Catalan dressing similar to mayonnaise), embutidos (sausages), pan con tomate (bread with tomato).

CASA JOANA   **12** F10
🚋 Major de Sarrià
Main line train: Sarrià
Major de Sarrià 59; tel. 203-10-36. Lunch 1–4 p.m., dinner 9–11 p.m. Closed Sunday and public holidays. Price: 1.500.-pts.
An interesting concept in no-frills food: you write your own order from a menu that tells you which products are frozen rather than fresh, then enjoy large, reasonably priced portions.

CONDUCTA EJEMPLAR   **21/22** K5/6
Ⓜ Girona   🚋 Bailem
Consell de Cent 403; tel. 231-51-12. Lunch 1–4 p.m., dinner 8.30 p.m.–midnight. Closed Sunday. Price: 1.200.-pts.
A predominantly young clientele comes here to dip into a wide assortment of salads and meat dishes.

119

EGIPTE   **21/29** J4
Ⓜ Liceu   🚋 Rambla
Jerusalem 3; tel. 317-74-80. Lunch 1–5 p.m., dinner 8.30 p.m.–midnight. Closed Sunday. Price: 1.200.-pts., lunch special 850.-pts.
Just behind the Boqueria market, off the Rambla, the ever-popular Egipte serves basic and well-prepared Catalan dishes. It has spawned a younger and trendier version near the Liceo, on Rambla de les Flors 79, serving much the same food in more modern surroundings.

LAIE   **21** K5
Ⓜ Pg. de Gràcia   🚋 Pg. de Gràcia
Pau Claris 85; tel. 302-73-10. Lunch 1 p.m. Closed in the evenings and on Sunday. Price: 2.000.-pts.
Features a library to enable more literary souls to feed the mind and stomach at the same time, all at a reasonable price.
A la carte: pate de montaña (pâté, mountain-style), carpaccio, filete a la salsa de pimienta (steak with pepper sauce).

LA MORERA   **28** J4   Ⓜ Liceu 🚋 Rambla
*Pl. San Agustí 1; tel. 318-75-55. Lunch 1–3.30 p.m., dinner 8.30–
11.45 p.m. Closed Sunday and public holidays. Price: 1.500.-pts., lunch
special 750.-pts.*
Much frequented by the theatre crowd—both performers and audience—
La Morera serves good quality, if basic dishes. The lunch special features five first courses, eight second courses and seven desserts to
choose from.
A la carte: la tarta de cebolla al graten (onion tart au gratin), las conchas
de vieiras rellenas de marisco (scallop shells stuffed with seafood), pulpitos encebollados (small octopuses with stewed onions).

TRAGARAPID   **21** J6   Ⓜ Diagonal
🚋 Av. Diagonal, Rbla. Catalunya   *Main line train: Provença*
*Passatge Consepció 5; tel. 487-01-96. Lunch 1.30–4.30 p.m., dinner 9
p.m.–1.30 a.m. Closed Sunday. Price: 2.000.-pts.*
The section of El Tragaluz which deals, as the name suggests, with customers wanting something quick and simple to eat. The whole place
smacks of design and trendiness.
A la carte: blinis de salmón (salmon blinis), potaje de garbanzos (chick-
pea casserole), pollo al cava (chicken in champagne).

120

EXTRA SPECIAL

The restaurants listed below have some special attraction, whether for
their decor, quality or price.

AGUT   **29** J3   Ⓜ Barceloneta 🚋 Pla del Palau
*Gignas 16; tel. 315-17-09. Lunch 1.30–4 p.m., dinner 9–11 p.m. Closed
Sunday evening and Monday, except public holidays. Price: 2.500.-pts.*
One of the better restaurants in the mid-price range. The Catalan cuisine served here is of excellent quality, judging by the queues. For the
same reason, the staff are in even more of a hurry to move you on.
A la carte: escalibada (aromatic grilled vegetables), arroz negro con
gambas (brown rice with prawns), conejo al ajillo (rabbit cooked with
garlic).

AMAYA   **29** J3   Ⓜ Drassanes   🚃 Rambla
*Rbla. Santa Mónica 20–24; tel. 302-61-38. Service 1 p.m–12.30 a.m.,
Sunday and public holidays lunch 1–5 p.m., dinner 8 p.m.–12.30 a.m.
Advance reservation recommended. Price: 4.000.-pts.*
Although this place is not very cheap, its Basque cooking is among the
best served in Barcelona. Service is very friendly.
A la carte: cocochas a las vasca (Basque barbels), chipirones del norte
(baby squid), and an assortment of fish.

ASADOR DE ARANDA   **5** J11   Ⓜ Av. Tibidabo   🚃 Balmes
*Av. Tibidabo 31; tel. 417-01-15. Lunch 1–4 p.m., dinner 9 p.m.–midnight.
Closed Sunday evening. Price: 4.000.-pts.*
Admire the modernist design of this town house while you choose from
a menu offering food from Catalunya and other parts of Spain. A few
tables are set out on the terrace.
A la carte: ensalada verde (green salad), pimientos (bell-peppers), mor-
cillas (black sausages), chorizo (spicy smoked sausage), cordero asado
(roast lamb), costillas a la brasa (roast ribs).

CAN MAJO   **29** K2   Ⓜ Barceloneta   🚃 Barceloneta
*Almirall Aixada 23; tel. 310-14-55. Lunch 1.30–4 p.m., dinner 9–
11.30 p.m. Closed Mondays, evenings on public holidays, all of August
and Holy Week. Price: 4.500.-pts.*
A relatively expensive but very popular fish establishment of quality.
A la carte: ajos tiernos y gambitas (tender garlic with shrimps), revoltillo
de marisco (mixture of seafood), arroz a banda (boiled saffron rice
served with angler-fish and shellfish).

121

LOS CARACOLES   **29** J3   Ⓜ Drassanes   🚃 Rambla
*Passatge Escudellers 14; tel. 302-31-85. Service 1 p.m.–midnight.
Advance reservation recommended. Price: 3.000.-pts.*
Classic Catalan cuisine at a reasonable price is served here. Diners are
surrounded by photographs of personalities, especially from the opera
world, who have frequented the restaurant.
A la carte: suquillo, lechón (suckling pig), corderito (young lamb), good
paella and bullabaise (fish stew).

EL CABALLITO BLANCO   **20** H6   Main line train: Provença
*Mallorca 196; tel. 253-10-33. Lunch 1–3.45 p.m., dinner 8.45–10.45 p.m.
Closed Mondays, evenings of public holidays, and all of August. Price:
2.500.-pts.*

Fairly basic dishes are served in this popular restaurant, where the interesting selection of cheese is a special feature.

CARBALLEIRA   **19** F5   Ⓜ Barceloneta 🚊 Barceloneta
Av. Reina Maria Cristina 3; tel. 310-10-06. Lunch 1–4 p.m., dinner 9–11 p.m. Closed Sunday evening and Monday. Price: 4.000.-pts.
Fish and shellfish cooked in the Galician style, are served in this tavern-type establishment next to the port.

LA DORADA   **12** H/J7   🚊 Aribau *Main line train:* Muntaner
Travessera de Gràcia 44–46; tel. 200-63-22. Lunch 1–4 p.m., dinner 8 p.m.–midnight. Closed Sundays and all of August. Price: 4.500.-pts.
The fresh fish available here could well have been flown in by private plane from the south of Spain. At slightly higher than average prices, you will be offered Andalusian cuisine to consume in an interior that resembles the inside of a sailing ship. La Dorada has a nationwide reputation.
A la carte: pescadito frito (Andalusian fried fish), dorada a la sal (gilt-head fish, baked in salt).

122   **ELCHE**   **28** H3   Ⓜ Paral.lel 🚊 Av. Paral.lel
Vilà i Vilà 71; tel. 241-30-89. Lunch 1–4 p.m., dinner 8.30–11.30 p.m. Closed Sunday evening. Advance reservation recommended. Price: 2.500.-pts.
Have an excellently prepared paella or fish dish here before going on to the show at El Molino (see Nightlife).
A la carte: arroz a banda (boiled saffron rice served with angler-fish and shellfish), arroz con costra (baked rice), fideuá valenciana (a Valencian noodle dish), salpicón de marisco (seafood salad), calamarcitos relleños (stuffed squid).

EL GRAN CAFÉ   **29** J3   Ⓜ Drassanes 🚊 Rambla
Avinyó 9; tel. 318-79-86. Lunch 1–4 p.m., dinner 9–11.30 p.m. Closed Saturday lunch, Sunday, public holidays and August. Advance reservation recommended. Price: 4.000.-pts., gourmet menu 5.500.-pts.
Catalan and French cuisine is served on both floors of this 1920s-style restaurant, where a pianist takes over in the evening from piped music.

LEOPOLDO 28 H4
Ⓜ Liceu 🚋 Rambla

Sant Rafael 24; tel. 241-30-14. Lunch 1.30–4 p.m., dinner 9–11 p.m. Closed Sunday evening, Mondays, all of August and Holy Week. Advance reservation recommended. Price: 4.500.-pts.

This restaurant's location in the city's red-light district probably explains its absence from most guides, but it provides good quality Catalan food at reasonable prices.

A la carte: albóndigas con sepia y gambas (forcemeat balls with cuttlefish and prawns), rabo de buey estofado (oxtail stew), and a selection of fish and seafood.

MADRID BARCELONA 21 J/K6
Ⓜ Pg. de Gràcia 🚋 Pg. de Gràcia

Aragó 282; tel. 215-70-26. Closed Saturday evening, Sunday, public holidays and August. Price: 2.500.-pts.

Reasonably priced Catalan cuisine, with hints of Madrid's cooking, appears on the menu of this traditional eating place for office workers, shoppers and tourists. Don't let the staff rush you through the courses.

A la carte: callos a la madrileña (Madrid-style tripe), calamares a la romana (breaded squid), sesos a la romana (brains a la romana), solomillo de buey (ox sirloin).

ELS PESCADORS 31 O3
Ⓜ Poble Nou

123

Pl. Prim 1; tel. 309-20-18. Lunch 1–4 p.m., dinner 8.30 p.m.–midnight. Advance reservation recommended. Price: 3.500.-pts.

Catalan cuisine, based on excellent fish dishes. It will be even more of a treat to eat on the terrace, which gives on to a shady square, once work on the Olympic Village is completed.

A la carte: caracoles a la brasa (roast snails), dorada al horno con patatas (baked gilthead with potatoes), sardinas a la brasa (roast sardines).

LA PUÑALADA 21 K6
Ⓜ Diagonal 🚋 Av. Diagonal

Pg. de Gràcia 104; tel. 218-47-91. Lunch 1–4 p.m., dinner 8.30 p.m.–midnight. Advance reservation recommended. Price: 3.000.-pts.

Slightly expensive and very comfortable, this traditional establishment specializes in Catalan cuisine with a French influence.

A la carte: paella La Puñalada de pescados y mariscos (house paella with fish and seafood), perdiz deshuesada a la col (boneless partridge with cabbage), esqueixada de bacalao (marinated codfish salad).

ELS QUATRE GATS　　**21** J4　　　　Ⓜ Liceu　🚌 Rambla
*Montsió 3 bis; tel. 302-41-40. Monday to Saturday 9 a.m.–2 p.m., Sunday
5 p.m.–2 a.m. Closed Sunday lunch. Price: 2.000.-pts.*
Picasso and his fellow artists and intellectuals whiled away the hours
here, when not at the canvas. The décor and paintings will evoke the
period.

SENYOR　　　　　　　　　　　　　　　　Ⓜ Barceloneta
PARELLADA　　**29** K3　　　　　　　🚌 Via Laietana
*Argenteria 37; tel. 315-40-10. Lunch 1–3.30 p.m., dinner 9–11.15 p.m.
Closed Sunday, public holidays and all of August. Advance reservation
recommended. Price: 3.000.-pts.*
A favourite for business people and personalities from the world of the
arts. A very pleasant and cool atmosphere make it a pleasure to eat here,
though everything seems to be taken rather seriously. Very
Catalunyan.
A la carte: ensalada de endivias (endive salad), caldereta de pescado
de Caldetas (fish soup from Caldetas), carpaccio de salmón (salmon
carpaccio).

LES SET PORTES　　**29** K3　　Ⓜ Barceloneta　🚌 Pla del Palau
*Pg. de Isabel II 14; tel. 319-30-33. Open 1 p.m.–1 a.m. Advance reser-
vation recommended. Price: 3.000.-pts.*
A venerable institution, little changed since it opened almost 160 years
ago. Reasonably priced, mainly Catalan food can be eaten in any of the
seven dining rooms at any hour of the afternoon or evening.
A la carte: arroz negro (brown rice), baked fish, zarzuela Set
Portes.(house dish of fish stew).

124

VELL SARRIÀ　　**12** F10　　🚌 Major de Sarrià　*Main line train:* Sarrià
*Major de Sarrià 93; tel. 204-57-10. Lunch 1.30–4 p.m., dinner
9 p.m.–midnight. Closed Sunday evening, Monday, all of August and
Holy Week. Advance reservation recommended. Price: 4.000.-pts.*
This old two-storey house converted into a restaurant, comes complete
with wooden beams, a terrace and a garden, where you can eat fine-
quality Catalan cuisine, including wild duck.
A la carte: canelones de marisco con girgolas (seafood cannelone), arroz Vell Sarrià con verduras, almejas y sepia (house rice dish with
vegetables, clams and cuttlefish), pollo con cigalas (chicken with
crayfish), fritura de setas del tiempo (grilled seasonal wild mushrooms).

ETHNIC

American

**CHICAGO
PIZZA PIE FACTORY**   **21** J/K 6

🚌 Pg. de Gràcia
Main line train: Provença

Provença 300; tel. 215-94-15. Service 12.30 p.m.–1 a.m. Price: 2.000.-pts.
Principally a take-away pizza establishment, but it also serves hamburgers, ribs and the rest, very rapidly.

HOLLYWOOD   **12** G8

Ⓜ Hospital Clínic
🚌 Villaroel, Av. Diagonal

Av. Diagonal 495; tel. 322-10-15. Service 1 p.m.–1.15 a.m. Price: 2.000.-pts.
Fast food, including hamburgers and other meat dishes, with décor to match its name.

STEAK & SALAD   **21** J7   Ⓜ Diagonal   🚌 Via Augusta   **125**
Dr. Rizal 20; tel. 217-05-47. Lunch 1–3 p.m., dinner 8–11.30 p.m. Price: 2.500.-pts.
Among the very first restaurants of its type to set up in Barcelona, it is still the place to go for meat prepared in typical North American fashion, in reasonably comfortable surroundings.

Argentinian

**LOS AÑOS
LOCOS**   **12** J8

🚌 Muntaner
Main line train: Muntaner

Mariano Cubí 85; tel. 209-69-15. Lunch 1.30–4 p.m., dinner 9 p.m.–midnight. Price: 2.000.-pts.
A good place to enjoy the most popular Argentine meat dishes.

EL CHURRASCO **21/22** K6   Ⓜ Pg. de Gràcia   🚃 Pg. de Gràcia
*València 324; tel. 258-96-31. Lunch 1–4 p.m., dinner 8.30 p.m.–midnight.
Closed Sunday. Price: 3.000.-pts.*
Provides everything you might expect from an establishment offering
Argentine-style food (although not exclusively) with ambience to match.

Asian

BALI **28** G3   Ⓜ Paral.lel   🚃 Av. Miramar de Camillas
*Montjuïc; tel. 241-36-09. Lunch noon–4 p.m., dinner 8 p.m.–midnight.
Price: 3.500.-pts.*
Indonesian food, with the accent on rijsttafel, but with influences from
other Asian cuisine. The restaurant is sited some way up Montjuïc and
has a terrace and garden, complete with tropical vegetation.

LA   Ⓜ Hospital Clínic
GRAN MURALLA **12/20** H7   🚃 Aribau
*Lluís Pellicer 7; tel. 230-00-49. Lunch 1.30–4 p.m., dinner 9–11.30 p.m.
Price: 2.000.-pts.*
Among the best Chinese restaurants in the city, and certainly one of the
oldest.

NUEVO SEOUL **20** J6   🚃 Balmes *Main line train: Provença
Enrique Granados 89; tel. 253-11-63. Lunch 1–4 p.m., dinner
8.30 p.m.–midnight. Price: 2.000.-pts.*
The Korean cuisine served at this establishment attracts a regular clientele, which indicates its quality.

French

CREPERIE   🚃 Pl. Molina
BRETONNE **13** J8   *Main line train: Pl. Molina
Balmes 274; tel. 217-30-48. Service 5 p.m.–1 a.m. Price: 600.-pts.*
French crèpes and pancakes are the speciality.

LA DENTELLERIE   **29** J3   Ⓜ Jaume I   🚌 Via Laietana
Ample 26; tel. 319-68-21. Tuesday to Saturday 8 p.m.–1 a.m. Closed lunch except on Saturday. Price: 2.500.-pts.
So close and yet so far from France—if you can't get across the border for the real thing, this traditionally decorated restaurant will serve the purpose.
A la carte: Alsatian salad, glazed duck salad and scallops provençal.

Indian

MAHARAJAH   **20** F6   Ⓜ Entença   🚌 Entença
Entença 137; tel. 426-35-59. Lunch 1–3.30 p.m., dinner 8.30–11.30 p.m.
One of the few Indian restaurants in Barcelona, this restaurant serves good food at moderate prices.
A la carte: classic curries and tandooris, mutton, fried breads and lassi (a yoghurt drink).

TAJ MAHAL   **20** H7   Ⓜ Hospital Clínic   🚌 Villaroel
Londres 89; tel. 322-32-33. Lunch 1.30–3.30 p.m., dinner 8.30–11.30 p.m. Closed Monday. Price: 2.500.-pts.
Specializing in tandoori dishes, but with a full complement of cuisine from the north of India.

127

Italian

QUEL FANTÁSTICO   Ⓜ Tarragona
LUNEDI!   **19/20** F6   🚌 Tarragona
València 26–28; tel. 425-39-12. Lunch 1.30–3.30 p.m., dinner 9–11 p.m. Closed Sunday evening. Price: 3.000.-pts.
Authentic Italian dishes, together with a list of Italian wines at ridiculously high prices compared to their Spanish equivalents.

TRAMONTI 1980   **12** G8   Ⓜ Entença   🚌 Entença
Av. Diagonal 501; tel. 410-15-35. Lunch 1–4 p.m., dinner 9 p.m.–midnight. Closed Sunday evening. Price: 3.000.-pts.
Fresh pasta dishes are served in bright, modern surroundings, to those who can't put up with the lesser Spanish version of the same.
A la carte: spaghetti con sugo di seppia, ravioli al uso di Pomagna.

Japanese

YAMADORI   **20** H6   🚊 Aribau
Main line train: Provença
Aribau 68; tel. 253-92-64. Lunch 1–3 p.m., dinner 8.30–11.30 p.m. Closed Sunday. Price: 3.800.-pts.
Popular not only with the many Japanese residents but with a growing number of Barcelona's other diners. Food is of a high quality without being over priced.
A la carte: sushi, sashimi, fried noodles with beef and vegetables, chicken shish-kebabs, stir-fried seafood and vegetables.

YASHIMA   **12** G7   Ⓜ Entença   🚊 Pl. Francesc Macià
Josep Tarradellas 145; tel. 419-06-97. Lunch 1–3.30 p.m., dinner 8.30–11.30 p.m. Closed Sunday and public holidays. Price: 5.500.-pts.
An up-market Japanese restaurant, with all the fixtures and fittings you might expect in an establishment of its class. Popular with international business people.
A la carte: fish soup, steamed crayfish ravioli, grilled fish, sushi.

Mexican

TIJUANA   **20** G7   Ⓜ Hospital Clínic   🚊 Villaroel
Compte Borell 296; tel. 439-11-09. Lunch 1–4 p.m., dinner 7 p.m.– 2.30 a.m. Price: 1.000.-pts.
Tex-Mex food at low prices.
A la carte: spicy tacos, Margarita.

North African/Middle Eastern

EL CUS-CUS   **12** J8   *Main line train:* Muntaner
Pl. Cardona 4; tel. 201-98-67. Lunch 1.30–3.30 p.m., dinner 8.30 p.m.–midnight. Closed Monday. Price: 2.500.-pts.
Cuisine from Algeria, and an ambience, complete with very tasteful décor, to match. Its name suggests the speciality.
A la carte: chek-kaka, pepper salad, lamb, tajine (sesame-seed paste).

LA ROSA Ⓜ Diagonal
DEL DESIERTO **21** J7 🚎 Via Augusta
Pl. Narcis Oller 7; tel. 237-45-90. Lunch 1–3.30 p.m., dinner 9–11.30 p.m. Price: 2.500.-pts.
The piped Arab music gives way to rather better live performances later in the evening. Good quality food, at modest prices, attracts a regular clientele.
A la carte: couscous, tajine (sesame-seed paste), harira soup, chicken with spring onions and raisins.

XIX KEBAB **20** H7 Ⓜ Hospital Clínic 🚎 Villaroel
Córcega 193; tel. 321-82-10. Lunch 1.30–4 p.m., dinner 9 p.m.–midnight. Closed Tuesday. Price: 3.000.-pts.
Food from the Middle East, with an emphasis on Syrian cuisine, gives this restaurant its uniqueness. The furnishings complement the cuisine.
A la carte: stuffed vine leaves, tabbula (cracked-wheat salad), stuffed aubergines.

EXCLUSIVE

129

BLAU MARÍ (See Eating Late at Night)

FLASH-FLASH TORTILLERIA (See Eating Late at Night)

NETWORK (See Eating Late at Night)

LA ODISEA Ⓜ Jaume I 🚎 Via Laietana
Copons 7; tel. 302-36-92. Lunch 1.30–4 p.m., dinner 9 p.m.–midnight. Closed Sunday, Saturday lunchtime, Holy Week and all of August. Price: 6.000.-pts., surprise menu 6.000.-pts.
The delight of a meal here is the number of unpretentious, but well-prepared dishes on the menu and the relaxed atmosphere.
A la carte: filete de lenguado al vino tinto (fillet of sole cooked in red wine), solomillo villete con hortalizas al calvados (sirloin with vegetables in calvados).

ROIG ROBI (see Excellent Addresses)

LA SOPETA   **20** H5   Ⓜ Universitat   🚌 Ronda Universitat
*Muntaner 6; tel. 323-56-32. Lunch 1.30–4 p.m., dinner 9–11.30 p.m.
Closed Sunday. Price: 3.000.-pts.*
Excellent Catalan-based dishes are served in this elegantly designed
restaurant that verges on the quaint.

LA VAQUERIA (See Eating Late at Night)

LA VENTA   **5** J11   🚌 Av. Dr. Andreu   *Main line train:* Av. Tibidabo
*Pl. Dr. Andreu, Tibidabo; tel. 212-64-55. Lunch 1.30–3.45 p.m., dinner
9–11.30 p.m. Closed Sunday. Price: 4.000.-pts.*
Near the foot of the funicular up to Tibidabo. The main feature of the
Venta is the view from its terrace over the rest of Barcelona.

TRAGALUX   **21** J6   Ⓜ Diagonal   🚌 Av. Diagonal
*Pje. de la Concepció 5; tel. 487-01-96. Lunch 1.30–4 p.m., dinner
9–11.30 p.m. Closed Sunday. Price: 5.500.-pts., sampling menu
6.000.-pts.*
The posh version of Tragarapid (see Economical), with high prices, flash
design—courtesy of Mariscal—and food of acceptable quality. You pay
to see and be seen here, at least for the moment.

130

UP & DOWN   **11** F8   Ⓜ Maria Cristina   🚌 Av. Diagonal
*Numància 179; tel. 204-88-09. Dinner 11 p.m.–2 a.m. Closed Sunday.
Price: 5.000.-pts.*
The main attraction of Up & Down appears to be its exclusivity, coupled
with the fact that it serves good food until well into the night. But prices
are high and admission depends on whether they like your face, which
can't be right.

EASY GOING

BALMORAL   **21** J7   Ⓜ Diagonal   🚌 Av. Diagonal
Av. Diagonal 488; tel. 218-30-39. Service 9 a.m.–8.30 p.m.
A tearoom restaurant and bar where the food is basic, but the clientele
is opulent. Come here in a group in order to overcome the sensation of
wide-open spaces. (See Nightlife: Discos Bars and Nightclubs).

LA BRIOCHE   **20** H7   Ⓜ Hospital Clínic   🚌 Villaroel
Casanova 189; tel. 322-00-27. Service 8 a.m.–8.30 p.m.
Mainly a place to eat croissants and other pastries filled with multifarious
delicious morsels, both sweet and savoury, especially at breakfast time.

LA FARGA   **21** J7   Ⓜ Diagonal   🚌 Av. Diagonal
Av. Diagonal 391; tel. 218-32-66. Service 9 a.m.–9 p.m.
Basically a tearoom, serving cakes and pastries at high prices on the
upper floor; downstairs is a good-quality cafeteria.

LAIE (See Economical)

LA JIJONENCA   **21** J5   Ⓜ Pg. de Gràcia   🚌 Rbla. Catalunya
*Rbla. Catalunya 35, tel. 301-91-96. Also at Diagonal 652. Service
9 a.m.–1.30 a.m.*
Well-established ice-cream makers turned restaurateurs. The Rambla
Catalunya branch features uncomfortable but trendy design seating on
the ground floor, and slightly more relaxed eating on the second floor,
complete with a terrace where nobody eats in summer because it's
too hot.

MAURI   **21** J6   🚌 Rbla. Catalunya   *Main line train:* Provença
*Rbla. Catalunya 102; tel. 215-09-98. Service 9 a.m.–9 p.m. Closed
Sunday afternoon.*
The décor, dating from the end of the last century, gives the restaurant
its special attraction, along with a wide variety of excellently produced
light meals served at the bar.

131

LA MECA   **27/28** F3   Ⓜ Paral.lel   🚌 Av. Paral.lel
*Parque de Montjuïc, Fundació Miró; tel. 329-07-68. Service 4–7 p.m.
Closed Monday, except public holidays.*
Combine culture with cuisine in the Miró Foundation, where the Meca
serves afternoon snacks.
A la carte: chocolate pastries and fresh fruit crumble with vanilla sauce.

LA PALLARESA   **29** J4   Ⓜ Liceu   🚌 Rambla
Petritxol 11; tel. 302-20-36. Service 9 a.m.–1.30 p.m. and 4.30–9 p.m.
The place to go for traditional pastries and light snacks, at breakfast time
or after an afternoon stroll.
A la carte: melindros (small cakes), hot chocolate.

VIADER **21** J4   Ⓜ Liceu 🚎 Rambla
Xuclà 4–6; tel. 318-34-86. Service 9 a.m.–1.30 p.m. and 5–9 p.m. Closed Sunday.
Snacks, pastries, breakfast and tea.

VILAPLANA **12** G8   🚎 Pl. Francesc Macià
Main line train: Bonanova
Pl. Gregori Taumaturg 4; tel. 201-13-00. Service 9 a.m.–2 p.m. and 5–9 p.m. Closed Sunday afternoon and Monday.
Good quality, if slightly expensive, standard international dishes can be eaten in this cafeteria. But the highlights are the excellent pastries.

EATING LATE AT NIGHT

132 From Midnight to 1 a.m.

BLAU MARÍ **29** J2/3   Ⓜ Barceloneta 🚎 Pg. Colom
Moll de la Fusta Edicle 2; tel. 310-10-15. Closed Monday except in summer.
One of the trendy places to eat, right next to the port, situated in the recently recreated quayside. Food or drinks on the terrace at night are the principal reason for a visit, as long as you don't mind the noise of traffic.
A la carte: bullabesa (fish stew), rice and fish dishes.

BRASSERIE FLO **21/22** K4   Ⓜ Urquinaona 🚎 Urquinaona
Junqueras 10; tel. 317-80-37.
A French-style brasserie, with all the bustle and business you would expect. It's especially good for seafood; many dishes are French-inspired but influenced by Catalan cuisine.

FLASH-FLASH   🚋 Balmes
TORTILLERIA   **13** J7   *Main line train:* Gràcia
La Granada del Penedès 25; tel. 237-09-90.
Some 70 different types of omelette are on the menu here, as well as rice dishes and hamburgers. The décor takes you back to the 70s.

MORDISCO   **21** J6/7   Ⓜ Diagonal   🚋 Av. Diagonal
Rosselló 265; tel. 218-33-14.
Open all day and into the night, Mordisco attracts a fashionable crowd, especially from the artistic fraternity, who tuck into unpretentious and well-prepared dishes.
A la carte: a variety of salads, scrambled eggs with prawns or salmon.

LA VAQUERIA   **12** G8   Ⓜ Les Corts
Deu i Mata 139–141; tel. 419-21-18. Closed Saturday lunch and Sunday.
There's a very relaxed atmosphere in this beautifully designed restaurant, where the accent is on Italian dishes.
A la carte: fried eggs, tortellini, estofado a la jardinera (stew).

TRAGARAPID (See Economical)

133

From Midnight to 2 a.m.

LA JIJONENCA (See Easy Going)

NETWORK   **12** G8   Ⓜ Diagonal   🚋 Av. Diagonal
Av. Diagonal 616; tel. 201-72-38.
Miniature television screens are at the table, and there's high-tech design to match. You choose from a menu featuring specialities from all over the world, or you can just have a drink.

**OLIVER
Y HARDY**   **11** F8   ⓜ Maria Cristina
🚇 Pl. Maria Cristina

Av. Diagonal 593; tel. 419-31-81. Monday to Saturday noon–4.30 a.m.
Not a cheap place for a late-night meal, but good quality food is served in a very comfortable atmosphere (especially on the large terrace). After midnight, the food service transfers to the nightclub part of the establishment (see Nightlife).
A la carte: ensalada de mariscos al vinagre de frambuesa (seafood salad with raspberry vinegar), salmonetes sin espina al vino tinto (boneless red mullet with red wine sauce), lubina en hojadre a la crema de puerros (haddock in puff pastry with creamy leek sauce).

From Midnight to 2.30 a.m.

**CAFÉ
DE LA REPÚBLICA**   **13/14** K9   ⓜ Lesseps
🚇 Pg. Sant Gervasi

República Argentina 83; tel. 210-23-03.
Mainly tapas, but a range of other dishes (including meat fondues) are provided to keep you going through the night.

134 **GADES**   **29** K3   ⓜ Jaume I, Barceloneta   🚇 Via Laietana
Esparteria 10; tel. 315-38-84.
A small and moderately priced restaurant that is more a place for a light meal than a substantial late-night dinner.
A la carte: a variety of salads, meat and cheese fondues, smoked salmon.

GIARDINETTO NOTTE   **13** J7   🚇 Balmes   *Main line train:* Gràcia
Granada del Penedés 22; tel. 218-75-36.
Mainly Italian food is served in this flashy restaurant that won a design prize for its décor. There's also a jazz piano bar.
A la carte: fettuccini al pesto, flan de rape con gambas (angler-fish flan with prawns).

MÀXIM'S   **12/20** H7   ⓜ Hospital Clínic   🚇 Aribau
Main line train: Provença
Aribau 230; tel. 209-97-96.
A whole range of fast food, as well as tapas, is on offer here.

TICKTACKTOE **21/22** K5   Ⓜ Pg. de Gràcia   🚌 Pg. de Gràcia
Roger de Llúria 40; tel. 318-99-47. Monday to Thursday 8 a.m.–2.30 a.m.,
Friday and Saturday until 3 a.m., music in the bar 7 p.m.–3 a.m.
A popular night spot for the trendies, where Catalan food is served late
as you sit among the drinkers and revellers playing snooker, or gazing
at the high-tech furnishings. Best to book, owing to popularity.

From Midnight to 4.30 a.m.

DRUGSTORE   🚌 Balmes
DAVID   **13** J7   *Main line train:* Gràcia
Tuset 17–19; tel. 209-69-58.
Mainly a pizza parlour, but other food is also available, with the big ad-
vantage being the very late opening hours. It's always packed with night
owls, even during the day.

BAR   🚌 Mandri/Gral. Mitre
MANDRI   **12** H10   *Main line train:* Muntaner
Mandri 60; tel. 417-11-29. Service 7.30 a.m.–2.30 a.m. Closed Saturday
afternoon, Sunday and all of August. Price: Glass of wine or mug of beer
125.-pts.
A bar for young trendies on their way out for the evening, especially in
the summer, but otherwise it's unremarkable.

BAR   Ⓜ Diagonal 🚌 Gala Placidia
ROBLE   **13** J7   *Main line train:* Gràcia
Luis Antúnez 7; tel. 218-73-87. Service 7 a.m.–midnight. Closed Sunday
and all of August. Price: Glass of wine 100.-pts., beer 110.-pts. Variety
of tapas at 225.-pts.
A disparate assortment of customers pass through here, eating, drinking and talking in typical café style.

BAR TURO   **12** H8   Ⓜ Muntaner   🚌 Pl. Francesc Macià
Main line train: Muntaner
Tenor Viñas 1; tel. 200-69-53. Service 9 a.m.–1 a.m. Closed Sunday and all of August. Price: Glass of wine 125.-pts. at the bar and 175.-pts. on the terrace. Glass of beer 175.-pts. at the bar and 250.-pts. outside. Average price of tapas 225.-pts.
Very high quality tapas are sold here, making Bar Turo a good staging post to restore energy before or during a night out.

BLAU MARÍ (See Eating Late at Night)

BODEGA SEPÚLVEDA   **20** H5   Ⓜ Universitat   🚌 Ronda Universitat
Sepúlveda 173; tel. 218-73-87. Service 9.30 a.m.–1 a.m., Saturday 12.30–4 p.m. and 7.30 p.m.–1 a.m. Closed Sunday, Holy Week and 4 August to 5 September. Price: Glass of beer 110.-pts., wine 75.-pts. Average price of tapas 350.-pts.
A busy and popular bar throughout the day and night, serving a good range of tapas.

CASA FERNANDEZ   **12** H8   Ⓜ Muntaner   🚌 Santaló
Main line train: Muntaner
136 *Santaló 46; tel. 201-93-08. Service 9.30 a.m.–2.30 a.m. Price: Glass of beer 175.-pts., wine 165.-pts.*
Late into the night, young and energetic people come here for tapas and a fine selection of beers from Spain and abroad.

CASA TEJADA   **12** H8   🚌 Calvet/Pl. Francesc Macià
Main line train: Muntaner
Tenor Viñas 3; tel. 200-73-41. Service 8 a.m.–2 a.m. Closed Sunday. Price: Glass of wine or beer 175.-pts.
Supposedly a classic tapas bar, but quite pricey.

CERVECERIA D'OR   **21** J5/6   Ⓜ Pg. de Gràcia   🚌 Pg. de Gràcia
Consell de Cent 339; tel. 215-64-39. Service 9 a.m.–2 a.m.
A wide range of beers are available, as well as good quality tapas, including some with a German touch.

JOSÉ-LUÍS   **13/21** J7   Ⓜ Diagonal
Av. Diagonal 520; tel. 200-83-12. Service 9 a.m.–1 a.m. Price: Pint of beer 225.-pts., glass of wine 175.-pts., montaditos 1.000.-pts.
An up-market tapas bar, complete with small terrace and good beer, plus an expensive restaurant where business diners and beautiful people pass the time at various points during the day.

MESON DEL JABUGO   **20** H7   Ⓜ Hospital Clínic   🚃 Villaroel
París 175; tel. 201-29-42. Service 9 a.m.–1 a.m. Closed Sunday and public holidays. Price: Glass of wine 125.-pts., pint of beer 175.-pts., ham-tapa 2.200.-pts.
As the name suggests, this is the place to sample a variety of Spanish hams.

CASA QUIRZE   Ⓜ Esplugues   🚃 Esplugues **137**
Laureà Miró 202, Esplugues de Llobregat; tel. 371-10-84. Lunch 1–4 p.m., dinner 9–11 p.m. Closed Saturday evening, Sunday, public holidays, all of August and Holy Week. Price: 4.000.-pts.
A rather special restaurant that has been in existence for over a century and a half. It is worth paying the relatively high prices for Catalan cuisine with a French touch.
A la carte: escarola con habitas y salmón a humado (endives with beans and smoked salmon), tronco de merluza donostiarra (Basque-style hake), assortment of game and seasonal mushrooms.

LAS BOTAS   🚃 Castelldefels   *Main line train: R.E.N.F.E.*
Av. Constitucion 326, Castelldefels; tel. 665-50-55.
A roadside restaurant, though not noisy, providing an excellent variety of mainly Catalan cuisine, with a speciality of meat dishes cooked over an open fire. Gargantuan portions are offered, and all at reasonable prices.

RESTAURANTS

GRAN CASINO
DE BARCELONA
Main line train: R.E.N.F.E.
Finca Mas Soler, Sant Pere de Ribes; tel. 893-36-66. Dinner 9 p.m.–1.30 a.m. Closed 23 December. Price: 5.000.-pts.

This restaurant is in the main gaming house of the region, about 40 kilometres (25 miles) from the city. After—or more wisely before—trying your luck at the tables, you can enjoy a good quality meal, based on international cuisine.

A la carte: supremas de salmón fresco con salsa de alcaparras (fresh salmon supreme in caper sauce), chuleton de Avila poele con mousse de foie-gras al roquefort (fried chop from Avila with Roquefort foie-gras mousse).

HISPANIA
Main line train: R.E.N.F.E
Ctra. Reial 54, Arenys de Mar; tel. 791-04-57. Lunch 1–4 p.m., dinner 8.30–11 p.m. Closed Tuesday and Sunday evening, Holy Week and all of October. Price: 3.500.-pts.

Some of the best Catalan cuisine available in the area around Barcelona can be found here. The quality of the ingredients is excellent, the wine list superb.

A la carte: judias con col (beans with cabbage), pulpitos salteados (salted octopus), buñuelos de bacalao (salted-cod fritters), langosta con patatas (lobster with potatoes), pollo en escabeche (chicken in a marinade).

138

LLICORELLA
Main line train: R.E.N.F.E.
Ctra. San Antonio 101, Cubelles; tel. 895-00-44. Lunch 1.30–4 p.m., dinner 8.30–11 p.m. Closed Monday and November. Price: 5.500.-pts.

A small hotel, set in peaceful gardens, houses this excellent restaurant serving mainly Catalan cuisine.

A la carte: supremas de lubina con salsa de erizos (haddock supreme in a sea-urchin sauce, estofado de salmón fresco con dátiles de mar (fresh salmon stew with mussels).

EL MOLINER
Ⓜ Cornellà 🚆 Cornellà
Ctra. d'Esplugues 154, Cornellà de Llobregat; tel. 375-70-53. Lunch 1–4 p.m., dinner 8.30–11 p.m. Closed Monday evening, public holidays, Holy Week and 2 weeks in August. Price: 4.000.-pts.

Set in a villa complete with terrace, El Moliner serves Catalan cuisine with French touchs in a relaxed atmosphere.

A la carte: ensalada de gambas con cangrejos de rio (shrimp salad with fresh-water crab), manos de cerdo rellenas de higos (pig knuckles stuffed with figs), pate de setas al perfume de tomillo (mushroom pâté with thyme).

RACO D'EN BINU   6 M12

Puig i Cadafalch 14, Argentona; tel. 797-01-01. Lunch 1–4.30 p.m., dinner 9–11 p.m. Closed Sunday evening and Monday. Advance reservation recommended. Price: 4.000.-pts.

Just 30 kilometres (19 miles) to the north of Barcelona by road, this established if quite pricey restaurant offers very good quality fish, shellfish and meat dishes, in a mainly Catalan style.

A la carte: surtido de flanes de legumbres (an assortment of vegetable flans), solomillo de ternera francés (French veal sirloin).

If you are staying near the centre of town, Barcelona might seem to be the "City That Never Sleeps", as traffic continues almost unabated and the Rambla is thronged with people out for the night, well into the early hours of the morning.

Catalans rarely entertain at home, preferring to go out to a restaurant or club with their friends. The bars which abound in Barcelona are an almost obligatory staging post for an evening out, either before or after a restaurant, a show or the disco.

The fashionable places to go vary from month to month, sometimes from week to week, as people search for a trendy new bar or disco. A few venues are always popular, while others make regular and radical changes to their decor in order to attract the customers. Some establishments that are relatively sober eating places for business people during the day, are transformed by night into swish discos. The trendiest places attract large queues outside, and reserve the right of admission: you could find yourself turned away on the basis of a doorman's whim.

There is usually a fair number of venues staging live music, and Barcelona is an obligatory stop for performers on tour. Rock, jazz and classical music are featured somewhere in the city every night.

The big treat for opera fans, of course, is to get hold of tickets for a performance at the Liceu, the city's famous opera house. A bigger treat is to attend an opera featuring one of Catalunya's home-grown stars, such as Carreras or Montserrat Caballé. Be warned, however, that tickets are very difficult to obtain.

Unlike many other cities, Barcelona has no tradition of ticket agencies for the reservation of seats at theatres, concerts and the like. However, there are often tickets for bigger concerts on sale in the ticket booths which can be found on the corner of Gran Via and Aribau, near the main university building. In addition, theatre tickets are usually available from branches of the Caixa de Catalunya savings bank. It is usually best to contact the theatre or venue directly. General information on cultural events is obtainable at the city's main culture information office on the Rambla at No. 99, telephone 301-77-75.

141

Light up your night at one of Barcelona's spectacular floor shows.

CINEMA

Barcelona's cinemas are generally modern, comfortable and reasonably priced—especially on Mondays or Wednesdays, when entry is cut-price. Most new, non-Spanish releases arrive in the city rapidly, and if the film is popular, it will be shown in several cinemas at the same time, including at least one where it can be heard in its original language version. Check the press or a listings magazine (such as the *Guia* which accompanies *El Pais* on a Friday) for cinemas offering "v.o.". It is customary to offer a tip to the usher or usherette: about 25 or 50 pesetas will do. The following is a list of the main cinemas.

CINEMA ALEX   **21** J6   Ⓜ Diagonal
(MULTICINE)   🚌 Rbla. Catalunya
Rbla. Catalunya 90; tel. 215-05-06. Daily 4 and 10.30 p.m. Price: 525.-pts., Wednesday 350.-pts.
In this four-screen cinema, at least one of the films showing is usually in its original language version.

CINEMA   Ⓜ Diagonal   🚌 Aribau
ASTORIA   **20** H7   *Main line train:* Provença
París 193; tel. 209-95-96. Daily 3.30 and 10 p.m. Price: 525.-pts., Wednesday 350.-pts.
New releases are screened, generally dubbed into Spanish.

142   **CINEMA BOSQUE**   **13** J8   Ⓜ Fontana   🚌 Av. P. Astúries
Rbla. Prat 20; tel. 217-26-42. Daily 6 and 10.05 p.m. Price: 525.-pts.
A large cinema showing films in Spanish.

CINEMA CAPSA   **21/22** K6   Ⓜ Pg. de Gràcia   🚌 Pau Claris
Pau Claris 134; tel. 215-73-93. Price: 500.-pts., Monday 375.-pts.
New releases, sometimes in their original version.

CINEMA   Ⓜ Diagonal
CASABLANCA   **21** J7   🚌 Av. Diagonal/ Gran de Gràcia
Pg. de Gràcia 115; tel. 218-43-45. Price: 525.-pts., Monday 350.-pts.
This small cinema regularly shows original language versions of films not newly released—some recent releases show for months, providing an opportunity to catch a film you missed at home.

CINEMA   Ⓜ Catalunya   🚌 Pl. Catalunya
CATALUNYA   **21** J5   *Main line train: Catalunya*
Pl. Catalunya 3; tel. 318-06-91. Daily 4 and 10 p.m. Price: 525.-pts.,
Wednesday 350.-pts.
New releases, usually dubbed into Spanish.

CINEMA   Ⓜ Gran Via/Catalunya
COLISEUM   **21** J5   🚌 Rbla. Catalunya
Gran Via de les Catalanes 595; tel. 301-00-91. Daily 4.15 and 10 p.m.
Price: 525.-pts.
A giant cinema, showing new releases.

CINEMA COMÈDIA   Ⓜ Catalunya
(MULTICINE)   **21** J5   🚌 Pg. de Gràcia
Pg. de Gràcia 13; tel. 318-23-96. Continuous projections from 4 p.m.
Price: 525.-pts., Wednesday 350.-pts.
Three-screen cinema, showing new releases.

THEATRE

The city's theatres are a mixed bunch, and Barcelona generally lacks
sufficient stages to accommodate all the productions that need them.
It is fair to say that theatre isn't the forte of this region, although some
of the most ambitious and avant-garde productions and groups establish
their reputation here. The theatres are at their best when taking part in
large-scale festivals. One such festival centres on the Grec Theatre and
attracts some of the best talent from Spain and around the world. Apart
from these festivals, virtually all theatre is performed in Catalan or
Spanish, although there are occasional visits by touring companies from
abroad.

143

C. DRAMÀTIC   Ⓜ Liceu
DE LA GENERALITAT   **28/29** J4   🚌 Rambla
Hospital 51; tel. 301-55-04. Tuesday to Saturday 9 p.m., Sunday 6 p.m.
In the heart of Barcelona just off the Rambla, this theatre is in an area
which is gradually moving up-market from being a red-light district.

CASINO L'ALIANÇA ⓜ Llacuna
DEL POBLE NOU **31** O3 🚃 Rbla. Poble Nou/Llull
Rbla. Poblenou 42; tel. 309-08-90/309-00-13. Weekdays 6 p.m.
Converted from a gaming establishment which gives it its name, this
theatre is in an area best known for its architectural design.

FUND. JOAN MIRÓ (see Children)
A small theatre and lecture hall within the permanent exhibition of this
famous artist's work.

GRAN TEATRE DEL LICEU (See Classical Music, Opera and
Modern Dance)
Better known for its performances of opera and ballet, the Liceu also
stages occasional theatrical productions.

INSTITUT DEL TEATRE, ⓜ Urquinaona
TEATRE ADRIÀ GUAL **21/22** K4 🚃 Rda. St. Pere
Sant Pere Més Baix 7; tel. 268-20-78.
A multi-stage theatre tucked away in a narrow side street. It is used reg-
ularly for smaller productions.

JOVE TEATRE ⓜ Diagonal
REGINA **21** J7 🚃 Via Augusta/Gran de Gràcia
*Sèneca 22; tel. 218-15-12. Tuesday, Friday, Saturday 10 p.m., Sunday
7 p.m.*
During the week, this theatre puts on productions for adults, at weekends it is taken over by children who come to see shows specially aimed
at them.

144

EL LLANTIOL **20** H4 ⓜ Paral.lel 🚃 Rda. St. Pau
*Riereta 7; tel. 329-90-09. Astrology and card-reading 6.30–9 p.m., café-
theatre Tuesday to Saturday midnight, Sunday 7 p.m.*
This establishment offers two types of entertainment under the same roof.
In one part, devotees can attend sessions with a resident astrologer and
card reader, while in the café-theatre, the show usually involves magicians, ventriloquists and similar acts.

SALA BECKETT **13** L8 ⓜ Alfons X 🚃 Escorial
*Alegre de Dalt 55; tel. 284-53-12. Tuesday to Saturday 10 p.m., Sunday
7 p.m.*
This small theatre regularly stages experimental productions or
readings.

TEATRE CONDAL **28** G4 Ⓜ Poble Sec, Paral.lel 🚌 Paral.lel
Av. Paral.lel 91; tel. 242-31-32. Tuesday, Thursday, Friday 10 p.m.,
Wednesday 5 p.m., Saturday 6 and 10 p.m., Sunday 7 p.m.
Music hall and comedies are usually on the bill here.

TEATRE Ⓜ Universitat 🚌 Pl. Universitat
GOYA **20** H5 *Main line train:* Catalunya
Joaquim Costa 68; tel. 318-19-84. Friday 10.30 p.m., Saturday 6.30 and
10.30 p.m., Sunday 6.30 p.m.
A regular venue for companies visiting from other parts of Spain, and
also the place to see dance performed every Monday.

TEATRE GREC **27** F4 Ⓜ Paral.lel 🚌 Paral.lel
Pg. Santa Madrona 36; tel. 325-10-93. Summer only.
An open-air theatre designed like an amphitheatre part of the way up
Montjuïc. It comes into its own every summer when the city holds its ma-
jor drama festival.

TEATRE Ⓜ Fontana
LLIURE **13/14** K8 🚌 Torrent de l'Olla/Gran de Gràcia
Montseny 47; tel. 218-92-51. Tuesday, Wednesday, Friday and Saturday
9 a.m., Thursday 5 p.m., Sunday 6 p.m.
One of Barcelona's highest-quality and best-established companies,
consistently producing innovative and exciting theatre, has its base here.

TEATRE MALIC (see Children)

145

TEATRE MUNICIPAL Ⓜ Paral.lel
MERCAT DE LES FLORS **19/20** F4 🚌 Palau dels Esports
Lleida 59; tel. 426-18-75/426-21-02. Tuesday to Saturday 10 p.m.,
Sunday 8 p.m.
The former flower market is now a popular theatre venue, and the site
for a range of prestigious productions from home and abroad, includ-
ing operas.

TEATRE 🚌 Rambla
POLIORAMA **21** J4 *Main line train:* Catalunya
La Rambla 115; tel. 317-75-99. Tuesday to Saturday 9 p.m., Sunday
6 p.m.
The place to visit for revue-type theatre, light comedies and the like.

TEATRE PRINCIPAL   **28/29** J3   Ⓜ Drassanes   Rambla
La Rambla 27; tel. 317-31-46.
Used occasionally as an adjunct to the Liceu, and the site of the city's oldest theatre, now long gone.

TEATRE ROMEA   **28/29** J4   Ⓜ Liceu   Rambla
Hospital 51; tel. 317-71-89. Tuesday to Saturday 9 p.m., Sunday 6 p.m.
This large and impressive theatre, built in the middle of the last century, usually puts on Catalan plays.

TEATRENEU-TEIXIDORS   Ⓜ Joanic
A MÀ   **13/14** K8   Escorial/Pi i Maragall
Terol 26; tel. 213-55-99. Tuesday to Saturday 9 p.m., Sunday and public holidays 7 p.m.
Usually a venue for smaller-scale productions, especially one-actor plays.

VILLAROEL TEATRE   **20** H5   Ⓜ Rocafort   Calàbria
Villaroel 87; tel. 451-12-34. Tuesday to Friday 10 p.m., Saturday 6.30 and 10 p.m., Sunday 5 and 8 p.m.
Regularly shows popular and longer-running productions.

CLASSICAL MUSIC, OPERA AND MODERN DANCE

146 There is probably almost as much classical music being performed in Barcelona as rock, and in addition to the fixed venues—concert halls, arts centres and churches—there's a variety of open-air concerts held around the city during the summer months. The Liceo remains the most exciting place to see opera and ballet, but a visit to the Palau de la Musica, with its suspended stone horses, should form part of any semi-cultural trip to Barcelona. Anything from jazz to oratorio might be heard there. For concert dates, check one of the regular city listings guides or contact the municipal tourist or cultural offices.

AUDITORI   Ⓜ Poble Sec/Roca
DE LA O.N.C.E.   **20** G5   Calàbria
Calàbria 66; tel. 325-92-00/423-86-63. Weekdays 7.30 p.m., Saturday times vary. Price: Free.
This auditorium, belonging to Spain's organization for the blind, regularly holds concerts that are open to everyone.

C. CÍVIC L'ARTESÀ   **13/14** K8   Ⓜ Fontana   🚌 Gran de Gràcia
Travessia Sant Antoni 6–8; tel. 218-44-85. Price: Varies from concert to concert.
A municipal cultural centre, slightly off the beaten track in the district of Gràcia.

C. CIVIC   Ⓜ Pg. de Gràcia
CASA ELIZALDE   **21/22** K6   🚌 Pg. de Gràcia/Pau Claris
València 302; tel. 215-97-80/215-99-02. Wednesday to Friday 7.30 p.m. Price: Free.
In this restored town house, now a municipal cultural centre, visitors can attend regular concerts, visit exhibitions, or walk through to the fine gardens behind the building.

CATEDRAL   Ⓜ Jaume I
DE BARCELONA   **29** K4   🚌 Via Laietana
Pla de la Seu 3; tel. 315-15-54.
A magnificent setting for hearing choral and orchestral works among the buttresses, trees and geese (see Sights: Churches).

CENTRE CULTURAL FUNDACIÓ   Ⓜ Verdaguer
LA CAIXA DE PENSIONS   **21/22** L6   🚌 P. St. Joan
Pg. Sant Joan 108; tel. 258-89-07/258-89-06.
The modernistic building is worth visiting, but the acoustics are not reckoned to be up to scratch.

147

CONSERVATORI SUPERIOR MUNICIPAL   Ⓜ Girona
DE MUSICA, AUDITORI EDUARD TOLRÀ   **21/22** K6   🚌 Bruc
Bruc 110; tel. 258-43-02/258-43-03. Price: Free.
As well as attending a concert in the city's conservatory of music, visitors can admire the fine modernistic style of the building.

ESGLÉSIA POMPEIA   Ⓜ Diagonal
PARES CAPUTXINS   **21** J/K7   🚌 Av. Diagonal/Via Augusta
Av. Diagonal 450; tel. 416-18-12.
A regular venue for classical concerts, often featuring the church's very fine organ.

ESGLÉSIA SANT FELIP NERI   **29** J4   Ⓜ Liceu
(see Sights: Churches)   🚌 Rambla
Pl. Sant Felip Neri 5; tel. 317-31-16/317-10-13.
A Baroque-style church where concerts are occasionally staged.

ESGLÉSIA SANTA ANA   **21** J4   Ⓜ Jaume I
(see Sights: Churches)   🚌 Via Laietana
Rivadeneyra 3; tel. 301-35-76.
Classical concerts are staged at irregular intervals at this Gothic church.

GRAN TEATRE DEL LICEU   **28/29** J3   Ⓜ Liceu   🚌 Rambla
Rbla. Caputxins 65; tel. 318-91-22/318-92-77. Monday to Saturday
9 p.m., Sunday 5 p.m. Price: 540–8.600.-pts.
Currently undergoing an extensive and controversial enlargement and
renovation, the Liceu is still the place to go for opera and ballet of the
highest calibre.

INSTITUT DEL TEATRE (see Theatres)
In addition to hosting theatrical productions, this venue occasionally puts
on classical concerts.

MERCAT DE LES FLORS (see Theatres)
A theatre that occasionally provides a venue for visiting opera companies.

148

PALAU D'ESPORTS   Ⓜ Espanya
SANT JORDI   **27** E4   🚌 Av. de l'Estadi
Minici Natal 5; tel. 426-20-89.
This recent, Olympic-inspired venue has been used to great effect and
apparent success by Pavarotti, and once the Games are out of the way,
some of the larger-scale and most popular concerts are expected to be
held here.

PALAU   Ⓜ Urquinaona
DE LA MÚSICA CATALANA   **21/22** K4   🚌 Via Laietana
Sant Francesc Paula 2; tel. 268-10-00. Weekdays 9 p.m., Sunday 11 a.m.

It's worth paying an admission fee just to see inside this masterpiece of modernistic architecture, recently restored. It is used as a venue for staging all types of live music.

PALAU 　　　　　　　　　　　　　Ⓜ Espanya
MUNICIPAL D'ESPORTS 　　　　🚋 Palau dels Esports
Lleida 40; tel. 424-27-76.
This sports complex just wasn't designed for sound, or for comfort during a concert, but it is used often.

PARANINF DE L'UNIVERSITAT 　　　　Ⓜ Universitat
DE BARCELONA　　**21** J5　　　🚋 Pl. Universitat
Gran Via de les Catalanes 585; tel. 318-99-26. Once a month, but not on any fixed day. Price: Free.
Regular concerts are held in the main city university's auditorium.

PARRÒQUIA　　　　　　　　　　Ⓜ Jaume I
SANTA MARIA DEL MAR　**29** K3　🚋 Via Laietana
Pl. Santa Maria 1; tel. 310-23-90. Price: Free.
One of the prettiest churches in the city, and therefore a pleasure to visit for music as well as sights.

SALA CULTURAL　　Ⓜ Catalunya　🚋 Pl. Catalunya
DE LA CAJA DE MADRID　**21** J5　*Main line train:* Catalunya **149**
Pl. Catalunya 9; tel. 301-44-94. Normally at 7.30 p.m. Price: Free.
Occasional concerts, as well as art exhibitons are held in this otherwise unremarkable building belonging to a savings bank.

SALO DE CENT　　　　　　　　Ⓜ Jaume I
(AJUNTAMENT)　　**29** J4　　🚋 Via Laietana
Pl. Sant Jaume s/n; tel. 302-42-00.
A very special place to hear a concert, within the medieval town hall and with a wealth of paintings and sculptures to admire at the same time.

TEATRE PRINCIPAL (see Theatres)
An occasional venue for classical concerts.

VELÒDROM MUNICIPAL D'HORTA
Ⓜ Montbau
(See Sights: Olympics) Pg. Vall d'Hebrón
This cycling stadium is used occasionally for large, open-air events. It makes a pleasant change from the centre of the city to listen to a concert here, though the venue's size makes it better suited to pop and rock performances.

POP AND ROCK MUSIC

Established Spanish bands, up-and-coming Catalan performers, and visiting stars from around the world all make regular appearances on Barcelona stages. However, the city has not been blessed with enough adequately sized venues, and this has resulted in popular acts having to perform in large basketball stadia with horrible acoustics. The Olympics have brought about two new important venues: the main Montjuïc Stadium for the megastars, and the Palau Sant Jordi for mere superstars. Discos and nightclubs generally account for the rest of the regular venues, along with some quite basic halls.

ARS
 Gral. Mitre
STUDIO **12/13** J9 *Main line train:* Putxet
Atenes 27; tel. 202-16-68. Daily 8 p.m.–4.30 a.m.

150 Mainly a music bar, the Ars is often the venue for live bands playing alternative music.

ARTÍCULO 26   **21** J5 Ⓜ Diagonal Gran de Gràcia
Gran de Gràcia 25; tel. 237-54-75. Monday to Thursday 11.30 p.m.–4.30 a.m., Friday to Sunday 6 p.m. to 6 a.m. Price: 1.500.-pts.
Live bands (especially of the salsa variety) play at this extremely popular venue regularly. The rest of the time, a disco takes over.

LA CIBELES   **21/22** K7 Ⓜ Verdaguer Còrsega
Còrsega 363; tel. 257-38-77/317-79-94. Thursday to Saturday 11.15 p.m.–4 a.m., Sunday 6.30–9.30 p.m. Price: 500–1.000.-pts.
More of a place to dance to salsa and other popular rhythms than a mere disco.

LA COVA Ⓜ Diagonal 🚌 Av. Diagonal/Rbla. Catalunya
DEL DRAC **13** J7 *Main line train: Gràcia*
Tuset 30; tel. 217-56-42. Daily 8 a.m.–2.30 a.m. Price: Free entry, drink 1.000.-pts.
Traditionally, the place where devotees went to hear jazz and Catalan pop and rock music. They still do. Live music is a regular feature, but it's a pleasant bar just to go for a drink.

ESTADI OLIMPIC DE MONTJUÏC **27** E3 Ⓜ Espanya
(See Sights: Olympics) 🚌 Av. de l'Estadi
Av. de l'Estadi 54; tel. 426-40-19.
After the Olympics, this is the place where the Michael Jacksons and the Rolling Stones of this world are expected to play in front of tens of thousands.

HUMEDAD 🚌 Av. del Princep d'Asturies
RELATIVA **13** J8/9 *Main line train: Pl. Molina*
Pl. Mañe i Flaquer 9; tel. 238-18-99. Daily 8.30 p.m.–3 a.m.; concerts weekends 8–10 p.m. Price: Drink 500.-pts.; entry to concert 300.-pts. including drink.
A music bar as well as a weekend venue for all kinds of live rock music. Bands from Barcelona and the rest of Spain play here and usually attract a younger crowd.

KGB **13/14** L8 Ⓜ Joanic 🚌 Pi i Maragall
Ca l'Alegre de Dalt 55; tel. 210-59-06. Monday to Saturday 10 p.m.–4 a.m. Sunday 6 p.m.–4 a.m. Price: Normally 1.000.-pts.
A massive converted warehouse, KGB houses a multicultural centre featuring live music, a disco and a loud and lively bar, all designed for the younger customer (or at least the young at heart).

151

OTTO 🚌 Travessera, Balmes
ZUTZ **13** J8 *Main line train: Gràcia*
Lincoln 15; tel. 238-07-22/238-06-63. Monday to Saturday noon–4.30 a.m. Price: 2.000.-pts. including drink.
A very popular disco, often providing the venue for live bands, from jazz to salsa to rock.

PALAU D'ESPORTS SANT JORDI (See Sights: Olympics)
Being used increasingly by medium megastars for rock concerts, this Olympic venue also hosts basketball games and other sporting events.

PALAU DE LA MÚSICA CATALANA (See Classical Music)
The modernistic Palau serves as a venue for all varieties of music, including rock, though its relatively confined stage space hampers the use of the vast amount of sound and lighting equipment with which most performers travel the world.

STUDIO 54   **28** H3   Ⓜ Paral.lel   🚌 Av. Paral.lel
Av. Paral.lel 64; tel. 329-54-54. Friday 5.30–9.30 p.m. and midnight–4.30 a.m., Saturday 6–9.30 p.m. and midnight–5 a.m., Sunday 6 p.m.–10 p.m. Price: Friday from 1.000.-pts., Saturday from 1.500.-pts., Sunday from 800.-pts.
Primarily a disco, Studio 54 is the venue for occasional rock concerts. A converted theatre, it has good acoustics and the stage is in full view.

VELÒDROM (See Sights: Olympics)
A cycling stadium that is used occasionally for large, open-air pop and rock performances (see Classical Music).

ZELESTE (see Discos and Bars)
A multicultural centre that has become a well-established venue for rock and other music. Bands usually play at weekends.

DISCOS, BARS AND NIGHTCLUBS

152

As mentioned previously, Barcelona is crammed to overflowing with bars, ranging from the cosy and quaint to the highly fashionable and expensive. They are all likely to be crowded, virtually every night, and if you want to sit down and make an evening of it, it's best to turn up reasonably early—around 10 p.m. As everywhere, most discos and nightclubs charge an admission fee, which often includes at least one drink. Some are for members only, though it is sometimes possible to arrange temporary membership. To avoid disappointment, telephone beforehand to find out how likely you are to gain entrance. At weekends, most discos and bars don't start to warm up before midnight, but then can become crammed rapidly.

AMARCORD   **21** J6   Ⓜ Diagonal   🚌 Pg. de Gràcia
Provença 261; tel. 215-72-49. Daily 7 a.m.–2 a.m.
A wide and exotic range of cocktails is among the main attractions of Amarcord. Sip one and try to work out just what was inspired by Fellini's film of this name.

ARS STUDIO (See Pop and Rock Music)
A music bar attached to a concert venue, which draws a varied crowd of Barcelona's clubbers.

ARTCAVA FUSINA   **29** K/L3   Ⓜ Jaume I   🚃 Via Laietana
Fusina 6; tel. 315-25-71. Daily 6 p.m.–1 a.m.
This combination of bar and art gallery has been installed in what was the Born market, an area rapidly gaining a fine reputation as a centre for the arts.

ARTICULO 26 (See Pop and Rock Music)
A disco, a venue for live music, and a place to meet people.

BALMORAL (See Restaurants)
A combination tearoom, restaurant and bar where the well-heeled enjoy a genteel atmosphere and some good basic dishes.

BAR DEL PÍ   **29** J4   Ⓜ Jaume I   🚃 Via Laietana
Pl. Sant Josep Oriol 1. Daily 9 a.m.–9.30 p.m.
A bar more likely to provide encounters with other tourists, although it does have a certain reputation as a meeting place for artists and intellectuals.

BERIMBAU   **29** K3   Ⓜ Jaume I   🚃 Via Laietana
Pg. Born 17; tel. 319-53-78. Daily 6 p.m.–3 a.m. Price: 550-pts.
A music bar, where you can sit, talk and drink cocktails to the sound of Brazilian rhythms.

153

BOADAS   **21** J4   Ⓜ Liceu   🚃 Rambla
Main line train: Catalunya
Tallers 1; tel. 318-95-92. Monday to Thursday noon–2 a.m., Friday to Sunday noon–3 p.m. and 6 p.m.–2 a.m.
It is generally standing-room-only in this established cocktail bar, which features an imaginative collection of drinks combining unexpected components. While you drink, take time to admire the décor, including pictures and messages from the famous.

BOIRA   **12** H8   🚃 Santaló   *Main line train:* Muntaner
Amigó 47; tel. 200-57-72. Daily 7.30 p.m.–2 a.m.
In addition to drinking, you can play a game of billiards, or just have a chat at Boira.

LA BOÎTE   **12** H7   🚌 Av. Diagonal
Av. Diagonal 477; tel. 419-59-50. Daily 10.30 p.m.–5 a.m.
Also known as Mas i Mas (more and more), this music bar features reg-ular live music from a variety of performers, and serves a selection of cold food to keep you going.

BOLICHE   **21** J7   🚌 Av. Diagonal
Av. Diagonal 508; tel. 416-11-90. Monday to Thursday 6 p.m.–3 a.m., Friday and Saturday 6 p.m.–3.30 a.m., Sunday 6 p.m.–2.30 a.m.
Boliche means bowling, but this is also a good place for a drink. And you don't have to arrive last thing at night for some atmosphere.

CAFÉ DE L'OPERA   **29** J3/4   Ⓜ Liceu   🚌 Rambla
Rbla. Caputxins 74; tel. 317-75-85. Winter: 9 a.m.–2 p.m., summer: 9 a.m.–3 a.m. Daily.
This is one of Barcelona's magnets for visitors, a place to have a cup of coffee or a drink at virtually any time of the day and watch the peo-ple go by on the Rambla. The clientele in summer is a mixture of stu-dents, tourists, gays and a few locals.

CENTRO CIUDAD   **21** J5   Ⓜ Pg. de Gràcia   🚌 Pg. de Gràcia
Consell de Cent 294; tel. 318-93-56. Monday to Thursday 8 p.m.–4 a.m., Friday and Saturday 6.30 p.m.–4.30 a.m.
Videos and billiards provide the extra entertainment in this popular bar-cum-disco, decorated in 1980s' style.

154

LA CIBELES (See Pop and Rock Music)
A dance hall with an orchestra that plays popular music to suit most tastes.

LA COVA DEL DRAC (See Pop and Rock Music)
An agreeable bar to visit for a drink. Live music is a regular feature.

COCO PRIVÉ   **21** J5/6   Ⓜ Pg. de Gràcia   🚌 Balmes
Balmes 51; tel. 454-76-12/323-68-20. Wednesday to Friday 6.30–9.30 p.m. and 11.30 p.m.–4 a.m., Saturday 6–9.30 p.m. and 11 p.m.–4 a.m., Sunday 6 p.m.–9.30 p.m. Performances Tuesday to Thursday 12.30 a.m., Friday and Saturday 11.30 p.m. and 1.30 a.m. Price: 1.000–3.000-pts.

At weekends this vast venue gets extremely crowded with run-of-the-mill disco-dancers.

DOS TORRES **12** G9/10

Tres Torres
Main line train: Provença

Via Augusta 300; tel. 205-16-08/203-98-99. Daily 1 p.m.–2.30 a.m.
A comfortable bar with a terraced garden, situated in an upland of Barcelona. At a price, you can come here to drink among the "thirty-something" crowd and stay relatively cool.

DRY MARTINI **20** H7

Aribau
Main line train: Aribau

Aribau 162; tel. 212-50-72. Monday to Saturday 6.30 p.m.–2.30 a.m.
As the name suggests, this is a cocktail bar of the more traditional kind, with a clientele to match.

FIBRA OPTICA **12** G8

Av. Diagonal

Beethoven 9; tel. 209-52-81. Daily 6 p.m.–9 p.m. and 11.20 p.m.–5 a.m.
This disco actually has to close its doors for two hours in the evening to prepare for the long haul through the night.

LA FIRA **20** H6

(M) Hospital Clínic   Aribau **155**

Provença 171; tel. 323-72-71. Monday to Thursday 7 p.m.–3 a.m., Friday and Saturday 7 p.m.–4 a.m., Sunday 6 p.m.–midnight.
As well as drinking here, the customer can admire all the fun of the fair (after which the bar is named), including merry-go-round horses and other disused attractions. Nostalgia is ever popular, so be prepared for the crowds, especially at weekends.

FUERA DE HORAS **13** J10

(M) Universitat   Balmes

Balmes 51. Weekends 6–11 a.m.
For the genuine die-hard, this club doesn't even open until well after most others have closed. Once past the door, however, you can carry on until most people are having their morning coffee break.

LA GASOLINERA   **20** H6   Ⓜ Hospital Clínic   🚋 Aribau
Main line train: Provença
Aribau 97; tel. 454-35-70. Daily 7.30 p.m.–2.30 a.m., Friday and Saturday until 3 a.m.
A music bar in what once was, apparently, a petrol station. A young clientele get to know each other or watch the videos on strategically placed screens.

GIMLET   **29** K3   Ⓜ Jaume I   🚋 Via Laietana
Rec 24; tel. 310-10-27. Monday to Thursday 7 p.m.–2.30 a.m., Friday and Saturday 7 p.m.–3 a.m.
A pleasantly relaxed bar, where there is no obligation to imbibe the drink after which it is named.

EL GRAN ENVELAT   **22** M5   Ⓜ Glòries   🚋 Gran Via
Gran Via de les Corts Catalanes 770; tel. 231-99-07. Tuesday, Wednesday and Friday 11 p.m.–5 a.m., Thursday, Saturday and Sunday 6–9.30 p.m.and 11 p.m.–5 a.m. Price: 600–1.000.-pts.
A dance hall for more mature customers, complete with a band playing all the favourite tunes.

HARLEM JAZZ CLUB   **29** J3   Ⓜ Jaume I   🚋 Via Laietana
Comtessa Sabradiel 8; tel. 310-07-55. Daily 7 p.m.–3 a.m. Price: Free.
Live jazz bands appear at the Harlem on certain nights, when, perhaps, too many people are concerned with the music rather than having a good time. But the club is lively during the rest of the week.

156

HUMEDAD RELATIVA (See Pop and Rock Music)
Even when there is no live band playing, the bar remains lively and loud.

IMPERATOR   **21** K7   🚋 Còrsega
Còrsega 327; tel. 237-43-22. Daily 6.30–9.45 p.m. and 11.30 p.m.–4 a.m., Friday and Saturday until 7.30 a.m. Price: 500–1.000.-pts.
A dance hall for those bored with pure disco music. Live bands are often featured and there's different pricing for men and women.

JIMMY'Z   **11** E9   Ⓜ Palau Reial   🚋 Av. Diagonal
Pl. Pius XII 4; tel. 339-71-08/339-78-62. Daily 10 p.m.–5 a.m.
Just behind the luxury Princesa Sofia Hotel on Diagonal, this recently opened disco (formerly named Regine's) combines a restaurant, bar

and private club—Blue—in one complex. It's all very exclusive and expensive.

KGB (See Pop and Rock Music)
As well as hearing the latest in live pop and rock, you can also have a drink in the bar of this converted factory. The most fashionable music is ever present.

MERBEYE   5 J11   *Main line train:* Tramvia Blau
Pl. Doctor Andreu s/n; tel. 212-64-55. Daily 11 a.m.–3 a.m.
Features include the interior design by Mariscal and others, and a terrace to help you wend your way through a hot night, while drinking cocktails or wine and nibbling tapas.

MIRABLAU   5 J11   *Main line train:* Tramvia Blau
Pl. Doctor Andreu s/n; tel. 418-58-79. Daily noon–5 a.m.
Take a late-night drink here and admire a magnificent view of the city from high above the noise and buildings. Two terraces allow you to sample the night air. Live music at weekends.

MIRAMELINDO   29 K3   Ⓜ Jaume I   🚊 Via Laietana
Pg. Born 15; tel. 319-53-76. Daily 8 p.m.–3 a.m.
A very popular bar, designed in colonial style, with jazz coming out of the speakers.

157

MIRASOL   12 H9   🚊 Gran de Gràcia
                                    Main line train: Gràcia
Pl. Sol 3; tel. 238-01-13. Daily 7 p.m.–2.30 a.m.
An extremely popular bar, with drinks and sandwiches on the menu.

NICK   Ⓜ Diagonal   🚊 Rbla. de Catalunya
HAVANNA   21 J6   *Main line train:* Provença
Rosselló 208; tel. 215-65-91. Monday to Thursday 6 p.m.–3 a.m., Friday to Sunday 5.30 p.m.–3 a.m.
A long-established disco bar that remains popular after its recent refurbishment. Glass, metal and uniformed staff have brought the customers back. An entire wall of TV monitors complete the high-tech image.

OLIVER Y HARDY (see Restaurants: Eating Late at Night)
Monday to Saturday noon–4.30 a.m.
This restaurant-cum-disco is so desperately trendy, it is often difficult to gain admission. But it's worth it once you're in.

OTTO ZUTZ (See Pop and Rock Music)
Everything moves at a frantic pace in this disco bar, including the customers. On the upper floor, you can admire the full-length mural while keeping an eye on the time shown by the large clock.

LA PALOMA   20 H5   Ⓜ Universitat   🚌 Rda. St. Antoni
Tigre 27; tel. 301-68-97. Thursday 6-9.30 p.m. and 11 p.m.–3 a.m, Friday and Saturday 6-9.30 p.m. and 11.30 p.m.–3.30 a.m., Sunday 6-9.30 p.m. and 11.30 p.m.–2.30 a.m. Price: 300–500.-pts.
La Paloma describes itself as the most camp dance hall in Barcelona. It comes complete with band.

QUARTIER   11 D10   🚌 Carr. Esplugues
Sta. Caterina Siena 28; tel. 203-82-26. Monday to Thursday 11 p.m.–4 a.m., Friday to Sunday 6.30–10 p.m. and midnight–5 a.m. Price: 400–700.-pts.
This disco is now a little out of fashion.

ELS QUATRE GATS   21 J/K4   Ⓜ Catalunya   🚌 Rambla
Montsió 3 bis; tel. 302-41-40. Daily 9 a.m.–2 a.m., Saturday until 3 a.m.
Historically, the meeting point for famous artists in Barcelona, Gats now has décor to match and is an interesting place to have a drink or snack while you look around.

SÍ SÍ SÍ   20 K7   Ⓜ Diagonal   🚌 Av. Diagonal
Av. Diagonal 442; tel. 217-57-73/237-56-73. Daily 7 p.m.–3 a.m.
A popular jazz bar where live bands can often be heard. Drinks are reasonably priced.

SHERLOCK   🚌 Gral. Mitre
HOLMES   12 H9   *Main line train:* Muntaner
Copèrnic 42–44; tel. 201-45-40. Daily 6 p.m.–1.30 a.m.
A well-established English-style bar, complete with everything you might

expect to find in British pubs. Booths help create a more intimate ambience.

SNOOCKER   **21/22** K5   Ⓜ Pg. de Gràcia   🚊 Llúria
Roger de Llúria 42; tel. 318-82-47. Weekdays 10 a.m.–2.30 a.m., Saturday 6 p.m.–2.30 a.m.
People queue up to play on the four snooker tables in this fashionable bar, while the rest watch the beautiful people or the videos, while drinking cocktails.

STUDIO 54 (See Pop and Rock Music)
Apart from providing one of the city's music venues, Studio 54 is a swish nightspot for dancing and drinking into the early hours.

SUTTON   **13** J7   Ⓜ Diagonal   🚊 Av. Diagonal
Main line train: Gràcia
Tuset 13; tel. 209-05-37. Sunday to Thursday 7 p.m.–4.30 a.m., Friday and Saturday 7–10 p.m. and 11 p.m.–5 a.m. Price: Weekday early evenings 1.800.-pts., evening 2.000.-pts., Friday and Saturday 2.300.-. pts., Sunday 1.500.-pts.
A disco and dance hall, with both live and recorded music. It caters for people wanting to dance to popular tunes, even though they are no longer teenagers. Not surprisingly, it remains very popular, especially at weekends.

159

TANGO   **20** G5   Ⓜ Rocafort   🚊 Calàbria
Diputació 94; tel. 325-37-70. Monday to Saturday 6–9.45 p.m. and 11.30 p.m.–4.30 a.m., Sunday until 5 a.m. Price: 400–1.200.-pts.
A place for dancing to tunes from the days before the disco beat.

TICKTACKTOE (See Restaurants: Eating Late at Night)
Monday to Thursday 8 a.m.–2.30 a.m., Friday and Saturday until 3 a.m., music in the bar 7 p.m.–3 a.m.
This popular nightspot offers food of good quality at lunchtime, although it can be a bit strange eating with all the décor of a disco around you. An "in" place to be seen at night, when people dance, drink or play snooker.

TORRES DE ÀVILA   **19** E4/5   Ⓜ Pl. Espanya
                                                  🚌 Poble Espanyol
Marquès de Comillas s/n, Poble Espanyol; tel. 424-93-09. Daily 10 p.m.–
4 a.m.
The twin towers of this expensive disco-bar house interior design (including work by Mariscal) that simply must be seen. It is an experience just to explore the nooks and crannies of this building. Lasers and other technology complete the picture.

UNIVERSAL   **12** H8   🚌 Santaló *Main line train:* Muntaner
Marià Cubí 184; tel. 200-74-70/201-46-58. Daily 7 p.m.–3 a.m.
Those who want loud music and those who prefer a quieter chat can all enjoy Universal, as it is split into two parts.

UP & DOWN   **11/12** F8   Ⓜ Maria Cristina 🚌 Av. Diagonal
Numància 179; tel. 204-85-03/209-17-00. Daily 11 p.m.–4 a.m.
One of the few posh establishments that has remained in fashion through thick and thin for several years. Members and mere customers are kept apart in the two halves of this restaurant and disco. You can almost smell the money. It is the place to see Barcelona's beautiful people at play, if you can get in.

VELÒDROM   **12** H7   Ⓜ Hospital Clínic 🚌 Muntaner
Muntaner 221–223; tel. 430-60-22. Daily 6 a.m.–1.30 a.m.
A bar where you can drink and take the opportunity to knock balls around
on the green baize.

160

VELVET   **21** J7   Ⓜ Diagonal 🚌 Balmes
                                   Main line train: Provença
Balmes 161; tel. 217-67-14. Monday to Saturday 7.30 p.m.–4 a.m.,
Sunday 5 p.m.–4 a.m.
One of the favourite venues to visit on a Barcelona bar-hopping tour. Velvet is popular with single people who enjoy 1960s' music. But it's worth going just to experience the infra-red-controlled toilets.

ZELESTE   **23** M/N4   Ⓜ Marina 🚌 Almògavers
Almògavers 122; tel. 309-12-04. Daily 11 p.m.–5 a.m. Price: Monday to
Thursday free, Friday and Saturday 700.-pts.
A popular disco is held here, and there's a regular live rock music slot.

ZSA-ZSA **20** H6/7   Ⓜ Hospital Clínic   🚌 Santaló
Rosselló 156; tel. 453-85-66. Monday to Saturday 7 p.m.–3 a.m.
This glass- and metal-dominated bar is one of the places to go for a good cocktail, and to see others there for the same purpose. If alone, just stare at the interior design, complete with constantly changing lighting, while you sip.

CABARET, VARIETY AND FLAMENCO

Top-flight cabaret rubs shoulders with music-hall variety shows in Barcelona, while in between are the strip joints, or the good-taste drag shows which maintain a fairly high standard of performance. Also, in spite of its distance from the origins of flamenco, the city attracts some excellent performers to its venues, with regular performances by leading stars in the field.

BAGDAD **29** J4   Ⓜ Liceu   🚌 Rambla
Nou de la Rambla 103; tel. 242-07-77. Monday to Saturday 11 p.m.– 1 a.m. and 1.15–3.15 a.m. Sale of tickets and reservation from 8 p.m.
A blue cabaret in the red-light district of town, where just about anything goes.

161

BARCELONA DE NOCHE **28** H3   Ⓜ Liceu   🚌 Rambla
Tàpies 5; tel. 441-11-67. Daily 11.45 p.m. and 1.30 a.m.
A drag cabaret of a reasonable standard, with a disco if you want to stay on after the show.

BELLE   🚌 Muntaner
ÉPOQUE **12** H7   *Main line train:* Muntaner
Muntaner 246; tel. 209-73-85. Daily 11.30 p.m. Price: Monday to Thursday 3.400.-pts. with drink, Friday and Saturday 3.900.-pts. with drink.
An arty cabaret, featuring women, men and a few in between.

BODEGA APOLO   **28** H3   Ⓜ Paral.lel   🚊 Paral.lel
Av. Paral.lel 59; tel. 441-40-05.
While the theatre of this name is in the process of reconstruction, the victim of Barcelona's move into the 21st century, this traditional music hall and variety show venue is reduced to more modest space.

BODEGA BOHÈMIA   **28** J3   Ⓜ Liceu   🚊 Rambla
Lancaster 2; tel. 302-50-61. Monday to Thursday 10.30 p.m.–3 a.m., public holidays and the evenings before holidays 11 p.m.–4 a.m.
Old-timers from the music hall, flamenco acts and other performing artistes can all appear on the bill here.

CORDOBÉS   **28/29** J3   Ⓜ Liceu   🚊 Rambla
La Rambla 35; tel. 317-66-53. Performances 10–11.30 p.m. and 11.30 p.m.–1.30 a.m daily. Price: 3.200.-pts.
A popular place to see and hear flamenco, though it has the reputation of being a tourist trap, rather than a venue for the true fan.

EL MOLINO   **28** G3   Ⓜ Paral.lel   🚊 Paral.lel
Vilà i Vilà 99; tel. 441-63-83. Performances Tuesday to Sunday 6 p.m. and 11 p.m., Saturday 10.15 p.m. and 1 a.m. Price: Tuesday to Friday 6 p.m. 900.-pts. with drink, Sunday 1.200.-pts. with drink, Tuesday to Friday and Sunday 11 p.m. 2.500.-pts. with drink, Saturday 11 p.m. 3.000.-pts. with drink.
One of the oldest established music-hall variety shows in town is held here. Until the venue's recent relaunch, the audience sat on wooden benches. The show is very popular, but sometimes very Catalan, complete with women, comedy acts and magicians. It's possible to join in with the fun even if you don't understand everything that is going on.

162

EL TABLAO   Ⓜ Pl. Espanya
DE CARMEN   **19** E4   🚊 Poble Espanyol
Poble Espanyol, Av. Marquès Comillas 25; tel. 325-68-95. Performances 11 p.m. and 12.45 a.m. Price: Meal and performance 4.300.-pts.
One of the best, or at least best-known, places in Barcelona to watch live flamenco of a high standard. This recently restored recreation of a typical Andalusian bar and restaurant features tapas as well as sit-down meals, plus flamenco at a reasonable price. Best to reserve beforehand, then relax with a drink in the Tablao or a nearby bar before moving on to the show.

LOS TARANTOS   **29** J3   Ⓜ Liceu   ⟨⟩ Rambla
Pl. Reial 17; tel. 317-80-98. Performances 10.15 p.m. and midnight.
Excellent flamenco is staged in this old established bar. Some say it is
the best in town, in spite of the venue's location in a square that is better visited during daylight.

TEATRE ARNAU   **28** H3   Ⓜ Paral.lel   ⟨⟩ Paral.lel
Av. del Paral.lel 60; tel. 442-28-04. Performances Monday, Tuesday,
Thursday, Friday and Sunday 6.30 and 11 p.m., Saturday 10.30
p.m.–1.15 a.m.
Cabaret of the music-hall variety, dancers, magic acts, comedy and
the rest. Best to book for a Saturday night out, as the Arnau is very
popular.

163

Barcelona has suffered for many years from a shortage of hotels, especially in the mid-price range. It is now doing something about it: a number of new hotels are being built in time for the Olympics, while many existing ones are being spruced up. However, the golden rule is still to book ahead whenever possible in order to be sure of a room. When one of the big international trade fairs is being held at the Montjuïc site of the Fira, rooms throughout the city are booked up entirely by exhibitors and visitors. That being said, the city can boast a fair selection of hotels and *pensiones*, most providing reasonably priced rooms within easy reach – by public transport or on foot – of the main attractions.

The bulk of Barcelona's budget hotels are to be found in the Barri Gòtic area, and along or just off the Rambla. As a general rule, hotels become increasingly up-market the further up the Rambla you go. The more expensive hotels are concentrated in the Eixample, which is a convenient district if you're travelling by car. The newest high-rise hotels are out along Diagonal, away from the city centre.

For a complete list of hotel accommodations in Barcelona, contact the Gremi d'Hotels de Barcelona (the Barcelona Hotels Association), Via Laietana 47; tel. 301-62-40; fax 301-42-92. Hotel reservations can be made upon arrival in Barcelona both at the airport and at Sants train station (8 a.m.–10 p.m.). Tourist offices will also provide hotel information, though they will not make reservations.

In the following pages, we offer a sampling of recommended establishments in Barcelona. The list is by no means exhaustive, but is designed to provide a few pointers to help you when making your choice. Hotels have been selected according to their facilities and location, and whether they offer something extra in the way of charm, picturesque setting or historic associations. The number of stars for each hotel is awarded under the Spanish grading system.

We have divided the hotels into the following price bands, based on the cost of a double room with bath or shower. Rates are exclusive of IVA (value-added tax), which ranges from 6% for budget hotels to 13% for four- to five-star hotels.

165

Lower-priced up to pts. 8.000
Medium-priced up to pts. 16.000
Higher-priced up to pts. 25.000
Top-priced above pts. 25.000

Flying the flag over Barcelona's elegant Ritz hotel.

UP TO 8.000-PTS

CATALUÑA**   **21** J4   Ⓜ Catalunya 🚌 Rambla
Santa Anna 22; tel. 301-91-50; fax 301-31-35. 40 rooms, single 4.505.-pts., double 7.971.-pts., breakfast 400.-pts.
Centrally located just east of the Rambla, this budget hotel has clean and comfortable rooms.

CORONADO*   **28** H3   Ⓜ Paral.lel 🚌 Paral.lel
Nou de la Rambla 134; tel. 242-34-48; fax 241-22-04. 26 rooms, single 3.180.-pts., double 6.800.-pts., breakfast 600.-pts.
This spotless budget hotel is in the charming neighborhood of Poble Seç – ideally placed for the Olympic village.

CORTÉS**   **21** J4   Ⓜ Catalunya 🚌 Rambla
Santa Anna 25; tel. 317-92-12; fax 301-31-35. 46 rooms, single 4.495.-pts., double 7.400.-pts., breakfast 400.-pts.
A small hotel with clean, modern rooms situated just off the Rambla in the old part of the city.

INGLÉS*   **29** J4   Ⓜ Liceu 🚌 Rambla
Boqueria 17; tel. 317-37-70. 28 rooms, single 2.940.-pts., double 6.150.-pts., breakfast 375.-pts.
A small hotel near the Boqueria market and the Liceu Opera House. Ask for one of the rooms at the back, which tends to be quieter and more peaceful.

166 **INTERNACIONAL***   **29** J3   Ⓜ Liceu 🚌 Rambla
La Rambla 78–80, tel. 302-25-66; fax 317-61-90. 60 rooms, single 6.000.-pts., double 7.000.-pts., breakfast 450.-pts.
With a superb location directly across from the Liceu Opera House, the Hotel Internacional is a hugely popular hotel of exceptional value. Rooms need to be booked well in advance.

LLORET*   **21** J4   Ⓜ Liceu 🚌 Rambla
La Rambla 125, tel. 317-33-66; fax 301-92-83. 52 rooms, single 4.400.-pts., double 6.800.-pts.
Another grand old hotel on the Rambla, the Hotel Lloret is a great favourite. The noise of traffic from the Rambla is its only drawback.

PASEO DE GRÀCIA***   **21** K6   Ⓜ Pg. de Gràcia   ▭ Pg. de Gràcia
Pg. de Gràcia 102; tel. 215-58-24; fax 215-37-24. 34 rooms, single 4.346.-pts., double 6.500.-pts., breakfast 350.-pts.
A new hotel on the Paseo de Gràcia. At least half the rooms have rooftop terraces with superb views.

SAN AGUSTÍN**   **28** J4   Ⓜ Jaume I   ▭ Via Laietana
Pl. Sant Agustí 3; tel. 318-16-58; fax 317-29-28. 70 rooms, single 4.950.-pts., double 7.425.-pts., breakfast 450.-pts.
This charming hotel was converted from a convent about 100 years ago. Its recently refurbished rooms have lost nothing of their old-world charm. Very good value for this price bracket.

TOLEDANO*   **21** J4   Ⓜ Catalunya   ▭ Rambla
La Rambla 138; tel. 301-08-72; fax 412-31-42. Parking, wheelchair access. 17 rooms, single 3.000.-pts., double 5.200.-pts.
Situated at the top of the Rambla near Plaça Catalunya, the Toledano is in a prime (albeit noisy) location. The rooms are basic but clean.

VIA AUGUSTA**   **13** J8   Ⓜ Diagonal   ▭ Via Augusta
Via Augusta 63; tel. 217-92-50; fax 237-77-14. 56 rooms, single 4.506.-pts., double 7.600.-pts., breakfast 450.-pts.
A modern hotel with a small garden.

UP TO 16.000-PTS

ALFA AEROPUERTO***
Zona Franca Mercabarna; tel. 336-25-64; fax 335-55-95. Parking. 60 rooms, single 9.444.-pts., double 12.200.-pts., breakfast 850.-pts.
Situated three kilometres from Barcelona's El Prat airport and approximately 20 minutes from the city centre, the Alfa Aeropuerto runs a free shuttle service to both (except on Sundays). Horseback riding, golf and tennis facilities nearby.

167

ARAGON***   **23** N6   Ⓜ Pl. de les Glòries   ▭ Independència
Aragó 569 bis, tel. 245-89-05; fax 447-09-23. Parking, wheelchair access. 72 rooms, single 9.500.-pts., double 15.900.-pts., breakfast 950.-pts.
Built in 1975 and recently renovated, the Aragon is a comfortable hotel located 500 metres from Sants train station. The rooms are air conditioned and equipped with TV, telephone and minibar.

ATENAS***   **23** O6   Ⓜ Fabra i Puig ▭ Meridiana
Av. Meridiana 151; tel. 232-20-11; fax 232-09-10. Parking. 166 rooms, single 9.500.-pts., double 15.900.-pts., breakfast 950.-pts.
A high-rise hotel located in a commercial area, the Atenas has comfortable, well-equipped rooms. The hotel features a rooftop swimming pool and terrace.

BONANOVA   ▭ Capità Arenas
PARK**   **11** F9   *Main line train:* Tres Torres
Capità Arenas 51; tel. 204-09-00; fax 204-50-14. Parking. 60 rooms, single 9.200.-pts., double 11.500.-pts., breakfast 550.-pts.
Pleasantly situated in a peaceful, well-heeled neighborhood near the university. Children's playground and gardens nearby.

CONDADO***   **12** H7   Ⓜ Aribau ▭ Aribau
Aribau 201; tel. 200-23-11; fax 200-25-86. Parking, wheelchair access. 88 rooms, single 12.800.-pts., double 16.000.-pts., breakfast 900.-pts.
Built in 1954 and recently renovated, the Condado is a comfortable hotel with rooms that are air conditioned and equipped with TV and telephone; some have balconies.

ESPAÑA**   **29** J4   Ⓜ Liceu ▭ Rambla
Sant Pau 9–11; tel. 318-17-58; fax 317-11-34. 84 rooms, single 4.500.-pts., double 8.700.-pts., breakfast 400.-pts.
An architectural gem, the España is a must for those in search of atmosphere. Even if the hotel is full, you should still make a point of dining in the Modernist splendour of the hotel's restaurant.

168 **EXPO HOTEL******   **19** F6   Ⓜ Tarragona
Mallorca 1–23; tel. 325-12-12; fax 325-11-44. Parking. 432 rooms, single 9.200.-pts., double 15.000.-pts., breakfast 1000.-pts.
Situated 20 metres from Sants train station, the Expo Residencia caters mainly to large tour groups. Facilities include a swimming pool, squash court, restaurant, bar and conference rooms.

GAUDÍ***   **28/29** J3   Ⓜ Liceu ▭ Rambla
Nou de la Rambla 12; tel. 317-90-32; fax 412-26-36. Wheelchair access. 71 rooms, single 7.700.-pts., double 11.000.-pts., breakfast 1.500.-pts.
Located across the street from Gaudí's Palau Güell, this hotel has comfortable, air-conditioned rooms with TV, telephone and radio.

GOTICO***   **29** K3   Ⓜ Jaume I   🚃 Via Laietana
Jaume I 14; tel. 315-22-11; fax 315-38-19. Parking. 70 rooms, single 8.645.-pts., double 12.950.-pts., breakfast 675.-pts.
An attractive hotel in the heart of the Barri Gòtic. The rooms are simple but tasteful with tile floors, white walls and wooden beams.

GRAN VÍA***   **21** J/K5   Ⓜ Girona   🚃 Bruc
Gran Via de les Corts Catalanes 642; tel. 318-19-00; fax 318-99-97. Parking, wheelchair access. 48 rooms, single 8.400.-pts., double 11.500.-pts., breakfast 750.-pts.
A delightful 19th-century town house teeming with old-world charm. The public rooms are richly furnished and decorated throughout with Art-Nouveau fittings.

GRAVINA***   **21** J5   Ⓜ Universitat   🚃 Pl.Universitat
Gravina 12; tel. 301-68-68; fax 317-28-38. Parking, wheelchair access. 60 rooms, single 8.900.-pts., double 13.900.-pts., breakfast 700.-pts.
Conveniently situated near Plaça Catalunya, the Gravina's attractive classic façade conceals a completely modern interior. The rooms are on the small side, but spotlessly clean.

MESON CASTILLA**   **20** J5   Ⓜ Universitat   🚃 Pl. Universitat
Valldonzella 5; tel. 318-21-82; fax 412-40-20. Parking. 60 rooms, single 5.400.-pts., double 8.100.-pts., breakfast 550.-pts.
Like so many Barcelona hotels, the Mesón Castilla has undergone extensive renovations and refurbishment. All the rooms are now air conditioned and furnished in traditional Castilian style.

METROPOL***   **29** J3   Ⓜ Drassanes   🚃 Rambla **169**
Ample 31; tel. 315-40-11; fax 319-12-76. Parking, wheelchair access. 68 rooms, single 7.000.-pts., double 10.800.-pts., breakfast 800.-pts.
Situated in old Barcelona near the harbour, this hotel is a good choice if you wish to get away from the bustle of Barcelona's main tourist areas. The rooms are modern and comfortable.

MITRE***   **13** J9/10   🚃 Gral. Mitre *Main line train:* Putxet
Bertrán 9–15; tel. 212-11-04; fax 418-94-81. Parking. 57 rooms, single 12.400.-pts., double 15.000.-pts., breakfast 725.-pts.
A modern, recently renovated hotel with rooms that are small but well equipped.

MONTECARLO***　　21 J4　　　　　　　Ⓜ Liceu 🚆 Rambla
La Rambla 124; tel. 317-58-00; fax 317-57-50. Parking. 73 rooms, single 7.095.-pts., double 11.900.-pts., breakfast included.
The main boast of the Montecarlo is its imposing entrance hall decorated with marble statues, gilded mirrors and chandeliers. The rooms, though perfectly clean and comfortable, rather pale in comparison.

NOUVEL*　　21 J4　　　　　　　Ⓜ Catalunya 🚆 Rambla
Santa Anna 18–20; tel. 301-82-74. 77 rooms, single 8.500.-pts., double 12.000.-pts., breakfast 400.-pts.
Situated on a pedestrian street just below Plaça de Catalunya, this hotel, with its attractive Art-Nouveau interior, is being refurbished in time for the Olympic games.

ORIENTE***　　29 J3　　　　　　　Ⓜ Liceu 🚆 Rambla
La Rambla 45–47; tel. 302-25-58; fax 412-38-19. 142 rooms, single 8.650.-pts., double 14.000.-pts., breakfast 750.-pts.
Barcelona's oldest hotel, the Oriente has managed to preserve its old-world glamour and style. The hotel ballroom is unique in the way it incorporates part of an old Franciscan monastery into its structure. The rooms are fairly ordinary, but nevertheless large, clean and comfortable.

PRINCIPAL**　　28 H/J4　　　　Ⓜ Pla del Palau 🚆 Pla del Palau
Junta del Comerç 8; tel. 318-89-70; fax 412-08-19. Parking. 55 rooms, single 4.900.-pts., double 8.800.-pts., breakfast included.
A friendly and efficiently run hotel located on a quiet street near Ciutadella Park.

REDING***　　21 J5　　　　　　Ⓜ Universitat 🚆 Universitat
Gravina 5–7; tel. 412-10-97. Parking. 44 rooms, single 9.500.-pts., double 11.500.-pts., breakfast 650.-pts.
A well-run establishment with bedrooms that are small but comfortable. The staff are particularly helpful and friendly.

170

REGENCIA COLÓN***　　29 K4　　　Ⓜ Jaume I 🚆 Via Laietana
Carrer Sagristans 13–17, tel. 318-98-58; fax 317-28-22. Parking. 55 rooms, single 5.400.-pts., double 13.900.-pts., breakfast 950.-pts.
Moderately priced in a prime location near the 13th-century cathedral, this recently renovated hotel is a good solid choice.

REGINA***　　21 J5　　　　　　Ⓜ Catalunya 🚆 Pl. Catalunya
Bergara 2; tel. 301-32-32; fax 318-23-26. 103 rooms, single 6.400.-pts., double 14.600.-pts., breakfast 950.-pts.

A comfortable and moderately priced hotel located just off Plaça de Catalunya. The rooms are air conditioned and equipped with TV and telephone; half of them have balconies.

RIALTO* **29** J3 Ⓜ Liceu 🚊 Rambla
Ferran 40–42; tel. 318-52-12; fax 315-38-19. Parking, wheelchair access. 128 rooms, single 9.150.-pts., double 13.500.-pts., breakfast 675.-pts.
Near Plaça de Sant Jaume in the Barri Gòtic, the Rialto is an attractive, comfortable hotel. The rooms are sizable, and have a distinctively Spanish feel to them.

SUIZO* **29** K3/4 Ⓜ Jaume I 🚊 Via Laietana
Pl. de l'Angel 12; tel. 315-41-11; fax 315-38-19. Parking, 48 rooms, single 10.800.-pts., double 13.500.-pts., breakfast 675.-pts.
Just off Vía Laietana on the edge of the Barri Gòtic, the Suizo enjoys a prime location. Its recently renovated rooms, each with its own balcony, are spacious, bright and cheerful.

WILSON* **12** H7 Ⓜ Diagonal 🚊 Av. Diagonal
Diagonal 568; tel. 209-25-11; fax 200-83-70. 55 rooms, single 6.500.-pts., double 13.000.-pts., breakfast 725.-pts
A clean and comfortable hotel, well placed for both the business and tourist areas. Rooms are air conditioned and equipped with TV and telephone.

UP TO 25.000-PTS

ALEXANDRA** **21** J6 Ⓜ Pg. de Gràcia 🚊 Pg. de Gràcia

171

Mallorca 251; tel. 487-05-05; fax 216-06-06. Parking. 75 rooms, single 17.500.-pts., double 25.000.-pts., breakfast 1.350.-pts.
A modern hotel with a reconstructed vintage façade, the Alexandra is the last word in quiet good taste. The rooms are spacious and well appointed; the staff attentive and efficient.

ARENAS** **11** E9 🚊 Capità Arenas
Main line train: Tres Torres
Capità Arenas 20; tel. 280-03-03; fax 280-33-92. Parking. 59 rooms, single 15.000.-pts., double 17.500.-pts., breakfast 925.-pts.
A comfortable hotel, recently renovated, the Arenas is situated in a residential district north of the city centre.

ASTORIA* 20** H7   Ⓜ Diagonal 🚋 Balmes
París 203; tel. 209-83-11; fax 202-30-08. Parking. 108 rooms, single 9.700.-pts, double 17.100.-pts., breakfast 975.-pts.
Well situated in the centre of Eixample just below Diagonal, this recently renovated 1950s' hotel is unpretentious but comfortable. The larger rooms have adjoining sitting room.

BALMES* 20/21** J6   Ⓜ Pg. de Gràcia 🚋 Pg. de Gràcia
Mallorca 216; tel. 451-19-14; fax 451-00-49. Parking, wheelchair access. 97 rooms, single 11.522.-pts., double 18.400.-pts., breakfast 975.-pts.
Built in 1989, the Balmes Hotel has its own little library, a garden, swimming pool, gym and sauna. The rooms are air conditioned and equipped with TV and video.

BALMORAL** 21** J7   Ⓜ Diagonal 🚋 Via Augusta
Via Augusta 5; tel. 217-87-00; fax 415-14-21. Parking. 94 rooms, single 12.650.-pts., double 22.000.-pts., breakfast 1.000.-pts.
Conveniently situated just off Avinguda Diagonal, the Balmoral is a quiet and comfortable hotel.

COLÓN** 29** K4   Ⓜ Jaume I 🚋 Via Laietana
Av. Catedral 7; tel. 301-14-00; fax 317-29-15. Parking. 151 rooms, single 12.500.-pts., double 19.500.-pts., breakfast 1.250.-pts.
With an unbeatable location right opposite the cathedral, this charming town-house hotel was one of Joan Miró's favourite haunts. Ask for one of the front rooms overlooking the cathedral plaza, where traditional sardanas are danced every Sunday.

172

CONDOR** 13** J8   Ⓜ Diagonal 🚋 Via Augusta
Via Augusta, 127; tel. 209-45-11; fax 202-27-13. Parking. 78 rooms, single 14.000.-pts., double 19.200.-pts., breakfast 1.200.-pts.
Conveniently situated just north of the city centre, the Hotel Condor is a business-orientated hotel offering all the facilities.

DANTE** 20** H6   Ⓜ Pg. de Gràcia 🚋 Pg. de Gràcia
Mallorca 181; tel. 323-22-54; fax 323-74-72. Parking, wheelchair access. 81 rooms, single 13.000.-pts., double 20.000.-pts., breakfast 1.100.-pts.
Situated near the city centre, one kilometre from Sants train station, the Dante has rooms that are small but well equipped.

DERBY****   **12** G7/8   Ⓜ Hospital Clinic
Loreto 21–25; tel. 322-32-15; fax 410-08-62. Parking. 116 rooms, single 15.288.-pts., double 22.000.-pts., breakfast 1.250.-pts.
A well-run hotel with comfortable air-conditioned rooms equipped with TV, telephone and minibar. The hotel features an English pub and piano bar.

DUQUES DE BERGARA****   **21** J5   Ⓜ Catalunya 🚋 Rambla
Bergara 11, tel. 301-51-51; fax 317-34-42. Parking. 56 rooms, single 14.900.-pts., double 23.900.-pts., breakfast 1.200.-pts.
A late 19th-century Modernist mansion, the Duques de Bergara was only recently converted into a hotel. The décor is a tasteful combination of old and new.

GRAN HOTEL CALDERÓN****   **21** J5   Ⓜ Catalunya 🚋 Rambla
Rbla. Catalunya 26; tel. 301-00-00; fax 317-31-57. Parking, wheelchair access. 244 rooms, single 17.600.-pts., double 24.200.-pts., breakfast 1.400.-pts.
A modern towering high-rise, the Gran Calderón offers stunning views over the whole city. Its facilities include indoor and outdoor swimming pools, sauna and exercise room.

HESPERIA****   **12** F/G10   🚋 Via Augusta
                                   Main line train: Tres Torres
Vergós 20; tel. 204-55-51; fax 204-43-92. Parking, wheelchair access. 139 rooms, single 13.500.-pts., double 19.625.-pts., breakfast 1.200.-pts.
Located in a quiet residential area, the Hesperia is a pleasant and comfortable hotel. The rooms are air conditioned and equipped with TV, telephone, hair dryer and minibar.

MAJÈSTIC****   **21** K6   Ⓜ Pg. de Gràcia 🚋 Pg. de Gràcia **173**
Pg. de Gràcia 70; tel. 215-45-12; fax 215-77-73. Parking. 336 rooms, single 18.000.-pts., double 23.800.-pts., breakfast 1.400.-pts.
A picturesque town-house hotel with a modern extension, rooftop terrace and swimming pool, as well as a prime position on the fashionable Passeig de Gràcia.

MASTER****   **20** G/H6   ⓂHospital Clinic
Valencia 105; tel. 423-62-15; fax 423-43-89. Parking. 84 rooms, single 15.600.-pts., double 21.200.-pts., breakfast 1.200.-pts.
Centrally located in a business district, the Hotel Master has air-conditioned rooms with satellite TV and minibar.

MIKADO***   **12** G10   🚊 Pg. Bonanova
P. de la Bonanova 58; tel. 211-41-66; fax 211-42-10. Parking. 66 rooms, single 11.900.-pts., double 18.900.-pts., breakfast 950.-pts.
Situated in a quiet residential area, the Hotel Mikado is recommended for longer stays. The rooms are air conditioned and equipped with TV, telephone and radio. Facilities include a restaurant, bar and solarium.

NUMANCIA***   **11/19** F4   Ⓜ Sants Estacio   🚊 Numància
Numància 72–74; tel. 322-44-51; fax 410-76-42. Parking. 140 rooms, single 11.900.-pts., double 16.700.-pts., breakfast 900.-pts.
Built in 1976 and recently renovated, the Numancia Hotel is located near Sants train station. The rooms are air conditioned with TV and telephone.

NUÑEZ-URGEL****   **20** H7   Ⓜ Hospital Clinic   🚊 Casanovas
Comte d'Urgell 232; tel. 322-41-53; fax 419-01-06. Parking. 121 rooms, single 11.500.-pts., double 20.000.-pts., breakfast 1.000.-pts.
A centrally located hotel with rooms that are air conditioned and equipped with TV, telephone and radio. Facilities include an international restaurant, bar, conference rooms and elevator.

PARK HOTEL***   **29** K/L3   Ⓜ Pla del Palau   🚊 Pla del Palau
Av. Marquès de l'Argentera 11; tel. 319-60-00; fax 319-45-19. Parking, wheelchair access. 95 rooms, single 12.450.-pts., double 16.500.-pts., breakfast 1.150.-pts.
Though unimpressive from the outside, the Park Hotel is tastefully decorated inside, and the staff are very helpful and friendly. Situated near the harbour, not far from the old railway station.

174

PARK PUXTET****   **13** J9   Ⓜ Gral Mitre   *Main line train:* Putxet
Putxet 68–74; tel. 212-51-58; fax 418-51-57. Parking. 141 rooms, single 11.500.-pts., double 19.900.-pts., breakfast 950.-pts.
A comfortable, modern hotel located two kilometres from Sants train station. The rooms are air conditioned and equipped with TV, telephone and minibar.

REGENTE****   **21** J6   Ⓜ Pg. de Gràcia   🚊 Rbla. Catalunya
Rbla. Catalunya 76; tel. 215-25-70; fax 487-32-27. Parking. 78 rooms, single 13.000.-pts., double 19.500.-pts., breakfast 1.100.-pts.
A charming Modernist town house in the Eixample, with a small rooftop swimming pool and panoramic views over Montjuïc.

RIVOLI RAMBLAS****   **21** J4   Ⓜ Liceu   🚃 Rambla
La Rambla 128; tel. 302-66-43; fax 317-50-53. Parking, wheelchair access. 87 rooms, single 19.200.-pts., double 24.000.-pts., breakfast 1.900.-pts.
With a prime location at the top of the Rambla, the Rivoli Ramblas is a swish, luxurious hotel. The rooms are spacious and elegantly decorated in shades of pastel. Facilities include a sauna, solarium and jacuzzi.

ROYAL****   **21** J4   Ⓜ Liceu   🚃 Rambla
La Rambla 117; tel. 301-94-00; fax 317-31-79. Parking. 108 rooms, single 17.500.-pts., double 21.800.-pts., breakfast 1.250.-pts.
Well situated at the top of the Rambla, the Hotel Royal offers all the amenities at a reasonable price. The rooms are tastefully appointed, if somewhat small.

SANT MORITZ****   **21** J/K5   Ⓜ Pg. de Gràcia   🚃 Pg. de Gràcia
Diputacion 262–264; tel. 412-15-00; fax 412-12-36. Parking, wheelchair access. 92 rooms, single 12.500.-pts., double 24.000.-pts., breakfast 1.300.-pts.
A modern hotel built in 1990, the Sant Moritz has comfortable and well-equipped rooms. Golfing facilities nearby.

AVENIDA PALACE*****   **21** J5   Ⓜ Universitat   🚃 Balmes
Gran Via de les Corts Catalanes 605; tel. 301-96-00; fax 318-12-34. 229 rooms, single 14.400.-pts., double 27.200.-pts., breakfast 1.400.-pts.
With a superb location between Passeig de Gràcia and Rambla de Catalunya, the Avenida Palace is an elegant hotel dating back to the 1950s. Its lobby is lavishly decorated, with marble columns and a grand double staircase. The rooms are comfortable and reasonably spacious. Facilities include a health club and sauna.

175

BARCELONA   Ⓜ Maria Cristina
HILTON*****   **12** H7/8   🚃 Pl. Maria Cristina
Av. Diagonal 589–591; tel. 419-22-33; fax 419-50-03. Parking, wheelchair access. 290 rooms, single 31.000.-pts., double 40.000.-pts., breakfast 2.000.-pts.
One of Barcelona's newest deluxe hotels, the Hilton is a citadel of comfort offering the complete range of facilities from conference rooms to limousines to babysitting services.

CONDES   Ⓜ Pg. de Gràcia
DE BARCELONA****   **21** K6   🚍 Pg. de Gràcia
Pg. de Gràcia 75, tel. 487-37-37; fax 487-14-42. Parking. 100 rooms, single, 17.900.-pts., double 28.000.-pts., breakfast 1.500.-pts.
A stately Modernist mansion dating back to the late 19th century, the Hotel Condes is one of Barcelona's most popular hotels. Particularly impressive is the marble-floored lobby, which incorporates all the features of the original courtyard. The rooms are modern, each with its own balcony.

DIPLOMATIC*****   **21/22** K5/6   Ⓜ Urquinaona   🚍 Pau Claris
Pau Claris 122; tel. 317-31-00; fax 318-65-31. Parking. 217 rooms, single 19.200.-pts., double 29.500.-pts., breakfast 1.750.-pts.
A comfortable hotel catering mainly to business travellers, the Diplomatic is conveniently situated in an elegant residential and commercial area.

GRAN   Ⓜ Les Corts
DERBY****   **12** G7/8   🚍 Pl. Francesc Macià
Loreto 28; tel. 322-32-15; fax 419-68-20. Parking. 38 suites, single suite 23.000.-pts., double suite 29.800.-pts., breakfast 1.250.-pts.
A modern Eixample hotel located near Plaça Francesco Macià. The rooms are very well equipped, each with its own adjoining sitting room; several have an extra bedroom as well. The only drawback is the hotel's location, which is well off the tourist trail.

HAVANA PALACE*****   **21/22** K5   Ⓜ Girona   🚍 Bruc
Gran Via de les Corts Catalanes 647; tel. 412-11-15; fax 216-08-35. Parking, wheelchair access. 149 rooms, single 23.600.-pts., double 31.000.-pts., breakfast 1.900.-pts.
A new luxury hotel situated in a business and commercial area. The air-conditioned rooms come with marble bath, cable TV and minibar. Facilities include a gym and sauna.

176

HOTEL DE LAS ARTES*****   **30** M3   Ⓜ Ciutadella
Pg. Carles I 19–21; tel. 488-28-54; fax 488-00-58. 456 rooms, single 27.000.-pts, double 34.000.-pts.
One of the hotels being built in time for the Olympic games, the Hotel de las Artes is Barcelona's newest *gran lujo* (super-deluxe) establishment. Set in a towering high-rise (the tallest building in Barcelona), the rooms have fabulous views over the whole city.

MELIÁ BARCELONA SARRIÀ*****   **12** G8   🚊 Trv. de les Corts
*Av. Sarrià 50; tel. 410-60-60; fax 321-51-79. Parking, wheelchair access.
312 rooms, single 23.000.-pts., double 30.000.-pts., breakfast 2.000.-pts.*
A modern, high-rise hotel offering the full range of facilities, with a picturesque setting in Sarrià.

LE MERIDIEN BARCELONA*****   **21** J4   Ⓜ Liceu 🚊 Rambla
La Rambla 111; tel. 318-62-00; fax 301-77-76. Parking. 210 rooms, single 28.400 to 42.900.-pts., double 41.000.-pts., breakfast 2.250.-pts.
Recently refurbished and upgraded, the Meridien (formerly the Ramada Renaissance) is now a top-rated luxury hotel, offering an extensive range of services and facilities.

PRESIDENTE*****   **12** H7   Ⓜ Diagonal 🚊 Av. Diagonal
Av. Diagonal 570; tel. 200-21-11; fax 209-51-06. Parking. 156 rooms, single 22.000.-pts., double 27.300.-pts., breakfast 1.500.-pts.
A well-established hotel for business travellers situated on one of Barcelona's main boulevards.

PRINCESA   Ⓜ Maria Cristina
SOFÍA*****   **11** E9   🚊 Pl. Maria Cristina
Pl. Pius XII 4; tel. 330-71-11; fax 330-76-21. Parking. 505 rooms, single 26.500.-pts., double 34.500.-pts., breakfast 1.700.-pts.
A modern towering high-rise in the new commercial area along Diagonal, the Princesa Sofía is better suited to business travellers than tourists. Its facilities are unbeatable, and include everything from conference rooms to swimming pools to banks, shops and restaurants.

RITZ*****   **21/22** K5   Ⓜ Girona 🚊 Pl. Tetuán
Gran Via de les Corts Catalanes 668; tel. 318-52-00; fax 318-01-48. Parking. 61 rooms, single 32.800.-pts., double 45.200.-pts., breakfast **177** *2.050.-pts.*
Extensive renovations have restored the Hotel Ritz to its former Belle-Epoque splendour. The rooms are spacious and utterly sumptuous, with marble fireplaces and Roman baths. Impeccable service.

SUITE   🚊 Santaló
HOTEL*****   **12** H9   *Main line train:* Muntaner
Muntaner 505; tel. 212-80-12; fax 211-23-17. Parking. 70 suites, single suite 18.500.-pts., double suite 29.900.-pts., breakfast 1.500.-pts.
A hotel made up entirely of suites – bedroom, sitting room and bathroom – that are modern, spacious and well equipped. Service is attentive and efficient.

Even if the amusement park in Tibidabo isn't your first port of call, sooner or later the children will have to be taken there, as by both night and day its giant and alluring Ferris Wheel is visible from many points of the city below. A visit to this highest point in Barcelona will be the pinnacle of any child's holiday, but there are also many other attractions to keep the young amused. Some of the more modern parks appear to have been designed with children in mind; Gaudí's creations are especially attractive, with shapes seemingly built to clamber over, through or around.

Several museums have special displays designed for children, while a trip out of town to see the miniature recreation of Catalunya in Torrelles de Llobregat provides a novel way of seeing the country without moving very far.

The Poble Espanyol, with its recreation of village and urban Spain, is an ideal and safe place to let the young run around the streets, and it also provides an educational insight into a variety of lifestyles and buildings.

In general, Barcelona is like the rest of Spain and other Mediterranean countries in that children are welcome in restaurants, shops and bars. There's a full complement of fast food establishments, both imported and home-grown, and restaurants will almost always be able to serve half-portions for accompanying children. Other customers are unlikely to tut at boisterous behaviour, unless the children are completely out of control.

However, there are a few drawbacks to life with a young child in the city. Barcelona is only gradually adapting to pushchairs, and the many cobbled streets, especially in the older parts of town, are definitely not user-friendly. The traffic is an additional hazard: even at pedestrian crossings you must keep your wits about you when you cross the street.

179

"Excuse me, which way to the Sagrada Família?"

INTERESTING THINGS TO SEE AND DO

CATALUNYA EN MINIATURA
(See Walks and Tours)   Ⓣ Numància/Sants
Torelles de Llobregat; tel. 656-41-61. Daily 9 a.m.–6 p.m.
These miniature representations of buildings from Barcelona and the rest
of Catalunya make for an interesting outing beyond the city.

PALAU REIAL   Ⓜ Palau Reial
DE PEDRALBES   11 D9   Ⓣ Av. Diagonal
Av. Diagonal 686; tel. 203-75-01. Daily 10 a.m.–8 p.m.
Apart from the gardens surrounding this former royal palace, several museums—amongst them the carriage museum, which is fun for older children—are concentrated in the area.

PARC   Ⓜ Espanya
ATRACCIONS MONTJUÏC   28 G3   Ⓣ Parc Montjuïc
Ctra. Montjuïc 26–50; tel. 242-31-75/241-70-24. Weekends noon–
9.15 p.m.
The big advantage of the amusement park on Montjuïc is that there are
other things to do in the same area, to suit all tastes. A variety of amusement park diversions are on offer.

PARC   Ⓜ Av. Tibidabo
ATRACCIONS TIBIDABO   5 J13   Ⓣ Av. Tibidabo/Tramvia Blau
Pl. Tibidabo 3; tel. 211-79-42/900-30-04-66. Weekdays 11 a.m.–8 p.m.,
weekends and public holidays until 9 p.m.
Great rivalry exists between Barcelona's two amusement parks, here and
on Montjuïc. Tibidabo has been relaunched recently with a whole set of
new attractions for children and adults. It's pricier than its rival, but the
more modern of the two. Fun and games can be had while overlooking
the city, especially on the roller coaster, which advertises itself as the
biggest in Europe, and Aeromagic, where you'll be suspended in gon-
dolas 25 metres (82 feet) off the ground.

180

PARC   Ⓜ Montbau
DEL LABERINT   7 O12/13   Ⓣ Pg. Valle d'Hebrón
Pg. Castanyers 1; tel. 428-39-34. Daily 10 a.m.–8 p.m.
Near the area of Horta, within the park of an aristocrat's estate, is the 200-
year-old Laberint, a maze fashioned out of yew hedges. Over the years
the labyrinth, the surrounding gardens and the palace dominating the
whole have been visited by various kings of Spain. Now they are very
popular with school outings and families.

PARC GÜELL   13/14 L9   Ⓜ Vallcarca   🚌 Crta. del Carmel
Olot 7. Daily 10 a.m.–8 p.m.
The colours, shapes and contours were obviously built into Gaudí's design for the park to please the young, who run and clamber around with enthusiasm.

PARC ZOOLÒGIC   29 L4   Ⓜ Ciutadella   🚌 Pg. Picasso
Parc de la Ciutadella, Pg. Picasso 15–21; tel. 309-25-00. Daily 10 a.m.–7 p.m.
The city zoo, within the Ciutadella park, features a host of monkeys, together with a show involving a killer whale and dolphins. Many unusual animals can be spotted amongst its 7,000 inhabitants. A special feature for children is a farm zoo, whose animals can be touched and stroked. A "Zoobus" departs regularly from Plaça Catalunya.

TURÓ PARC –   🚌 Pl. Francesc Macià
POETA EDUARDO MARQUINA   12 G8   *Main line train:* Muntaner
Av. Pau Casals 1. Daily 10 a.m.–8 p.m.
A city park with plenty of space for children to run around. A small lake and a skateboard "run", incorporating everyday street obstacles, are among the attractions to keep young ones out of mischief. Puppet shows on Sundays at lunch time are also a popular feature.

PLANETARIUMS

FUND.   🚌 Gral. Mitre
MEDITERRANIA   12 G10   *Main line train:* Sarrià
Planetari de Barcelona, Escoles Pies 103; tel. 211-64-16. Weekdays 8 a.m.–1 p.m. and 3–6 p.m. Closed in August. **181**
The city's main planetarium is very popular with children, who appreciate the interactive approach to astronomy (see Museums). Closed until September 1992.

MUSEU DE LA CIENCIA (See Museums)
The planetarium and many of the museum's displays are specifically aimed at keeping children—and adults—interested and occupied.

WORKSHOPS AND LEISURE ACTIVITIES

Most of the following run special activities or mount seasonal displays specifically for children. Since these change regularly, ask for information from one of the city tourist offices, or contact the museum directly.

INST. BOTÀNIC
DE BARCELONA   **19** D/E4

Ⓜ Paral.lel
🚇 Av. Paral.lel

Av. Montanyans 25; tel. 325-80-50/325-81-04. Monday to Saturday 9 a.m.–5 p.m., Sunday until 2 p.m.
A research institution, attached to the Botanical Gardens on Montjuïc (see Walks and Tours: Leisurely Walks). Important investigative work is carried out here.

MUSEU ARTS, INDUSTR.
I ATRACCIONS POPULARS   **19** E4/5

Ⓜ Espanya
🚇 Marqués de Comillas

Av. Marqués Comilla 25; tel. 423-69-54/423-01-96. Tuesday to Sunday 10 a.m.–1 p.m. Book in advance.
Another of the attractions inside the Poble Espanyol on Montjuïc, the museum contains a wide breadth of exhibits from all over northern Spain, especially Catalunya. Among them are wooden toys, lead soldiers and the paraphernalia of a chemist's shop over the centuries.

MUSEU DE CERA DE BARCELONA (See Museums)
Regular updates of the 300 or so waxworks contained in this exhibition take place. The children won't notice some of the more approximate versions of their heroes.

MUSEU D'AUTÒMATES DEL TIBIDABO (See Museums)
Here you can play the original amusement arcade machines, though they might seem very basic compared to their modern equivalents.

182 ### MUSEU D'HISTÒRIA DE LA CIUTAT (See Museums)
The section that explains and details the changes in urban life that have taken place since the 14th century is a popular attraction.

MUSEU DE LA CIENCIA (See Museums)
"Please do touch" is the instruction in this well-planned museum, and there are special sessions for children, in various languages. Previous attractions have included the opportunity to see and hold reptiles (to overcome any fear you might have of the creatures) and an exhibition

of holograms, complete with a one-metre (three-foot) tarantula. Among the more than 300 exhibits are a human gyroscope and a special section for children between the ages of three and seven.

MUSEU DE LES ARTS D'ESPECTÀCLE – INSTITUT TEATRE (See Museums)
Costumes, props and models from the world of theatre, dance, opera and cinema.

MUSEU Y CENTRE D'ESTUDIS DE L'ESPORT "DR. MELCIOR COLET" (See Museums)
Sporting memorabilia from this century, mainly from Catalunya, now with more emphasis on the Olympics.

OBSERVATORI FABRA   **5** J12   Ⓜ Montbau   🚌 Pg. Valle d'Hebrón
Ctra. Observatori F,M 820; tel. 417-57-36. Reserve in advance.
The Observatory is due to reopen in mid-1992 with a new programme of attractions. Consult the tourist office for details.

MAGIC AND PUPPET SHOWS

With a stupefying lack of logic, many of the following establishments take a break from putting on shows just when children—and their parents—need them, namely, during the holidays.

EL LLANTIOL   **20/28** H4   Ⓜ Sant Antoni   🚌 Rda. Sant Antoni
Riereta 7; tel. 329-90-09. Sunday 11.30 a.m.
Clowns and magic shows are a regular feature in this café-theatre.

FUNDACIÓ JOAN MIRÓ   **28** F/G3   Ⓜ Espanya   🚌 Av. de l'Estadi **183**
Av. Miramar 71–75; tel. 329-19-08. Saturday 5.30 p.m., Sunday 11.30 a.m. and 1.30 p.m.
Clowns, puppets and children's theatre appear regularly in the Foundation's small auditorium.

TEATRE MALIC   **29** K/L3   Ⓜ Jaume I   🚌 Via Laietana
Fussina 3; tel. 310-70-35.
The emphasis here is on children's theatre, with occasional puppet and marionette shows.

TURÓ PARC –
POETA EDUARDO MARQUINA   **12** G8   🚌 Calvet Muntaner
Av. Pau Casals 1; tel. 301-61-00. Sunday noon–1.30 p.m.
Regular puppet shows, usually on Sundays at lunch time.

CINEMA

Several of Barcelona's cinemas have special matinées for children. They normally take place on Sundays and public holidays, at the Lauren or Verdi (see Nightlife), usually from about 11.30 a.m. or noon. Check the weekend paper for the programme, or the "Para Niños" box in the cinema section of the *El País Guia* on Friday. Most will be films dubbed into Spanish or Catalan, but there is usually a fair sprinkling of cartoons where language is less important for younger children.

CINE SAVOY   **21** J/K6   Ⓜ Diagonal 🚌 Pg. de Gràcia
Pg. de Gràcia 86; tel. 215-37-76. Children's screenings at weekends at 4.30 p.m., also Sunday and public holidays 11.30 a.m.
Regular children's matinées.

FILMOTECA INFANTIL,   Ⓜ Gràcia
FILMOTECA DE LA GENERALITAT   **12** H8   🚌 Travessera
Trav. de Gràcia 63; tel. 317-35-85. Children's screenings on Sunday at noon.
Like its "adult" equivalent, the Sunday matinées for children usually feature older films, often classics.

FUNDACIÓ   Ⓜ Espanya
JOAN MIRÓ   **28** F/G3   🚌 Av. de l'Estadi
Av. Miramar 71–75; tel. 329-19-08. Saturday 5.30 p.m., Sunday 11.30 a.m. and 1.30 p.m.
Holds a regular season of theatre and shows especially designed for children, usually in Catalan or Spanish.

JOVE TEATRE ⓜ Diagonal
REGINA   21 J7 🚌 Gran de Gràcia
Séneca 22; tel. 218-15-12. Weekends 6 p.m.
A prolific producer of children's theatre in Catalan or Spanish, with
frequent visiting companies, but with a long summer break between
seasons.

PARC ATRACCIONS MONTJUÏC, ⓜ Espanya
AMFITEATRE   28 G3 🚌 Av. de l'Estadi
Ctra. Montjuïc 26–50; tel. 242-31-75.
Regular but poorly scheduled theatre, magic shows and the like are held
in the Amphitheatre of the amusement park.

TEATRE MALIC, ⓜ Jaume I
TEATRE INFANTIL   29 K/L3 🚌 Via Laietana
Fussina 3; tel. 310-70-35.
Many children's theatre companies come to the Malic. Dramatized his-
torical tales performed with marionettes or puppets are another feature.

BOOKS

The following bookshops have good sections of literature for children,
though they are not necessarily just for the young.

ALCORA I DELFIN (See Shopping)
Although its speciality is books on art, design and photography, this well-
established shop offers a good selection of children's reading.

LLIBRERIA COOPERATIVA ⓜ Diagonal
ABACUS   20 J7 🚌 Av. Diagonal
*Còrsega 269, tel. 415-14-44. Monday to Saturday 9.30 a.m.–1 p.m. and
4–7.30 p.m. Also at Ausias Marc 16–18, tel. 217-81-66.* **185**
If you make friends with a teacher or someone else in the profession,
discounts are to be had here on books, toys and other educational
material.

LLIBRERIA ⓜ Catalunya
ELS TARTESSOS   21 J4 🚌 Rda. Sant Pere
*Canuda 35; tel. 301-81-81. Monday to Saturday 10 a.m.–2 p.m. and
4.30–8 p.m.*

A bookshop-cum-gallery with a good children's section in addition to photography books.

LLIBRERIA   🚊 Rambla
LLAR DEL LLIBRE   **20/21** J4   *Main line train:* Catalunya
Elisabets 6; tel. 318-27-00. Monday to Saturday 9 a.m.–1.30 p.m. and 4–7.30 p.m.
Although mainly a bookshop specializing in the sciences, it also stocks a good range of books aimed at children.

LLIBRERIA ONA   **21/22** K5   Ⓜ Tetuán 🚊 Pl. Tetuán
Gran Via de les Corts Catalanes 654; tel. 318-19-79. Monday to Saturday 9.30 a.m.–1.30 p.m. and 4–8 p.m.
Almost exclusively books in Catalan on sale here, along with recorded music by Catalan artistes.

ELS TRES TOMBS   **21** J/K6 Ⓜ Pg. de Gràcia 🚊 Pg. de Gràcia
Pg. de Gràcia 76, tel. 215-16-48. Monday to Saturday 10 a.m.–8.30 p.m. Also at Trav. de Gràcia 96, tel. 218-92-86.
A paradise of toys and books for children. It also includes a selection of disguises for parties or fiestas.

TOYS

CAVALL   🚊 Balmes
DE CARTRÓ   **12** H/J9   *Main line train:* Putxet
Rda. Gral. Mitre 158, tel. 418-06-76. Monday to Saturday 10.10 a.m.–1.30 p.m. and 4.10–8 p.m. Also at Av. Infanta Carlota 124, tel. 321-52-95; Pg. de Gràcia 55–57, tel. 215-94-01.
Specializes in traditional, well-made toys, many carved from wood. Beautiful dolls are another highlight.

186

HOBBY-MODELS   **19** E7   Ⓜ Sants 🚊 Numància
Galileo 93; tel. 339-15-94. Monday to Saturday 10 a.m.–1.30 p.m. and 4.30–8.30 p.m.
As the name suggests, this shop specializes in kits, model railways, slot-car racing and a whole range of other hobbies.

JUGUETES PALAU   **21** J5   Ⓜ Catalunya 🚊 Balmes
Balmes 4, tel. 318-14-73. Monday to Saturday 10 a.m.–1.30 p.m. and 4.30–8 p.m. Also at Pelai 34, tel. 317-36-78.
Kits and models, electric trains and slot-car racing, and computers.

TAMBOR   **12** H8   🚊 Calvet *Main line train:* Bonanova
Tenor Viñas 4–6; tel. 200-11-39. Monday to Saturday 9.30 a.m.–1.30 p.m. and 4.30–8 p.m.
An emporium of modern toys, including electronic games and a bewildering assortment of dolls that do everything imaginable.

TIC-TAC   **12** H7   Ⓜ Diagonal 🚊 Av. Diagonal
Av. Diagonal 550; tel. 200-63-13/209-59-78. Monday to Saturday 9.30 a.m.–1.30 p.m. and 4.30–8 p.m.
Two floors of toys, games, sports equipment, models and the rest.

BOUTIQUES

BEBELIN   **21** J6   Ⓜ Catalunya 🚊 Pg. de Gràcia
Pg. de Gràcia 39, tel. 215-83-54. Monday to Saturday 10 a.m.–1.30 p.m. and 4–8.15 p.m. Also at Tenor Viñas 5, tel. 209-97-53.
Mother-to-be, baby, and toddler clothes are sold here, along with baby equipment.

BISCUIT   **20** H5   Ⓜ Urgell 🚊 Gran Via
Gran Via de les Corts Catalanes 535, tel. 323-68-08. Monday to Saturday 9.30 a.m.–2 p.m. and 4.30–8.30 p.m. Also at Rbla. Catalunya 66, Bulevard Rosa T. 52, tel. 215-81-70.
Clothing for children between 0 and 12, at reasonable prices.

187

CACHAREL   **12** H9   🚊 Gral. Mitre *Main line train:* Putxet
Gral. Mitre 139, tel. 418-81-21. Monday to Saturday 10 a.m.–1.45 p.m. and 4.30–8 p.m. Also at Pg. de Gràcia 55, tel. 215-92-98.
An expensive boutique catering for 4- to 14-year-olds.

CACHE-CACHE   **21** K6   Ⓜ Pg. de Gràcia 🚊 Pg. de Gràcia
Pg. de Gràcia 62; tel. 215-40-07. Monday to Saturday 10.30 a.m.–8.30 p.m.
Supplies clothing for babies, and children up to 14 years.

L'HEDRA   **13/14** K7   🚊 Gran de Gràcia *Main line train: Gràcia Trav. de Gràcia 154; tel. 218-49-90. Monday to Saturday 10 a.m.–1 p.m. and 5–8 p.m.*
Bright and colourful clothes for the up to 10 year olds, at a reasonable price.

MIKIMA   **12** H8   🚊 Calvet *Main line train: Muntaner Calvet 60; tel. 209-29-27. Weekdays 10.30 a.m.–1.30 p.m. and 4–8.30 p.m., Saturday 10.30 a.m.–1.30 p.m.*
Classical clothes for the up to 12 year olds, all in the best possible taste.

MULLOR   **21** J6   🚊 Rbla. Catalunya *Main line train: Provença Rbla. Catalunya 102 bis; tel. 215-12-02. Monday to Saturday 10 a.m.–1.30 p.m. and 4.30–8 p.m.*
A rather trendy boutique catering for babies and children up to 3 years old.

NIÑOS-NIÑAS   **11/12** F9   Ⓜ Maria Cristina 🚊 Pl. Manuel Girona *Manuel de Falla 35; tel. 203-21-71. Monday to Saturday 10 a.m.–2 p.m. and 5–8 p.m.*
Very reasonable prices in a store decorated like a child's room to make under-8s feel at home.

PRENATAL   **21** J5   Ⓜ Catalunya 🚊 Gran Via *Gran Via de les Corts Catalanes 611 bis, tel. 302-05-25/318-02-33. Monday to Saturday 10 a.m.–1.30 p.m. and 4.30–8 p.m. Also at Pi 3–5, tel. 302-10-95/317-54-07; Buenos Aires 20–22, tel. 321-97-57.*
A virtual department store, with clothes and equipment for mothers-to-be, babies and toddlers.

188

PRIMER PLANO   **11** F8   Ⓜ Maria Cristina 🚊 Av. Diagonal *Av. Diagonal 613, Bulevard Rosa T. 51 . Monday to Saturday 10 a.m.–1 p.m. and 4–8 p.m.*
Very trendy, and full of children's designer clothes to suit every occasion.

SPORT-MENUT   **20** H6   🚊 Mallorca *Main line train: Provença Provença 222; tel. 323-42-28. Monday to Saturday 10.30 a.m.–1.30 p.m. and 5–8.30 p.m.*
Colourful and fashionable children's clothes.

SUGAR-PEPE   🚌 Muntaner
ISUS   **12** H10   *Main line train:* Putxet
Camp 78–81; tel. 417-11-74. Weekdays 9 a.m.–1.30 p.m. and 3–7.30 p.m., Saturday 9 a.m.–1.30 p.m.
Reasonably priced clothes, many of which are in-house designs.

TEENAGE FASHION

The following selection of shops and boutiques cater for both teenagers and those in their early twenties.

10h.30   **21** J4   Ⓜ Catalunya   🚌 Pl. Catalunya
Duc de la Victoria 6; tel. 318-34-42. Monday to Saturday 10.30 a.m.–2 p.m. and 4.30–8.30 p.m.
The latest designs are copied and are therefore reasonably priced. They are sold together with the inevitable selection of jeans.

ACE   **12** H9   🚌 Muntaner *Main line train:* Putxet
Muntaner 519; tel. 418-88-90. Monday to Saturday 10.30 a.m.–2 p.m. and 4.30–9 p.m.
Clothes for the smart young man, complete with designer suits and accessories.

ALAIN MANOUKIAN (See Shopping: Fashion)
As well as clothes for young women, the beautiful fashions on sale here look good, if a little classical, on teenagers.

ALOE   **28** H/J4   Ⓜ Liceu   🚌 Rambla
Junta del Comerç 2; tel. 318-82-34. Monday to Saturday 10 a.m.–1.30 p.m. and 5–8 p.m.
The Indian look which you thought had almost disappeared turns up here—cotton clothes at low prices.

189

ARAÑA   **12** H8   🚌 Santaló *Main line train:* Muntaner
Amigó 48. Monday to Saturday 9.30 a.m.–2 p.m. and 4–8.30 p.m.
A branch of this chain of shops which offers well-priced if not especially fashionable clothes for teenagers.

BANG   **13/14** K8   Ⓜ Lesseps   🚊 Trav. de Dalt
*Pérez Galdós 47; tel. 218-76-74. Monday to Saturday 10 a.m.–2 p.m. and
5–8 p.m.*
Extremely good prices are set for the remaindered but good-quality
clothes.

CANADÁ   **12** H9   🚊 Muntaner   *Main line train:* Muntaner
*Muntaner 392; tel. 201-27-41. Monday to Saturday 9.30 a.m.–2 p.m. and
4.30–8.30 p.m.*
Leaning more towards the youthful business person than the fashionable teenager, but nevertheless appealing.

CHIC   **12** H8   🚊 Pl. Francesc Macià   *Main line train:* Muntaner
*Mestre Nicolau 20. Monday to Saturday 10 a.m.–1.30 p.m. and 5–
7.30 p.m.*
Very well-priced clothes for the young, including some garments from
past designer collections.

DO. BARCELONA   **12** G8   🚊 Calvet   *Main line train:* Muntaner
*Mestre Nicolau 14; tel. 209-80-13. Monday to Saturday 10 a.m.–2 p.m.
and 4.30–8.30 p.m.*
Catering for teenagers and young women, this boutique carries designs
by the likes of Verinno and Bamboo.

DON   🚊 Rbla. Catalunya
ALGODÓN   **21** J6   *Main line train:* Provença
Rbla. Catalunya 102 bis; tel. 215-67-34.
Cotton clothes, aimed at the younger set, go for a song here.

190 **DONALDSON**   **11** F8   Ⓜ Maria Cristina   🚊 Av. Diagonal
*Av. Diagonal 609–615 tda. 90; tel. 419-17-00. Monday to Saturday
10 a.m.–1.30 p.m. and 4.30–8 p.m.*
For the older child or younger teenager, as well as adults who don't mind
sporting clothes adorned with Disney characters.

GROC (See Shopping: Fashion)
Elegant clothes for younger people well up with today's fashion are sold
along with garments for adult men and women.

HIC ET NUNC   **21** J6   Ⓜ Pg. de Gràcia   🚌 Pg. de Gràcia
Pg. de Gràcia 55; tel. 215-77-25. Monday to Saturday 10 a.m.–2 p.m. and 5–8 p.m.
Exclusive young fashion, retaining a classic touch in spite of often bright colours.

I O   **12** H8   🚌 Calvet *Main line train:* Muntaner
Ferrán Agulló 18; tel. 201-14-99. Monday to Saturday 10 a.m.–2 p.m. and 4.30–8.30 p.m.
Very fashionable, mainly Italian designs aimed at the teenager or younger woman fill this boutique. Prices are high.

JEAN PIERRE BUA (See Shopping: Fashion)
In among the international designer clothes are expensive and exclusive things for the younger fashion-conscious girl.

JUAN   🚌 Santaló/Muntaner
MAS   **12** H8   *Main line train:* Muntaner
Trav. de Gràcia 36; tel. 201-55-50. Monday to Saturday 9.30 a.m.–2 p.m. and 4–8.30 p.m.
Reasonably priced designer clothes for the teenager or young-at-heart. The look is different, if quite staid.

BABY-SITTERS

AGENCIA   🚌 Calvet
MADOSMAS   **12** H8   *Main line train:* Muntaner
Sagués 11–13; tel. 200-93-78.

BABY AND HOME   **11** E7   Ⓜ Sants 🚌 Av. de Madrid
Av. de Madrid 168–2B; tel. 411-18-77.

BIKSA   Ⓜ Badal
INTERNACIONAL   **10/11** C7   🚌 Badal/Santa
Bonvei 2; tel. 333-19-16/334-73-31.

191

CANGURSERVEIS   **23** 05   Ⓜ Glòries 🚌 Llacuna
La Llacuna 162; tel. 401-97-97.

SERVI-NENS   **13** J8   🚌 Balmes *Main line train:* Pl. Molina
Via Augusta 120; tel. 218-23-87.

W hen Barcelona's sights, sounds and heat begin to wear you out, head for one of the leafy retreats listed below. Either a park or a shady square will do the trick. Walks in the city are, in any case, the best way to see Barcelona, and since most areas are relatively compact, a stroll around them won't place too much of a strain on the feet. Otherwise, a number of sightseeing tours by coach are available.

The best panoramic views of the city come from a trip on the cable-car up to Montjuïc from the port area; while the ultimate, latest attraction is a short trip by helicopter over the main Olympic sites.

LEAFY RETREATS

The city's leafy retreats are few and far between, and in some cases are almost bereft of leaves, in keeping with the trend towards city parks that concentrate on concrete. However, once you've found one to relax in, it's almost possible to forget that all around you the noisy traffic and activity of a busy city carry on. Here is a selection of the main retreats to head for.

CEMENTIRI DE MONTJUÏC   27 D2   🚌 Pg. Cementiri
Mare de Déu Port s/n. Daily 10 a.m.–7 p.m.
It might be thought that a cemetery is an odd place to wander around, but Barcelona's principal last resting place is both fascinating and, by definition, peaceful. Many of the victims of Spain's bloody Civil War lie within the neatly stacked tombs, which boast a wealth of art-deco and modernistic design, as well as a superb view out to sea over the city's port. Not at all a depressing place to visit, the Cementiri is testament to the Mediterranean practice of treating death with openness and optimism.

A freewheeling tour through Barcelona's spectacular hinterland.

JARDINES DE PEDRALBES 11 D9

Ⓜ Palau Reial
🚌 Palau Reial

Av. Diagonal 686. Daily 10 a.m.–8 p.m.

During the the Olympics, the Pedralbes area will be taken over almost entirely by visiting VIPs and the Spanish Royal Family. But at other times, the gardens surrounding the former palace (see Sights: Monuments) are a perfect place for a stroll under the trees, along the paths and in the shadow of the mountains. Make sure you don't miss Gaudí's wrought-iron dragon gate, part of the work he carried out for his patron, Güell.

MONTJUÏC 27 D/E 2/3

Ⓜ Espanya

Once the excitement of the Olympics has subsided, this mountain over-looking Barcelona should return to its primary role as a place in which to relax and get away from the city. The various attractions include the-atres, palaces, museums, bars, restaurants and an amusement park, as well as the installations built for the Games. When you get tired of these, take a leisurely stroll in the Institut Botànic (see Museums), with its large selection of exotic plants; or the Jardí Joan Maragall, which com-bines flora with sculptures. The imposing castle on top of Montjuïc is also to be recommended as part of a day away from the city grind (see Sights: Monuments).

PARC DE L'ESCORXADOR 19/20 F6

Ⓜ Espanya 🚌 València

Aragó 1. Daily 10 a.m.–8 p.m.

A city park, named rather unromantically and a little unimaginatively af-ter the slaughterhouse which stood on the site. The Escorxador is dom-inated by the totem-pole-like Miró sculpture which is so often seen in pic-tures and is now clearly associated with Barcelona. The park is a pleasant break from the city's main exhibition centre.

PARC DE LA CIUTADELLA 29 L3

Ⓜ Ciutadella
🚌 Pg. Picasso

Pg. Picasso 15–21. Daily 10 a.m.–8 p.m.

Within a stone's throw of the sea, the Ciutadella Park is a perfect place in which to escape the hustle and bustle of the city. The fort which had stood on the site from the early 18th century was finally demolished in 1869; it had had a bloody history as a place where Catalan nationalists were imprisoned or executed. The park was one of the main sites for Barcelona's Universal Exposition in 1888, and the whole area was re-landscaped for the event. It now includes the recently renovated Arc del Triomf, the Catalan Parliament, the zoo and the Museu d'Art Modern (see Museums).

PARC DE L'ESPANYA INDÚSTRIAL   19 E6   Ⓜ Sants ⊞ Watt
Watt 24–34. Daily 10 a.m.–8 p.m.
Dominated by a series of edifices that resemble air-traffic-control buildings, this park stands on the site of a former factory right next to Barcelona's main railway station at Sants. The combination of a lake, fountains and sculptures make it a cool and beautiful place for a walk. And it is infinitely more preferable to wait for a train here than in the busy station.

PARK GÜELL   13 L9   Ⓜ Vallcarca ⊞ Crta. de Carmel
Olot 7. Daily 10 a.m.–8 p.m.
Named after Gaudí's most famous benefactor, the park which stands high above the city is one of the "musts" for visitors to Barcelona. The original intention was for it to become an unusual housing estate: Gaudí was effectively given the plot at the beginning of the century and was asked to create whatever he wanted. He worked on it sporadically for almost 15 years (his house, converted into a museum, stands in the park). The result is a large collection of Gaudí's favourite themes, using broken glass, ceramics, colours and curves to create all the paraphernalia of a park, including the famous serpentine benches. Evidently, Güell's original intention failed, and the whole area was converted into a park in 1923. The 86 columns of the Saló de les Cent Columnes (Hall of a hundred columns—Gaudí never seems to have finished projects he started) were supposed to enclose the estate's market. Close inspection of the roof will reveal depictions of the goods which would have been sold there, such as bottles, glasses and plates.

TIBIDABO   5 J12/13   Ⓜ Av. Tibidabo
⊞ Av. Tibidabo/Tramvia Blau   *Main line train:* Funicular
As well as Barcelona's favourite amusement park (see Children), Tibidabo mountain provides the city's best panoramic view. On a clear day, it is possible to catch a glimpse of distant mountains and even sometimes Mallorca; but it's more likely you'll be prevented from seeing very far by the low cloud—not smog, say the city authorities, but the product of Barcelona's high levels of humidity. The mountain is the highest point in the city. As such it became the site for the monumental

195

figure of Christ (at the Church of the Sagrat Cor) which oversees Barcelona's spiritual welfare; and also for the main television transmitter, which deals with the city's more worldly requirements. On a hot day, this sometimes seems to be the only area in Barcelona that still has a breeze blowing through it, especially in the evening. The most enjoyable of the several ways of reaching Tibidabo combines the Tramvia (tram) with the Funicular; this enables you to get maximum benefit from the view as you mount the 542-metre (1,779-foot) peak.

LEISURELY WALKS

All the following walks can be safely undertaken within the space of an hour or two, depending on how many times you feel forced to stop to examine something more closely. The suggestions here will provide a good idea of the breadth of the city's architecture, sights and sounds, without being too fatiguing. As in any tourist city, normal precautions should be taken when wandering around—carry a minimum amount of cash, and keep the rest of your vital documents (such as your passport) in a money belt.

BARCELONETA   **29 K2**   Ⓜ Pla del Palau/Barceloneta
The look of this traditional if rather shabby section of Barcelona, right on the seafront, has changed considerably with the alterations associated with the Olympics, and with the application of the Spanish law that prohibits buildings to be within a certain distance of the shoreline. As a result, a whole string of very popular restaurants lining the beach fell to the bulldozer, changing forever the character of the area. The restaurants are promised to re-emerge in the swanky, new "Paseo Marítimo"—promenade—which will stretch from Montjuïc to the new Olympic Village and beyond. Their demolition means that an entirely new stretch of urban beach has re-emerged. The combination of the Ciutadella Park, the green areas behind the Olympic Village, and the relatively long stretch of beach, make Barceloneta a beautiful, peaceful and popular attraction right inside the city. And rest assured, other fine restaurants have remained, further back from the shoreline.

BARRI GÒTIC 29 J/K 3/4

Ⓜ Jaume I/Liceu   🚋 Via Laietana/Rambla
Main line train: Catalunya

The history of Barcelona is encapsulated in this relatively small district which can be explored during a leisurely stroll. Start from the Plaça de Sant Jaume, and the historical centre of the city is laid out in front of you. In the square, opposite each other physically and these days politically, stand the palaces which house the city and regional administrations, the Ajuntament and the Generalitat. From here it is only a short walk to the cathedral, and next to it the museum of the city's history, both of which are worth a visit. Almost opposite the cathedral is the building housing the Col.legi d'Arquitectes, with Picasso's original design decorating the front. Throughout the Barri Gòtic are the squares, churches and build-ings—such as the Palau Reial (Royal Palace) and the church of Santa Agata—which give the area its fame and attraction. No trip to Barcelona is complete without a visit to this district.

LA RAMBLA 21/29 J3/4

Ⓜ Liceu   🚋 Rambla
Main line train: Catalunya

There are actually five Ramblas stretching seamlessly from Plaça de Catalunya to the Monument a Colom (Columbus Monument). The Rambla is a pedestrianized, tree-lined boulevard that teems with people during the warmer months. Recent changes make it possible to walk all the way from Diagonal, down the Rambla de Catalunya to the sea. Starting at the Rambla de Canaletes, you first encounter the newspaper kiosks (which stock papers and magazines from around the world) before reaching the first stalls selling a variety of birds and small animals, all piled together in cages on the Rambla dels Ocells. Moving on from the noise of the birds, you'll next encounter stalls brimming with cut flowers on the Rambla de les Flors, and to the right, the entrance to the Boqueria Market, which sells fresh food (see Markets). The main concentration of bars and cafés begins on the Rambla dels Caputxins, overlooked by the opera house, the Liceu, on the right. A little further down on the left is the entrance to the Plaça Reial. As you arrive at the port end of the Rambla, at the Rambla de Santa Mònica, there are fewer kiosks, and the boulevard is wider, but somehow a little less charming. The remaining "down-market" members of this area's population—traditional in any port city—have been gradually moved on. Nevertheless, the golden rule to remember when wandering along the Rambla during the day, is to be sensible with valuables, especially bags and cameras. The simplest way of dealing with people who might accost you on the street, or as you sit at a table (where you should keep your possessions at your feet), is a firm and repeated "no, gracias".

197

LA RIBERA   **29** KL/3   Ⓜ Jaume I   🚃 Via Laietana/Pla del Palau
Between the Barri Gòtic and the Ciutadella Park is the area known as
the Ribera, which includes some of the most attractive Gothic architecture
in the city. Especially noteworthy are the church of Santa Maria del Mar
and the buildings along the twisting narrow streets named after the trades
of workmen who used to operate near the church. The Ribera area is
physically cut off from the Barri Gòtic by the Via Laietana, a busy road
created at the beginning of the 20th century as a main route from the
sea into the newer part of the city. An obvious destination during a walk
around these streets is the Museu Picasso, though another attraction is
the clothing and textile museum opposite (for both, see Museums). A
dominant feature of the area is the former market of El Born, now converted into a multicultural centre where live music, theatre and exhibitions take place.

L'EIXAMPLE   **21/22** K5/6   Ⓜ Pg. de Gràcia   🚃 Pg. de Gràcia
Main line train: Provença
With the Gran Via to the south, Diagonal to the north and Passeig de
Gràcia to the east, the Eixample district was considered to be the modern section of the city—until building work started in the area around the
Olympic Village on the seafront. The name of the district, which means
"broadening" or "expansion" in Catalan, describes the process which
led to the massive growth of the original city over a twenty-year period
from the 1860s. It follows a grid pattern, which enables you to find your
way around the area with ease. Some of Barcelona's principal streets
were created during this period. The jewels in the crown, of course, were
the buildings put up in the district, forming what is known as the Quadrat
d'Or (Golden Quarter). They include some of the finest work of modernist
architects such as Gaudí, Domènech and Puig. In a single block on
Passeig de Gràcia stands beautiful work by all three: the Casa LLeó
Morera by Domènech at No. 35 (containing the city's tourist authority),
the Casa Amatller by Puig at No. 41, and the Casa Batlló by Gaudí next
door (for all, see Sights: Town Houses). Further towards Diagonal and
on the other side of the Passeig de Gràcia is the fine Gaudí-designed
Casa Milà or La Pedrera, the cake-like building, which is among the best-
known images of Barcelona (See Sights: Town Houses). A stroll down
the Passeig de Gràcia, with its top-class shopping, or the Rambla de
Catalunya, recently renovated and very shady, will allow you to gain at
least a partial picture of the district.

198

PUERTO   Ⓜ Drassanes   🚃 Rambla
Starting from the Monument a Colom, a stroll around the port area has
again become relatively easy and will reveal the changes that have taken

place to the fabric of the city. Just back from the monument are the royal shipyards, containing the fascinating Maritime Museum (see Museums) and the Port Authority, naval and military headquarters, all dominated by the modern and ugly Torre Colom (Colombus Tower). The Moll de la Fusta remains a very pleasant quayside walk, well away from the traffic, with a view around the immediate port. A new stretch of bars and restaurants have been built here. Negotiating the frustratingly long spiral walkways remains an exercise of patience, especially as pushchairs and wheelchairs fall foul of the designer-cobblestones. Beyond the Moll de la Fusta, in sight of the twin towers of the Olympic Village, lies the new marina, with 800 moorings for the richest inhabitants of the apartments behind, together with the latest arrivals in bars and restaurants. The "Paseo Marítimo" continues much further, past Barceloneta (see above) and beyond.

BOAT RIDES

GOLONDRINAS   **29** J2/3   Ⓜ Drassanes 🚃 Rambla
Moll de la Fusta; tel. 412-59-44. October to June: Monday to Saturday 11 a.m.–6 p.m. (Sunday and public holidays until 7 p.m.); July to September: daily 10.30 a.m.–9 p.m.
This trip by boat around the port of Barcelona, as far as the breakwater, leaves from the quayside at the Moll de la Fusta, near the Monument a Colom. The intention is to provide a cheap, water-bus type of tour, similar to those available on the river in Paris. It's best to book in advance, as the tours are quite popular.

COACH TOURS

AUTOBÚS TURÍSTICO NÚMERO 100
End June to mid September 9 a.m.–7.30 p.m., every half-hour.
Run by the city authorities, this bus tour travels around many of the most interesting sights of Barcelona, leaving every 30 minutes. There is no running commentary from a guide, although a tourist office representative is on the bus. Nevertheless, the two-hour round trip represents a remarkably cheap way of visiting 16 of the main attractions in a short space of time. One feature of the tour is that a visitor can choose to get off at any of the stops, spend some time looking around, and then get

199

back on the next bus to carry on with the tour. In addition to the tour, the price of a ticket—for a full or half day—gives free travel on the Tramvia Azul, the Tibidabo Funicular and the Montjuïc Teleférico, plus discounts to various attractions. The scheme is only in operation during the summer.

GAUDÍ-PICASSO

A tour that is specifically designed for visitors wanting to take in the best-known artistic and cultural sights of Barcelona. It encompasses the Eixample area, the Park Güell, the Sagrada Família and the Museu Picasso, the most visited museum in the city. Check with the tourist information office (see Practical Information) for details.

PANORÁMICA Y TOROS

Every Sunday during the bullfighting season, this excursion combines a tour around the city with a visit to a fight. In Catalunya, bullfighting has almost died out through lack of interest (except among tourists and the odd die-hard), but it remains popular in other parts of Spain, perhaps as an exhibition of patriotism in the face of foreign disapproval. Ask at the tourist information office (see Practical Information) for details.

PANORAMICA DE NOCHE Y FLAMENCO

After a night-time tour around the streets of the city by coach, this excursion ends with a visit to a flamenco show (a tradition best witnessed in its place of origin, in the south of Spain, unless you have no other opportunity). Ask at the tourist information office (see Practical Information) for details.

VISITA DE LA CIUDAD

A commercially operated guided tour of the city that includes visits to the Barri Gòtic and the Poble Espanyol. Check with the tourisit information office (see Practical Information) for details.

200 OTHER MEANS OF TRANSPORT

CARRUATGES DE ALQUILER   28 H/J3

Portal de la Pau; tel. 421-88-04.
Only a few of these horse-drawn carriages still exist, and the main concentration is at the bottom of the Rambla, near the Columbus Monument

(though a few operate on Montjuïc, where the traffic is lighter, and in the Ciutadella Park). Most drivers display their price somewhere on the carriage, but if they don't, ask what the cost will be before getting in and find out how long the journey will take.

FUNICULAR AL TIBIDABO 5 J12

Av. del Doctor Andreu s/n; tel. 211-79-42. Daily 7.15 a.m.–9.45 p.m. Price: 325-pts.

This fascinating form of transport, in a carriage which mounts Tibidabo at a 45-degree angle, takes visitors to the top of the 542-metre (1,779-foot) mountain, after connecting up with the Tramvia Blau.

HELICOPTER

Tel. 325-78-66.

The latest and most original way to see the city and especially the main Olympic sites around Montjuïc. This ten-minute tour by helicopter was mounted jointly by the city tourism authority and a commercial firm. Ask at a tourist office (see Practical Information) for details.

TELEFÉRICO AL CASTILLO DE MONTJUÏC 28 G2

Crta. Miramar 40; tel. 317-55-27. Open July to September: daily noon–8.30 p.m.; September to June: Sunday and public holidays 11 a.m.–2.45 p.m. and 4–7.30 p.m. Price: 450-pts.

High above the port and all the way up to the castle dominating Montjuïc, the cable-car ride provides some breathtaking views of the city, starting from what appears to be a small version of Blackpool Tower. Alternative ways up Montjuïc for those with a fear of heights are being provided by escalators; and eventually, the metro is to go there. The journey right to the top of Montjuïc is actually in two parts—the Transbordador from the port to Miramar, and the Telefèric up to the castle on the mountain.

TRAMVIA BLAU 5/13 J10

Av. Tibidabo 2; tel. 241-28-00. Daily 7.05 a.m.–9.35 p.m. Price: 200-pts.

The last remaining tramway in Barcelona, the Tramvia rises high above the city from the end of the Generalitat railway line at Av. del Tibidabo, at the foot of the mountain. On the way up, the line passes some beautiful houses and attractive bars and restaurants, before connecting with the Funicular railway to take passengers even further up Tibidabo to the amusement park.

Getting away from the city for a while will allow you to gain a better picture of the surrounding region, and there are many interesting places within easy reach of Barcelona, either by road or public transport. Beaches along the coast, north and south of the city, are a good alternative to the crowded Barceloneta, although they are not recommended during weekends in the summer, when city dwellers flock to them in their thousands. In fact, the weekend is probably the best time for a leisurely exploration of the city.

Apart from the sights in the immediate vicinity suitable for a half-day outing, there are plenty of attractions towards the interior, away from the crowded coast. A few suggestions are listed in this section, and the regional tourist authorities, the tourist offices run by the Generalitat (see Practical Information), have a wealth of information in English.

There is a surprising range of countryside to be seen, varying according to whether you travel north or south of Barcelona. Towards Tarragona, the earth is drier and the vines and olive trees are more frequent; while nearer Girona to the north, lie the rolling hills and lush open countryside of the Empordà. To the north-west, around the provincial capital of Lleida, the interior of the "real" Catalunya is characterized by the foothills and mountains of the Pyrenees and by its many small villages and twisting roads.

The co-principality of Andorra can be visited in a day, with an early start and a late return, but it is well worth a more leisurely trip taking in some of the northern reaches of this rich and varied region.

The following are some suggestions for a break from the city.

THE OUTSKIRTS

CAVA SANT SADURNI D'ANOIA
Transport: by car, take the Sant Sadurní exit of the A2 motorway. R.E.N.F.E. trains from Barcelona-Sants Central Station. Coaches are run by the "Hispano Llacunense" company from Urgell/París (tel. 891-25-61).

Sant Sadurní d'Anoia, approximately 40 kilometres (25 miles) south of Barcelona, is at the centre of the region in which *cava*, the sparkling wine that is possibly Catalunya's most famous export, is made. Producers

Sitges: vibrant and colourful neighbour of Barcelona.

were forced under European Community agreements to drop "Champan" from its labels, but most people continue to refer to *cava* in terms reserved for its better-known northern rival. Similar production techniques have been used for many centuries, and several *cava* producers welcome visitors to view the traditional *Champenoise* process employed and to sample the results (for free). The two biggest producers in the region are Freixenet and Codorniu—a museum dedicated to the latter stands in Sant Sadurní d'Anoia—but there are other major wineries challenging them. Nearby, Vilafranca del Penedès, the capital of the region, houses the Museu del Vi, dedicated to wine-making.

COLONIA GÜELL
Monday to Friday 10.15 a.m.–1.15 p.m. and 4–6 p.m., Sunday 1 0 a.m.–1.30 p.m. Transport: by car, take the N340 turn-off to Santa Coloma de Cervelló from the A2 motorway. By train, take the Ferrocarril from Pl. Espanya to Santa Coloma de Cervelló

The Colonia is well worth a visit to see one of Gaudí's greatest works for his closest patron, the industrialist Eusebi Güell. Gaudí was commissioned to design and build a special church within the workers' village that Güell had constructed around his textile factory. Only the crypt and some of the outside buildings were finished, but the techniques and materials used in their construction, between 1898 and 1908, served Gaudí well when he took on the much larger project of the Sagrada Família cathedral. It is alleged that the architect never used modern tools, but relied on rule of thumb and simple plumb lines when working on the church. The result is a magnificent construction that resembles a forest glade, complete with graceful, arching columns which seem like trees, strengthening a curved roof with branch-like supports. The beautiful stained-glass windows and the modernist-design pews complete the picture. The textile factory is long closed, and the church is used as a conference centre and concert hall as well as for its original religious purpose.

MINIATURA
Daily 9 a.m.–7 p.m. Price: 250.-pts. children, 600-pts adults. Transport: by car, Torrelles de Llobregat is 17 kilometres (11 miles) south of Barcelona. The "Tisa" coach company runs a service from Viriato/ Numància.

204

Miniatura offers an opportunity to walk around the buildings and cities of Catalunya without wearing out your shoes. It is claimed that this model city is the biggest of its kind, with 170 perfectly detailed miniature representaions. Especially noteworthy is a selection of buildings designed by the architect Gaudí, including the Sagrada Família; and there's also the Columbus Monument, along with the other main buildings in Barcelona. It's a lot easier than walking around the real thing, if not quite so much fun.

MONESTIR DE MONTSERRAT

Tel. 835-02-51. Abbey open daily 6 a.m.–8 p.m.; choir singing: daily at 1 p.m. and 6.45 p.m.; Shrine to the Virgin: daily 8–10.30 a.m. and noon–1.30 p.m. and 3–6.30 p.m.; museum: daily 10.30 a.m.–2 p.m. and 3–6 p.m. Transport: by car, Montserrat is along the motorway, 60 kilometres (38 miles) to the north-west of Barcelona. By train, take the Ferrocarril from Pl. Espanya. Organized coach trips, run by Pullmantur (tel. 318-02-41) and Julia Tours (tel. 422-11-00), depart daily at 9.30 a.m., return at 2.30 p.m. From 1 April to 30 August departure also at 3.30 p.m., return at 8 p.m. Price 3.675.-pts.

The spectacular mountains around the monastery at Montserrat form a perfect setting for this austere 19th-century architectural jewel, situated high above the surrounding countryside. It can be seen from afar, if you arrive by motorway, or spectacularly if you arrive by train and take the funicular to a point 1,000 metres (3,280 feet) up the mountain. The original monastery buildings were destroyed by French troops at the beginning of the 19th century, when the monks, hermits and animals were forced to flee. Now the monastery is clearly a tourist trap as well as a place of religious devotion. The main attractions are the 12th-century representation of La Moreneta, the black Madonna; the hair-raising trip by funicular almost vertically up the mountain; and the heavenly chants of the monks' and children's choir, from a music school founded in the 13th century. Somehow, among all the tourists, the monks carry on with their daily tasks. Many devoted pilgrims still undertake an annual walk here from all points of the country as a sign of their faith, and several visit Montserrat for a retreat.

SITGES

Transport: by car, Sitges is 37 kilometres (23 miles) south of Barcelona on the C246. By train, take R.E.N.F.E. from Barcelona-Sants Central Station or from Pg. de Gràcia.

Within half an hour by train of Barcelona, the town of Sitges is well known to British visitors—it was one of Catalunya's first "resorts"—and remains a popular destination for motorized tourists. At the end of the last and the beginning of this century, the town was a magnet for artists and intellectuals, establishing a reputation as a cultural centre. A smallish place, it features twisty, relatively unspoiled streets, leading down the hill to clean if crowded beaches, the best of which is the tiny Sant Sebastià to the left of the parish church as you look out to sea. Otherwise, the town is a mixture of tourist traps, typical bars, and museums. There's a semi-permanent carnival atmosphere, which comes to a head during the pre-Lent season, and which is one of the attractions for the regular gay community and visitors. Further down from the main beach is a long promenade of villas and hotels, of many different styles, which gives the resort its very British character.

FURTHER AFIELD

ANDORRA

Transport: by car, Andorra is a 200-kilometre (125-mile) trip along the C1410, the C1313 and the C145. Coaches are run by the "Alsina Graells" company; Rnda. Universitat 4, 08004 Barcelona; tel. 302-65-45. Price: weekdays 1.805.-pts., public holidays 2.060.-pts. Departure 6.30 a.m. and 2.45 p.m. By taxi, contact "Taxis Simorra"; Vilamarí 10, 08015 Barcelona; tel. 325-22-05. Price: 3.000.-pts, departure 9 p.m. Organized day trip Monday, Tuesday and Friday from Barcelona at 6.30 a.m., return 10 p.m. Price: 5.000.-pts. Two-day trip from Barcelona on Saturday at 6.30 a.m., return Sunday at 10 p.m. Price: from 6.500.-pts. Both tours organized by Pullmantur (tel. 318-02-41) and Julia Tours (tel. 422-11-00).

Administered jointly by the French President and the Bishop of the Seu d'Urgell in Catalunya, Andorra is probably best known by visitors as the place to buy duty-free goods on the way between France and Spain.This tax-free haven with its excellent ski slopes and resort areas is, in fact, a very small country, with a population of approximately 20,500. Andorra was busy making money, mainly from smuggling, while the rest of the world got on with wars and soring out frontiers. Today, the country depends on tourism, banks and shopping—a year-round trade. A trip here by coach takes the visitor through some spetacular countryside, with the mountains of the Pyrenees to the fore. Take care not to excede the legal limits on duty-free goods, however, as random checks are often carried out.

COSTA BRAVA

Transport: by car, the Costa Brava is reached along the A19 and NII. By train, R.E.N.F.E. from Barcelona-Sants Central Station. Coaches are run by the "Sarfa" company; Pl. Duc de Medinaceli 4; tel. 318-94-34. Organized trips from 1 May to 30 September daily except Sundays. Departure from Barcelona at 9 a.m., return 6 p.m. Price: 6.435.-pts. Organized by Pullmantur (tel. 318-02-41) and Julia Tours (tel. 422-11-00).

The Costa Brava—literally "wild coast", in reference to its rugged nature and its number of coves and inlets—stretches from the French border at Port-Bou to the town of Blanes, about 60 kilometres (40 miles) north of Barcelona. In spite of its reputation in many parts of the world, the Costa is not all mass tourism (for that go to Tossa, Lloret or L'Estartit). A major part of the coast remains rugged while, in other places, it has become a refuge for the rich. Much of it has survived unscarred by skyscraper hotels. If you are touring by car, the coast road up from Barcelona, though frustrating in places, provides some beautiful views of the sea. An alternative is a coach tour, or a trip by train to some of the prettier towns, like Begur, Palafrugell, Aiguablava and Sant Feliu.

FIGUERES AND PORTLLIGAT

Museum: October to 30 June daily 11 a.m.–4.45 p.m.; June to 30 September daily 9 a.m.–8 p.m. Price: 400.-pts. Transport: by car, about 200 kilometres (125 miles) to the north of Barcelona along the A7. By train, R.E.N.F.E. from Barcelona-Sants Central Station, or from Pg. de Grácia. Coaches are run by the "Asser" company from Norte-Vilanova station.

Near the French border are two important landmarks in the life of the famous surrealist artist Salvador Dalí. Dalí's house stands on the coast overlooking the sea at Portlligat, only a short walk from the small and picturesque town of Cadaqués. Inland, in the region's capital at Figueres, is the Museu Dalí, Spain's second most visited museum after Madrid's Prado. Formerly the town's theatre, now converted into a work of art in itself, the museum contains a wide selection of pieces produced by Dalí, including some of his most famous paintings and "objects". Dalí wanted the museum to be in constant change, in keeping with his surrealist philosophy, but this has not happened (in spite of some superficial reshuffling) since Dalí's death in 1989. Owing to its popularity, extremely long queues form during the summer months, so it's best to go when the sun keeps at least some people on the beach.

207

GIRONA

Transport: by car, Girona is 100 kilometres (62 miles) to the north of Barcelona along the A7. By train, R.E.N.F.E. from Barcelona-Sants Central Station, or from Pg. de Grácia. Coaches are run by the "Asser" company from Norte-Vilanova station.

Girona is the main city in the northern region of Catalunya. Its medieval centre overlooks the Onyar River and contains the impressive cathedral and the Gothic Sant Feliu church, both of which are worth visiting. The archaeological museum housed in the third major church, Sant Pere de Galligants, traces Girona's history, including its Jewish influences; these can also be seen in the Jewish Quarter. A walk along the ancient city walls is both fascinating and invigorating. And a visit to the 700-year-old Arab baths—not actually Moorish but built in that style—is also to be recommended. If you have time, a look around the more modern part of the city on the other side of the river provides a contrast to the cobbled streets and the medieval buildings. Alternatively, take a leisurely walk around the large Parc de la Devesa, or sample one of the several fine restaurants in the town.

MONASTERIO DE POBLET

Tel. 977-87-02-54. Summer: daily 10 a.m.–12.30 p.m. and 3–5.30 p.m.; winter: Monday to Saturday 10 a.m.–12.30 p.m. and 3–6 p.m., Sunday until 5.30 p.m. Transport: by car on the A2 motorway, exit Montblanc.
Santa Maria de Poblet is the first of the three famous Cistercian monasteries founded in the 12th century in the area surrounding Montblanc. A beautiful and cool place to visit on a hot day, the well-maintained monastery is proof of the wealth and influence of the Church. As well as being a working monastery, Poblet is also the final resting place of several kings of Catalunya and Aragon from the 12th to the 15th centuries. Although the monastery was sacked in 1835, when the monks were forced to abandon the buildings and the royal tombs were virtually destroyed, the remains of the tombs were saved and returned to the monastery in 1953, after clever restoration work.

MONASTERIO DE SANTES CREUS

Daily 10 a.m.–1 p.m. and 3.30–6 p.m. (in summer until 7 p.m.). Transport: by car take the A2 motorway, exit Valls Vila-rodona.
The third of the Cistercian monasteries is found in a peaceful valley near the River Gaià. Although it was built around the same time as Poblet, it features remarkably different styles, which makes it feel a little less austere than its bigger rival. Two of the country's kings decided to be buried

here rather than at Poblet, and their tombs were not sacked in the 19th century. At the foot of Pere the Great's tomb lies the king's famous admiral, Roger de Llúria, who is reputed to have brought his monarch's bath-like urn—thought to be unique in Spain—back from one of his trips to the Orient.

SANTA MARIA DE VALLBONA

Tel. 977-33-02-66. Monday to Saturday 10.30 a.m.–1.30 p.m. and 4.30–6 p.m. Transport: by car on the A2 motorway, exit Montblanc.

The Cistercian nunnery at Vallbona de les Monges is smaller than Poblet, but is also very much a working community. The nuns dedicate several hours a day to spiritual communion and to their daily tasks. The peace and quiet, as well as the excellent examples of church architecture, archives and religious tapestries, make it a pleasure to visit. Look out for the lantern hanging over the main part of the church, made at the end of the 13th and beginning of the 14th centuries; its octagonal shape allows light to be thrown around the church.

TARRAGONA

Transport: by car, Tarragona lies about 100 kilometres (60 miles) to the south of Barcelona, along the C246 and the N340. By train, R.E.N.F.E. from Barcelona-Sants Central Station, or from Pg. de Grácia. Coaches are run by the "Hispania Reus" company from Pl. de Sant Joan/Diputació (tel. 977-30-11-34).

Tarragona contains perhaps the best and most numerous examples of Roman remains in this region, as well as a collection of fine beaches. Its Roman origins date from 218 B.C. and the city boasts a wealth of museums and sights, including a fine amphitheatre, aqueduct and an excellent archaeological museum. The old part of the city is gradually being renovated, with the creation of pedestrian streets and the rebuilding of some of the edifices. This makes it a good place for a leisurely stroll. And Tarragona is more relaxed than Barcelona, to suit its more southerly location. The train journey between the cities hugs the coast past cliffs and beaches, and is an experience in itself, while by car the trip is likely to be more frustrating, especially at the weekend when traffic becomes unbearable. While in Tarragona, try to visit the delta of the River Ebre, with its abundance of wildlife.

CONSULATES

Australia: Gv. Carles III 98, 08028 Barcelona; tel. 330-94-96.
Canada: Via Augusta 125, 08021 Barcelona; tel. 209-06-34.
Eire: Gv. Carles III 94, 08028 Barcelona; tel. 330-96-52.
Great Britain: Av. Diagonal 477, 08036 Barcelona; tel. 322-21-51.
South Africa: Gv. Corts Catalanes 634, 08010 Barcelona; tel.318-07-97.
U.S.A.: Via Laietana 33, 08003 Barcelona; tel. 319-95-50.

EMERGENCIES (SEE ALSO CONSULATES)

The police emergency number in Barcelona is 092; outside the city, dial 091.

Ambulance	La ambulancia
Careful!	Cuidado
Fire!	Fuego
Help!	Socorro
Police!	Policia
Stop!	Deténgase
Stop thief!	Al ladrón

LOCAL TRANSPORT

General information on public transport (underground, urban buses, inter-urban and long-distance services etc.) may be obtained by telephoning 412-00-00.

Bus. In general, buses run from 6.30 a.m. to 10 p.m., although some lines also operate until dawn or up to midnight. Night buses run on the principal routes between 10 p.m. and 4 a.m. There's also the **Aerobús** linking Pl. Catalunya and the airport; and the **Tombus** covering the commercial area.

The Palau Nacional at dawn.

Metro. There are four underground lines and two corporation railway lines. The entrances to the underground stations are marked with a red diamond outlining the word "metro". Plans of the network showing connections with other lines and with the railway lines are on display in the vestibule and on the platform at all stations. Trains run from 5 a.m. to 11 p.m. Monday to Thursday, 5 a.m. to 1 a.m. Friday, Saturday and the day before public holidays, and 6 a.m. to midnight on Sundays and public holidays. Single fares are 90-pts and a T-2 ticket for 10 journeys is 760-pts.

Bus and metro combined fares. Single ticket: 100-pts. T-1 ticket for 10 journeys: 510-pts. One-, three- and five-day passes permitting unlimited use of Barcelona's bus and underground system cost 300, 850 and 1.200-pts. respectively.

Taxis are black with yellow trim and there are plenty on the streets at all hours. Taxis bear the initials SP (*servicio público*) on front and rear bumpers. Fares are low by London or New York standards: most rides cost 300–400-pts. For general information, telephone "Taxi card" on: 412-20-00.

Taxi companies. Barnataxi, tel. 357-77-55
Taxi Radio Móvil, tel. 358-11-11
Tele Taxi, tel. 392-22-22
Radio Taxi, tel. 490-22-22

MONEY MATTERS

Currency. The monetary unit of Spain is the *peseta* (abbreviated pts.).
Banknotes: 1.000, 2.000, 5.000 and 10.000 pesetas.
Coins: 1, 5, 10, 25, 50, 100, 200, and 500 pesetas.
A five-peseta coin is called a *duro* and prices are sometimes quoted in duros, e.g., 10 duros = 50-pts.

Exchange. All branches of Bancos y Caixas have currency exchange offices as do the branches situated in tourist areas. Your hotel will be able to change money for you without difficulty, and there is also a currency exchange office in El Corte Ingles, Pl. Catalunya 14, tel. 302-12-12.

Banking hours. Monday to Friday 8.30 a.m.–2 p.m., Saturday 8.30 a.m.–1 p.m. (closed on Saturday in summer). Currency exchange offices in the city centre are open in the afternoon until 4.45 p.m.

The following currency exchange offices are open on public holidays:

La Caixa, Barcelona-Sants Central Station. Open daily 8 a.m. to 10 p.m., tel. 490-77-70. Closed 25 and 26 December and 1 and 6 January.

Banco Bilbao Vizcaya, Barcelona-Sants Central Station. Open 8.15 a.m. to 10 p.m., closed between 2 and 4 p.m. on public holidays in winter. Tel. 409-26-95.

Banca Exterior de España, Barcelona Airport. Open daily 7 a.m. to 11 p.m., tel. 370-10-12.

Eurocheques are not common in Spain; you are advised to use them only to withdraw cash. However, credit cards are widely accepted. Always remember to take your passport with you when changing money.

POST AND TELEPHONE

Central post office. Pl. Antoni López 1, 08002 Barcelona; tel. 318-38-31. Open Monday to Friday 8 a.m.–10 p.m., Saturday 10 a.m.–8 p.m. There are branches in most districts of the city, though most close between 2 p.m. and 4 p.m., and only stay open to 6 p.m.

Telex and business services. Àngel Baixeras, D 2°; tel. 301-29-27.

Telephones. Fontanella 2; tel. 318-61-00. Open Monday to Saturday 8.30 a.m. to 9 p.m. Barcelona-Sants Central Station (vestibule); open daily 7.45 a.m. to 10.45 p.m.

Public telephones with instructions for use are found throughout the city. An urban call to the surrounding area costs 15-pts. for three minutes; inter-urban calls cost upwards of 25-pts. The country code for Spain is 34, the area code for Barcelona is 93. If phoning from outside Spain, drop the 9 in the area code.

Telephone information. tel. 003. City telephone information tel. 010. **213**

TOURIST OFFICES

Before your trip, you might like to gather more information from a Spanish tourist office. Some addresses:

Australia. International House, Suite 44, 104 Bathhurst St., P.O. Box A-675, 2000 Sydney NSW; tel. 02-264-79-66

Canada. 102 Bloor St. West, 14th floor, Toronto, Ont., M5W 1M8; tel. 416-961-31-31

United Kingdom. 57–58 St. James's St., London SW1A 1LD; tel. 071-499-1169

United States. Water Tower Place, Suite 915 East, 845 North Michigan Ave., Chicago IL, 60611; tel. 312-944-0216/230-9025
The Gallery Bldg., Suite 4800, 5085 Westheimer Rd., Houston TX 77056; tel. 713-840-7411-13
8383 Wilshire Blvd., Suite 960, 90211 Beverly Hills, CA 90211; tel. 213-658-7188/93
665 5th Ave., New York, NY 10022; tel. 212-759-8822

Barcelona. Many of the staff in the city's tourist offices can speak English. Ask them for a programme of events for the month of your visit. The main tourist offices are:

City Tourist Offices (*Of. Informació Turística i Ciutadana*). Barcelona-Sants Central Station. Open daily 8 a.m. to 8 p.m.; tel. 490-91-71.
Av. Reina Maria Cristina 2–16. Open daily 8 a.m. to 8 p.m.; tel. 326-52-35.

Regional Tourist Offices (*Of. Turisme Generalitat*). Barcelona Airport. Open Monday to Saturday 9.30 a.m. to 8 p.m., Sunday 9.30 a.m. to 3 p.m.; tel. 325-58-29.
Gv. Corts Catalanes 658. Open Monday to Friday and Sunday 9 a.m. to 7 p.m., Saturday 9 a.m. to 1.30 p.m.; tel. 301-74-43.

MAP SECTION

Key

Scale 1 : 15 000

Terreno urbanizado
Bebaute Fläche
Built-up area
Terrain bâti

Bosque; campo de deportes
Wald; Sportplatz
Wood; playing ground
Forêt; terrain sportif

Parque; cementerio
Park; Friedhof
Park; cemetery
Parc; cimetière

Autopista
Autobahn
Motorway
Autoroute

Arteria principal
Hauptverkehrsstr.
Great passage way
Route principale

Calle de direccion unica
Einbahnstr.
One way street
Sens unique

Limites municipales
Gemeindegrenzen
Borders of settlements
Limites de commune

Distritos Postales
Postzustellbereiche
Postal Districts
Arrondissements postaux

Ferrocarril con estación
Eisenbahn mit Bahnhof
Railway with station
Gare de chemin de fer

Estación de Metro
U-Bahnlinie mit Haltestelle
Underground with station
Ligne et station de Métro

Escola
Schule
School
École

Museo
Museum
Museum
Musée

Hospital
Krankenhaus
Hospital
Hôpital

Correos; policia
Postamt; Polizei
Post office; police
Bureau de poste; police

Iglesia
Kirche
Church
Église

Teatro
Theater
Theatre
Théatre

Piscina; parking
Schwimmbad; Parkplatz
Swimming pool; parking
Piscine; parking

Surtidor de Gasolina; estacion de Servicio
Tankstelle; Werkstatt
Filling station; service station
Poste d'essence; station-service

Overall map p. 2: numbers in blue refer to map pages

Copyright by Falk-Verlag · Hamburg · Germany

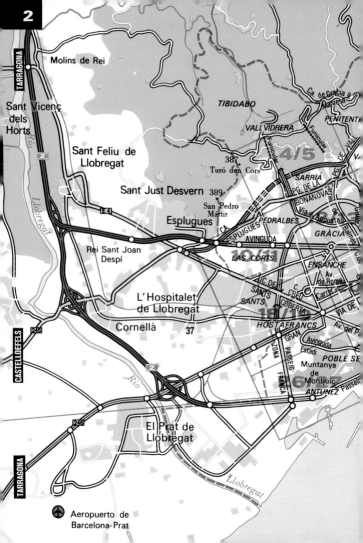

TERRASSA GIRONA

C'an Sant Joan

Poyơ • 303

Santa Coloma
de Gramenet

TORRE BARO

LES REQUETES

VIA FAVENCIA

PG. DE

TRINITAT

VALLDAURA

8

de Sant Andreu

BON
PASTOR

Turó Matas
170

MATARÓ/GIRONA

34

E4

33

HORTA

RCA

CARMEL

AGUINARDÓ

15

SAGRERA

6/17

VERNEDA

CLOT

C/ DE CARRIL C/DE

C/ DE GUIPÚZCOA

Badalona

Sant Adrià
de Besòs

DIAGONAL

C/ Aragó

CORTS CATALANES

22/23

24/25

C/ Calle de

Pedro IV

C/Calle de

POBLE
NOU

Pln de
atalunya

Parc
de la
Ciutadella

30/31

Passeig

de Colom

2/29

Transbordador
Aéri

BARCELONA

M A R

M E D I T E R R À N I A

N

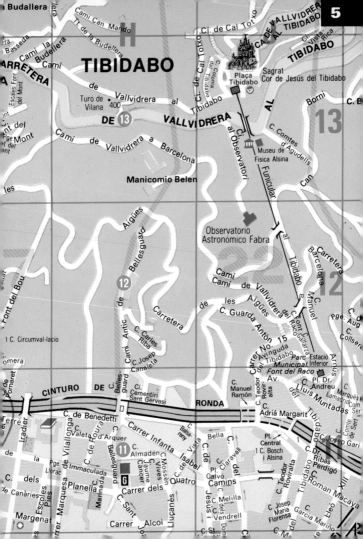

Budallera

Camí Can Mando

Cami la Budellera

Budellera

Camí

Tt. de la Budellera

Ci. de Cal Totxo

Ci. de Cal Toxto

CA DE VALLVIDRERA AL TIBIDABO

C. Vista Rica

TIBIDABO

CARRETERA

Escales Font del Mont

Font del

Poe Mont

del

ant

TIBIDABO

de

Vallvidrera

al

Turó de
Vilana • 400

DE

13

Colonia del Tibidabo

Plaça Tibidabo

Sagrat
Cor de Jesús del Tibidabo

Borni

C. B

al

Tibidabo

VALLVIDRERA

C. Comtes d'Agudells

13

Camí

de

Vallvidrera a Barcelona

Ci. al Observatori

Museu de
Física Alsina

Funicular

Can

Manicomio Belen

Aigües

Observatorio
Astronómico Fabra

Bellesguard

de

12

Camí

Camí

de

Vallvidrera

de

les

Aigües

C. Guarda Antón

Tibidabo

al

Carretera

Barcelona

C. Manuel

22

12

Pge. Aug

C. Collser

Font del Bou

Carretera

Camí Antic

C. Carles
Riba

C. Josep
Canaleta

1 C. Circumval-lacio

omera

Carrer No. 15

Avinguda
Tibidabo

Parc
Municipal
Font del Raco

C.
Tron
del
Raco

Galarza

Estació
Inferior

Arnús

Pl. Dr.
Andreu

Av.

Tibidabo

C. Marquès
Lamadrid

Com
Ser

CINTURO DE

Bellesguard

Ci.
Cementiri
Sant Gervasi

RONDA

C. Teodor
Roviralta

C. Manuel
Ramón

Adriá Margarit

Lluís Muntadas

C. Josep Gari

Comte de

Terrer

tradier

C. de Benedetti

C. Valeta d'Arquer

Carrer Infanta Isabel

Balle-
rany

Vista

Bella

C.

de

Pl.
Central
1 C. Bosch
i Alsina

C. Dr.
Ribas
Perdigó

de

la

Pge. de
Immaculada

Pl. de
Llorac

Planella

C. Marquesa de Vilallonga

Bellesguard

11

C. Almadén

Mossen
Vives

C. Jaume
Cáncer

Quatre

C. de

C. Claravel

Pl. Calvó
Camins

C. Teodor
Roviralta

Tibidabo

C. Roman Macaya

G

Carrer dels

Jesús

C. de
Jesús

C. Melilla

C. dels
Vendrell

Heo

García Mariño

Escales
Pies

C.
de Canàries

Marinada

C. Sant Joan

Lluçanès

C. Josep
Maria
Florensa

C.

M

Margenat

Carrer Alcoi

Carrer dels

C. Si

N · O

CERDANY[O]

13

Cami de

Parc les Heures

13

Parc del Laberint

C.F. Virgen del Camino

C. Constantí

C. Dos rius

C. Castellar

C. Matadepera

Desvalls

C. Mura

Muntanyola

Cr. Notari

Harmonia

Ritme

C. Dansa

C. Cançó

C. Pantomima

C. Lírica

C. Museu

C. Mímica

C. Sant Cebrià

Hospital de Sant Miquel Fundació Alba

Velódromo Municipal

Velòdrom d'Horta

Radrenn-bahn

Camí Notari

Pge. dels Castanyers

C. Germans

11

C. Can Gloria

Can Pallai

C. Harmonia

C. Berruguete

Pl. Herrera el Vell

12

VALL D'HEBRON

CARRETERA DE HORTA

12

Cem d'H

Scala

LA

C. Juan de Mena

C. Jorge

C. Ventura Rodriguez

II CINTURÓ DE

C. Sitjar

Pare Mariana

Pl. Concha Espina

C. Berruguete

Plaça de Rafael

PASSEIG DE VALLDAURA

C. de Rembrandt

Plaça Botticelli

bron

Parc de la Unitat

Venècia

Carrer

de

Ca. de Sant

Ra. de Manrique

I Pge. Marques Castellbell

C. Marcel·li

Pge. de Venècia

C. Enseyança

Can Travi

Carrer

C. Lloret de Mar

C. Campoamor

Carrer

Sant Gaudenci

Carrer Porrera

Carrer

C. Pintor Josep Pinós

del

Dr.

Coimbra

Coimbra

C. Fontanet

Plaça Fatima

Ramon Vinadé

Plaça Ciutadella

C. Consorts Bernuy

Alt

1 Pge. Alt de Mariner

2 Pge. Guardiola

3 C. Rajoler

4 Pge. Galla

C. Capcir

Purissima

C. Torello

Genis a Horta

C. Braganca

Pge. St. Jaume

C. Platans Carrer

de Lisboa

Alarcon de Avila

Plaça de Castellnou

C. J.

C. Pge. de

Ciutadella

C. St. Tomàs

C. Palafox

C. Rectoria

Salses

C. Sant Bernabé

C. Baix

Combinació

C. Sant

11

C. Mestre Daimau

de Feliu i Codina

Congrès

Hedilla

Puig

Pge. de Farnes

Pt.

C. de Farnes

C. Argimon

Andalet

C. de Farnes

Serrallonga

Lusitania

Beatriu Isabel de Portugal

Pge. isabel

de Lisboa

Dante

Carrer de Ivissa

Carrer d'Horta

C. Riveró

C. de Plana Bda

C. Crehuet

Alt 1

C. de Mariner

Pere Pau

Baix de Mariner

C. Marti Alsina

del Vent

Pge. de Fabra

Xavier

Pl. St. F

C. de Cornudella

C. Camps Marces

Moratin

Carrer d'emp

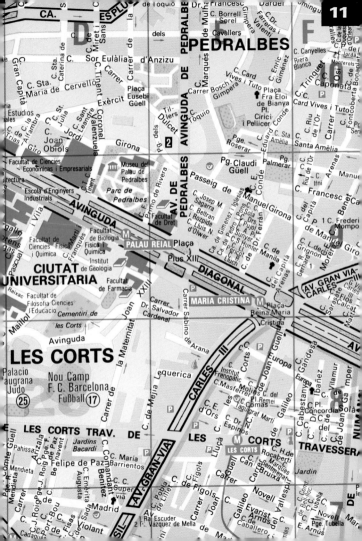

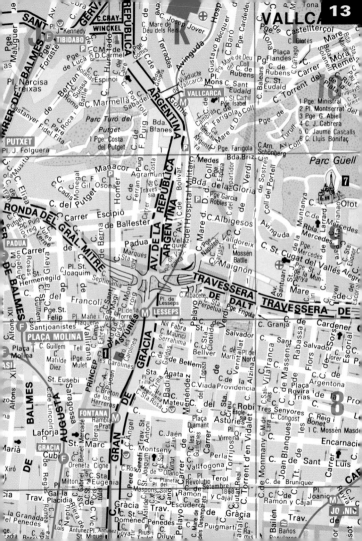

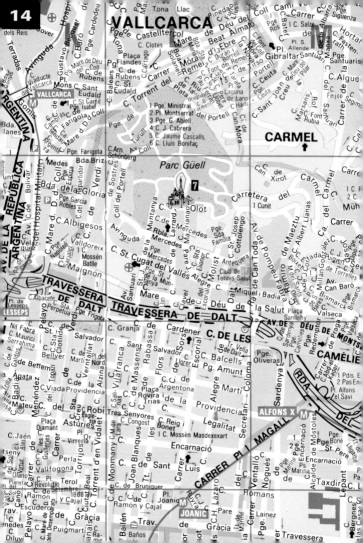

17

9

1 C. Baga
2 C. Brocá
3 C. Clará
4 C. Fiol
5 C. Mollet
6 C. Odena
7 C. Sto D. Savio

8 C. Beat Domènec Savi
9 C. Collbató

C. Sta. Calonge

Carrer de Quito

Carrer de Valparais

C. de Tucumán

Caracas

d'Asuncion

Carrer de Guayaquil

Carrer

de

de

Potosí

Carrer

Carrer de Maracaibo

Ciutat

Carrer de Cuzco

BON PASTOR

Carrer de Lima

Pge. Lima

Carrer de

Carrer de

C. Augusto Cesa
Sandino

Pl. Fra Juniper Serra

C. de Lima

Costa Daurada

C. Vilamajor

C. de Mollerussa

Passeig

CINTURO DEL LITORAL

Besós

STA COLOM. DE GRAMENE

C. San Ernesto

Carrer

C. de Térre

Claramunt

Carrer

PONT DEL MOLINET

AV. DE LA GENERAL

Santander

Rec de Nova

Av. del Ferrocarril

Passeig de la Verneda

AV. DE LA GENERAL

AV. Pius XII

BADALONA

VERNEDA

1 C. Sant Isidre
2 C. Orella

A. Molins

JOAN XXIII

AV. ALFONS

AV. DE MARGALL

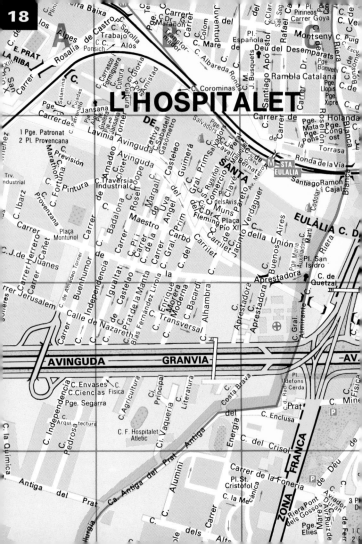

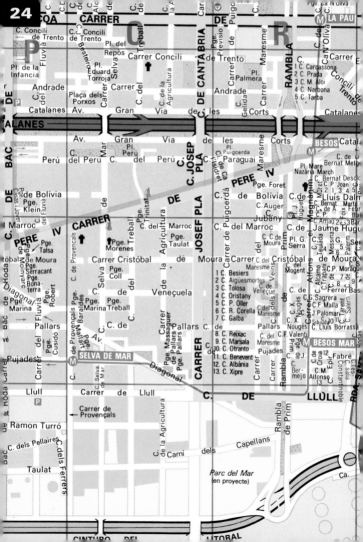

GUIPUSCOA

MATARO

SANT DE ADRIÀ BESÓS

SANT CATERINA

Av. de les Corts Catalanes
C. de les Corts Catalanes

Av. de les Corts Catalanes
Pl Pius XII

C. CRISTOFOL DE MOURA

C. DE TORRASSA

Carrer de Ponent

Pl. Mossos d'Esquadra

Avinguda   Eduard Maristany

Av. Eduard   Maristany

NTURO DEL LITORAL

Planta   Incineradora d'Escombreries

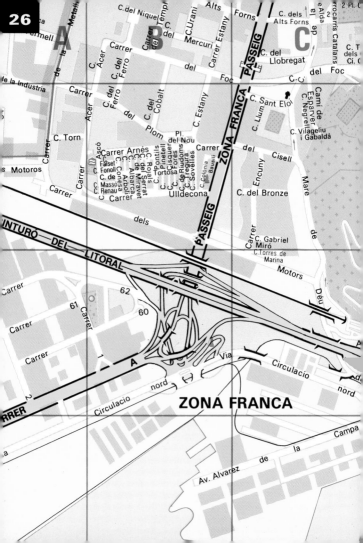

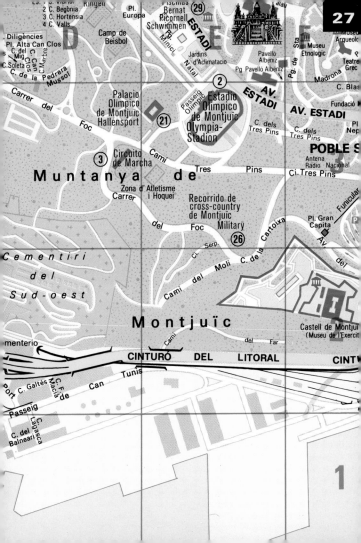

2 C. Begònia
3 C. Hortènsia
4 C. Valls

Ringen

Pl.
Europa

Camp de
Beisbol

Píscinas
Bernat
Picornell
Schwimmen

(29)

ESTADI

Museu
Arqueol

C. del
C. de la Pedrera

Diligències
Pl. Alta Can Clos
C. del
Mig
C.Soleta

Jardins
d'Aclimatacio

Pg.
Minici

C. Natal

Pavelló
Albeniz

Pg. Pavelló Albeniz

Pg. de Sta.

Museu
Etnologic

**AV.
ESTADI**

Teatre
Grec

Carrer
del

Foc

Palacio
Olimpico
de Montjuic
Hallensport

(2)

Passeig
Olimpic

**Estadio
Olimpico
de Montjuic
Olympia-
Stadion**

AV. ESTADI

Madrona

C. Blas

Fundació

(21)

C. dels
Tres Pins

C. dels
Tres Pins

Pl.
Nep

POBLE S

(3)

Circuito
de Marcha

Camí

Antena
Radio Nacional

M u n t a n y a   d e

Tres   Pins

Cl. Tres Pins

Zona d'Atletisme
i Hoquei

Carrer

Recorrido de
cross-country
de Montjuic
Military

Funicular

del

(26)

Pl. Gran
Capita

_C e m e n t i r i_

Foc

Cl. Serp.

Av.

del

_d e l_

C. del Moli

C. de la Cartoixa

_S u d - o e s t_

Camí del Moli

M o n t j u ï c

Castell de Montjuïc
(Museu de l'Exercit

Camí

del   Far

menterio

CINTURÓ   DEL   LITORAL

CINT

Tunis

C. Galtés
C. F. Macià

Can

Port

de

Passeig

C. del
Balneari

Lagasca

1

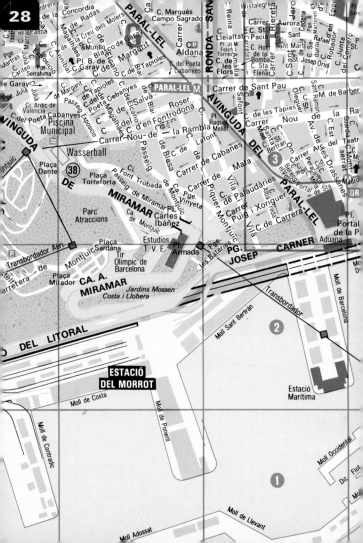

K2
1 C. Paredes
2 C. Magatzems
3 C. Monjo
4 C. del Baluard
5 C. la Sal
6 C. Mariners
7 C. Safareigs
8 C. Atlàntida
9 C. Sant Josep
10 C. Escuder
11 C. dels Pescadors
12 C. Comte de Sta. Clara
13 C. de Sevilla
14 C. Mestrança
15 C. Meer
16 C. Pontevedra
17 C. de Vinarós
18 C. Grau i Torras
19 C. de Guiter
20 C. de Vila Joisa
21 C. Alcanar
22 C. Dr. G. i Partagàs
23 C. de Salamanca
24 C. Proclamació
25 C. Sta. L. de Marillac
26 C. A. Barceló
27 C. Sòria

1 C. B. Mall
2 C. M. Boe
3 C. Conrer
4 C. Havana
5 C. Geli
6 C. Medite
7 C. Cerme

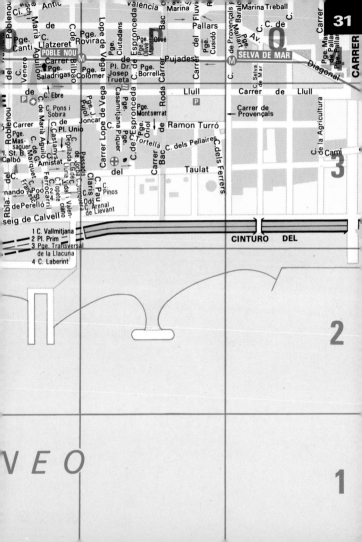

CARRER

Ci.
Antic
de
Pge.
Canti
Llatzeret
C. de
Rovira
Pge.
de
Lope
Ciutadans
Vega
de
Esponceda
Olivé
Pge.
Marignany
Bac
Marina
Fluvi
València
Marina Treball
Pallars
Provençals
Pge.
Cusidó
Av.
C. de
Pge. Mas
de Pallar
Pge. de Pallar

POBLE NOU
Carrer
de
Bilbao
Pge.
Colomer
Pge.
Saladrigas
de
de
Olivé
Pujades
SELVA DE MAR
Diagonal
C.
Pl. Dr.
Josep
Trueta
Pge.
Borrell
Carrer
C.
Selva
de Mar

de
Venero
P
C.
Ebre
C. Pons i
Sobira
de
Maria
C. Aguiló
Pge.
J.
Pujol
Lope
de
Vega
Joncar
de
Casamitjana
Piquer
Llull
P
Carrer
de
Llull
Carrer de
Provençals

Roda
de
Pge.
Montserrat

Carrer
Poblenou
Pge.
Mas-
saquer
Pl. St. B.
Calbó
de
Maria
Aguiló
de
Amistat
C. Castanys
Pl. Unió
Degollada
de
C. de C.
C. Lluna Vidal i Valenc
Passadís C. Junquera
Carrer
Lope
de
Vega
Clariss
C.
Pau
Pge.
Oriol
C. d'Esponceda
C. de
Tortellà
C. d'Oriol
Ramon Turró
C. dels Pellaires
C. dels Ferrers
C.
de la Agricultura
Cami

3

del
Ferrocarril
Pge.
de
Franc
nando de
Poo
C. Llopet
ciano
Odó
C. Pinos
C. Arenal
de Llevant
C. Marquet
Pou
Taulat

Rbla.
de Perelló
eig de Calvell

1 C. Vallmitjana
2 Pl. Prim
3 Pge. Transversal
de la Llacuna
4 C. Laberint

CINTURO
DEL

2

V E O

1

METRO

L1 Metro Línia 1
L3 Metro Línia 3
L4 Metro Línia 4
L5 Metro Línia 5

Ferrocarrils
Tramvia Blau
Funicular
Telefèric

L4
L1
L3
L5

Sabadell Terrassa Manresa
Granollers, Vic, Puigcerdà
Cornellà, Vic, Puigcerdà, Girona, Port Bou

Sta. Coloma
Baró de Viver
Trinitat Vella
Torras i Bages
Sant Andreu
Llucmajor i Bages
Fabra i Puig
Sagrera
Roquetes
Congrés
Navas
Clot
Verneda
Joan XXIII
Sant Roc
La Pau
Besòs Mar
Besòs
Selva de Mar
Poblenou
Llacuna
Bogatell
Ciutadella
Barceloneta

Gorg, Pep Ventura
Mataró, Arenys, Port Bou

Montbau
Vall d'Hebron
Penitents
Vallcarca
Lesseps
Fontana
Joanic
Hospital de Sant Pau
Vilapicina
Horta
Virrei Amat
Maragall
Guinardó
Alfons X
Camp de l'Arpa
Sagrada Família
Verdaguer
Gràcia
Diagonal
Passeig de Gràcia
Girona
Tetuan
Monumental
Marina
Glòries
Encants
Arc de Triomf
Jaume I
Urquinaona
Catalunya
Universitat
Liceu
Drassanes
Passeig de la Rambla
Miramar
Tibidabo
Av. del Tibidabo
Les Tres Torres
El Putxet
Pàdua
Putget
Molina
Sant Gervasi
Muntaner
La Bonanova
Sarrià
Reina Elisenda
Peu del Funicular
Vallvidrera Superior
Peu del Funicular

Sant Cugat Sabadell Rbla. Terrassa

Zona Universitària
Palau Reial
Maria Cristina
Les Corts
Plaça del Centre
Entença
Hospital Clínic
Provença
Sants-Estació
Rocafort
Urgell
Tarragona
Espanya
Poble Sec
Paral·lel
Parc de Montjuïc
Castell

Collblanc
Badal
Plaça de Sants
Hostafrancs
Mercat Nou
Ildefons Cerdà
Santa Eulàlia
Torrassa
Florida
Pubilla Cases
Can Vidalet
Can Serra
Can Boixeres
Sant Ildefons

Gornal
Bellvitge
Av. Carrilet
Sant Josep
Baldiric
Almeda
Cornellà
Rbla. Just Oliveras
Gavarra

Feixa Llarga
L'Aeroport Vilanova

Martorell Vilafranca
Manresa Igualada

L5 Cornellà

A

Abacería Central 98
Ace189
Adolfo Dominguez 67
Agencia Madosmas 191
Agut 120
Airo 91
Ajuntament de Barcelona 9
Alain Manoukian 68, 189
Alcora i Delfín 79, 185
Alexandra 171
Alfa Aeropuerto 167
Alfredo Villalba 68
Alguero 87
Alice Ramon 84
Aliword 91
Alma, D' 68
Aloe 189
Altair Força 80
Amarcord 152
Amaya 121
Ana Ros 77
Ancien Bijou, L' 77
Andorra 206
Anec, L' 91
Antic Hospital de la Santa Creu 11, 62
Antic Mercat del Born 62
Antifaz Comic 80
Antiga 77
Antigüedades Noirjean 77
Aragon 167
Aramis 68
Araña 189
Arc de Triomf 11
Arce 68

Arenas 171
Arkupe 77
Arpi 101
Ars Studio 150, 153
Artcava Fusina 153
Articulo 26 150, 153
Artisan Perfumerier, L' 86
Artur Ramon 77
Asador de Aranda 121
Astoria 172
Aswani Parsram 101
Atenas 168
Atlan 78
Atlas 101
Atri 88
Auditori de la O.N.C.E. 146
Augusta 91
Autobús Turístico Número 100
Avenida Palace 175
Avenida, La 66
Azulete 109

B

B.D. Ediciones de Diseño 89
Baby and Home 191
Bagdad 161
Bagués 84
Baixas 91
Balagué 80
Bali 126
Balmes 172
Balmoral (Tearoom) 130, 153
Balmoral (Hotel) 172
Balsa, La 113

Bang 190
Bar del Pí 153
Bar Mandri 135
Bar Roble 135
Bar Turo 136
Barcelona de Noche 161
Barcelona Hilton 175
Barceloneta 196
Barcelonina de Vins i Espirits, La 92
Barri Gòtic 195
Baztan 113
Bebelin 187
Bel Air 113
Belle Époque 161
Benetton 68
Berimbau 153
Beverly Hills 101
Biblioteca de Catalunya 11
Biksa Internacional 191
Bilbao 118
Biscuit 187
Blau Marí 132
Boadas 153
Bodega Apolo 162
Bodega Bohèmia 162
Bodega Sepúlveda 136
Body Shop, The 86
Boira 153
Boîte La 154
Boliche 154
Bonanova Park 168
Bopan 92
Born Market 39
Bosch 80
Bossa Art 101
Botafumeiro 109
Botas, Las 137

Botet 101
Brasserie Flo 132
Brioche, La 131
Brusi. Tin i Montse 92
Bulevard Rosa 66
Burradas 76

C
C. Civic Casa Elizalde 147
C. Cívic l'Artesà 147
C. de Tir de Mollet, Camp de Tir Olímpic de Mollet del Vallés 35, 36
C. Dramàtic de la Generalitat 143
Caballito Blanco, El 121
Cacharel 187
Cache-Cache 187
Café de l'Opera 154
Cafe de la Academia 118
Café de la República 134
Caixa's Science Museum, La 40
Camarasa 92
Camilla Hamm 78
Camp de Tir Amb Arc de la Vall d'Hebron 31
Camper 68
Can Caralleu 38
Can Jaume 118
Can Majo 121
Can Melic 38
Can Punyetes 118
Can Travi Nou 114

Canadá 190
Cangurserveis 191
Canilla, La 102
Caracoles, Los 121
Carballeira 122
Carmen Rubio 69
Carruatges de Alquiler 200
Carruatges 51
Cartier 84
Casa Almirall 80
Casa Amatller 25
Casa Batllo 25
Casa Bellesguard 25
Casa Calvet 26
Casa de l'Ardiaca 11
Casa de les Punxes 26
Casa del Bacalao 92
Casa dels Canonges 12
Casa Fernandez 136
Casa Fuster 26
Casa Isidro 109
Casa Joana 119
Casa Lleo Morera 26
Casa Milà (La Pedrera) 27, 40
Casa Pepe 92
Casa Quirze 137
Casa Tejada 136
Casa Viçens 27
Casa-Museu Gaudí 43
Casals 92
Casino l'Aliança del Poble Nou 144
Castell de Montjuïc 12
Castello 87
Castells 80
Cataluña 166

Catalunya en Miniatura 180
Catedral de Barcelona 20, 147
Cava Sant Sadurni d'Anoia 203
Cavall de Cartró 186
Celia Cosmetic Center 86
Celler de Gelida 93
Cementiri de Montjuïc 193
Centre Cívic Casa Elizalde 62
Centre Cultural Fundació Caixa de Pensions de Barcelona 62, 147
Centre Municipal de Pilota de la Vall d'Hebrón 36, 38
Centro Ciudad 154
Cerveceria d'Or 136
Charcutería Molina 93
Charo 69
Chemisse 69
Chic 190
Chicago Pizza Pie Factory 125
Chicoa 114
Choses 69
Christian Dior Monsieur 69
Churrasco, El 126
Cibeles, La 150, 154
Cinc d'Oros 80
Cine Savoy 184
Cinelandia 81
Cinema Alex (Multicine) 142
Cinema Astoria 142
Cinema Bosque 142
Cinema Capsa 142

Cinema Casablanca 142
Cinema Catalunya 143
Cinema Coliseum 143
Cinema Comèdia (Multicine) 143
Circuit d'Hípica del Montanyà 36
Coco Privé 154
Col·legi Oficial d'Arquitectes de Catalunya 12
Colmado Murrià 93
Coloma, La 114
Colón 172
Colonia Güell 204
Complex Esportiu Can Caralleu 37
Concepcio 98
Condado 168
Condes de Barcelona 176
Condor 172
Conducta Ejemplar 119
Confit 93
Conservatori Superior Municipal de Musica, Auditori Eduard Tolrà 147
Conti 69
Contribuciones 76
Cordobés 162
Coronado 166
Corte Inglés, El 66, 86
Cortés 166
Costa Brava 207
Cova del Drac, La 151, 154

Cr. Castelldefels, Canal de Regates de Castelldefels 38
Cravane 69
Creperie Bretonne 126
Crisol 81
Cristal Park 114
Croissant 93
Crònica 81
Cus-Cus, El 128

D
D. Barcelona 102
Da Giorgio 93
DAE 89
Dama, La 110
Dante 172
Dentellerie, La 127
Derby 173
Desii 93
Diamantissimo 84
Diez 69
Diplomatic 176
Do. Barcelona 190
Documenta 81
Don 102
Don Algodon 70, 190
Don Carlos 70
Donaldson 70, 190
Dorada, La 122
Dorado Petit, El 110
Dos i Una 102
Dos Torres 155
Drugstore David 94, 135
Dry Martini 155
Duques de Bergara 173

E
E.M. Beisbol l'Hospitalet, Estadi Municipal de Beisbol de Hospitalet, L' 32
E.M. Beisbol Viladecans, Estadi Municipal de Beisbol de Viladecans 32
E.M. la Romareda, Estadio Municipal de Fútbol la Romareda 33
E.M. Nova Creu Alta, Estadi de la Nova Creu Alta de Sabadell 33
Edelsa 81
Efectos Especiales 70
Egipte 119
Eixample, L' 198
Elche 122
Emporio Armani 70
En Linea Barcelona 89
Encants de Sant Antoni, Els 99
Encants, Els 78, 99
English Bookshop, The 81
Enric Majoral 84
Escribá Pastisseries 94
Església Capilla del Palau 21
Església Castrense Parc de la Ciutadella 21
Església Mare de Déu de Betlem 21

Església Mare de Déu de la Mercé 21

Església Pompeia Pares Caputxins 147

Església Sant Agustí 22

Església Sant Felip Neri 22, 148

Església Sant Jaume 22

Església Sant Josep i Santa Monica 22

Església Sant Miquel del Port 23

Església Sant Pau del Camp 23

Església Sant Pere de Puel-les 23

Església Sant Sever 23

Església Santa Ana 24, 148

Església Santa Maria de Montalegre 24

Església Santa Maria del Mar 24

Església Santa Maria del Pí 24

Església Sants Just i Pastor 24

España 168

Esposició de Pintors de la Sagrada Familia 99

Estadi de Fútbol Club Barcelona 33

Estadi de Luis Casanova 33

Estadi de Sarrià del Reial Club Deportiu Espanyol 33

Estadi Eqüestre (Miniestadi del Futbol Club Barcelona) 35, 36

Estadi Olímpic de Montjuïc 12, 31, 151

Estany de Banyoles 36

Exclusive 102

Expo Hotel 168

F

Fancy Men 70

Fantasy Shop 70

Farga, La 94, 131

Farreras 71

Feria de l'Artesanat 100

Fibra Optica 155

Figueres and Portlligat 207

Filmoteca Infantil, Filmoteca de la Generalitat 184

Finisterre 110

Fiorucci – Naf Naf 71

Fira, La 155

Flash-Flash Tortilleria 133

Fleca Balmes 94

Flores Prats 100

Foix de Sarrià 94

Font de Canaletes 13

Font Màgica de Montjuïc 13

Forn de Pa Barril 94

Fortuño 100

Frontó Colom 36

Fuente, La 95

Fuera de Horas 155

Fund. Joan Miró 144

Fund. Mediterrania 181

Fundació Antoni Tàpies 44

Fundació Joan Miró 44, 183, 184

Funicular al Tibidabo 201

Furest 71

Futbol Club Barcelona 35

G

Gabinet Postal 44

Gades 134

Galeria d'Art Ambit 57

Galeria d'Art Artur Ramon 58

Galeria d'Art Barbié 58

Galeria d'Art Carles Taché 58

Galeria d'Art Ciento 58

Galeria d'Art Comas 58

Galeria d'Art Dau al Set 59

Galeria d'Art Fernando Alcolea 59

Galeria d'Art Ignacio de Lassaleta 59

Galeria d'Art Joan Prats 59

Galeria d'Art Kreisler 59

Galeria d'Art la Pinacoteca 60

Galeria d'Art Maeght 60
Galeria d'Art Manel Mayoral 60
Galeria d'Art René Metras 60
Galeria d'Art Sala Dalmau 60
Galeria d'Art Sala Gaspar 61
Galeria d'Art Sala Gaudí 61
Galeria d'Art Sala Nonell 61
Galeria d'Art Sala Parés 61
Galeria d'Art Sala Vayreda 61
Galeria d'Art Theo 62
Galerías Preciados 67, 86
Galeries Maldà 67
Gales 71
Galuchat 78
Galvany 98
Gasolinera, La 156
Gaudí 168
Gaudí-Picasso 200
Giardinetto Notte 134
Gimeno 102
Gimlet 156
Giorgio Armani 71
Girona 208
Godiva 95
Golondrinas 199
Gonzalo Comella 71
Gorria 115
Gotico 169
Gràfiques el Tinell 103
Gran Café, El 122
Gran Casino de Barcelona 138

Gran Colmado, El 95
Gran Derby 176
Gran Envelat, El 156
Gran Hotel Calderón 173
Gran Muralla, La 126
Gran Teatre del Liceu 13, 144, 148
Gran Vía 169
Gravina 169
Grec '92 40
Gres 89
Groc 72, 190
Gucci 72
Guided Tours of the City 40

H
Habitat 89
Happy Books 81
Harlem Jazz Club 156
Havana Palace 176
Hedra, L' 188
Helados Italianos 95
Helicopter 201
Herboristería Guarro 95
Herder 82
Héroes 72
Hesperia 173
Hic et Nunc 191
Hispania 138
Hivernacle 14, 63
Hobby Art 103
Hobby-Models 186
Hogar del Libro 82
Hollywood 125
Horno de Montserrat 95

Hospital de la Santa Creu i de Sant Pau 14
Hotel de las Artes 176
Humedad Relativa 151, 156

I
I O 191
Idea Mueble 89
Imperator 156
Imprenta del Carrer Paris, L' 103
Inglés 166
Inicial G 103
Insòlit 90, 103
Institut Botànic de Barcelona 51, 182
Institut del Teatre 148
Institut del Teatre, Teatre Adrià Gual 144
Institut Nacional d'Educació Física de Catalunya 39
Intercambio 76
Internacional 166

J
Jardines de Pedralbes 194
Jaume de Provenza 111
Jazz Collectors 88
Jean Pierre Bua 72, 191
Jean Pierre Victim's 72
Jijonenca, La 131

Jimmy'z 156
Joaquín Berao 84
Jocs & Games 103
José-Luís 137
Jove Teatre Regina 144, 185
Juan Mas 191
Juguetes Palau 187

K
Kayfi 72
KGB 151, 157
Konema 104
Kristel 87

L
Laie 82, 119
Lasierra 96
Leopoldo 123
Librería de la Empresa 82
Librería Francesa 82
Liles, Les 78
Llantiol, El 144, 183
Llibreria Anglesa 82
Llibreria Cooperativa Abacus 185
Llibreria els Tartessos 185
Llibreria Llar del Llibre 186
Llibreria Ona 186
Llicorella 138
Lloret 166
Llotja del Mar 14
Loewe 72
Look 83
Los Años Locos 125
Los Tarantos 163
Lucca 78

M
Madrid Barcelona 123
Magnífico, El 96
Maharajah 127
Majèstic 173
Manual Alpargatera, La 73
Maria Pilar 73
Masimo Dutti 73
Master 173
Matricula 73
Mauri 96, 131
Màxim's 134
Meca, La 131
Meliá Barcelona Sarrià 177
Merbeye 157
Mercat de la Boqueria 14, 98
Mercat de les Flors 148
Mercat de Numismàtica i Filatelia 100
Mercat Gòtic d'Antiguitats 79
Meridien Barcelona, Le 177
Meson Castilla 169
Meson del Jabugo 137
Metropol 169
MG 73
Mikado 174
Mikima 188
Milla 83
Miniatura 204
Mirablau 157
Miramelindo 157
Mirasol 157
Mitre 169
Modo 90

Moirée 73
Moliner, El 138
Molino, El 162
Monasterio de Poblet 208
Monasterio de Santes Creus 208
Monestir de Montserrat 205
Monestir de Pedralbes 14
Montecarlo 170
Montjuïc 194
Monument a Colom 15
Mordisco 133
Morera, La 120
Mots 83
Mullor 188
Museu Arqueòlogic 45
Museu Arts, Industr. i Atraccions Populars 182
Museu Clarà 45
Museu d'Art de Catalunya 40, 45
Museu d'Art Modern 45
Museu d'Arts Decoratives 46
Museu d'Autòmates del Tibidabo 51, 182
Museu d'Història de la Ciutat 46, 182
Museu d'Història de la Medicina de Catalunya 46
Museu d'Història del Calçat 47
Museu de Carruatges Fúnebres 52

Museu de Cera de Barcelona 52, 182
Museu de Ceràmica 47
Museu de Geologia (Museu Martorell) 52
Museu de la Catedral 47
Museu de la Ciencia 52, 181, 182
Museu de la Holografia 53
Museu de la Música 47
Museu de la Zoologia 53
Museu de les Arts d'Espectàcle 53
Museu de les Arts d'Espectàcle – Institut Teatre 183
Museu de les Arts Gràfiques 48
Museu del Fútbol Club Barcelona 53
Museu del Perfum 54
Museu del Temple Expiatori 48
Museu Etnogràfic Andino-Amazònic 54
Museu Etnològic 48
Museu Frederic Marès 48
Museu Galeria de Catalans Il.lustres 49
Museu i Laboratori de Geologia del Seminari 54
Museu Marítim 49

Museu Mentora Alsina 55
Museu Militar 49
Museu Monestir de Pedralbes 49
Museu Palau Reial de Pedralbes 50
Museu Picasso 50
Museu Taurí 55
Museu Tèxtil i de la Indumentària 50
Museu Verdaguer 51
Museu y Centre d'Estudis de l'Esport "Dr. Melcior Colet" 55, 183

N
Neichel 111
Network 133
Nick Havanna 157
Niños-Niñas 188
Norma Comics 83
Nou Disc 88
Nou i Vell 76
Nouvel 170
Novecento 79
Novecientos 83
Nuevo Seoul 126
Numancia 174
Nuñez-Urgel 174

O
Observatori Fabra 183
Odisea, La 129
Oliver y Hardy 134, 158
Oriente 170
Oriol 85
Orotava 111
Otto Zutz 151, 158

P
P. Club Patí de Vic, Pavelló del Club Patí de Vic 34
P.B. Joventut Badalona, Pavelló del Club de Bàsquet Joventud de Badalona 32
P.M. Esports Granollers, Palau Municipal d'Esports de Granollers 34
P.M. Sant Sadurní, Pavelló Municipal Agrícola de Sant Sadurní 34
P.M.E. de Badalona, Palau Municipal d'Esports de Badalona 32
P.O.M. de Reus, Pavelló Municipal d'Esports de Reus 35
Palau Berenguer Aguilar 15
Palau Blau Grana 35, 37
Palau d'Esports Sant Jordi 15, 34, 38, 148, 151
Palau Dalmases 16
Palau de la Generalitat 16
Palau de la Metalurgia 33, 35
Palau de la Música Catalana 16, 148, 152
Palau de la Virreina 16, 63

Palau de Lloctinent 17
Palau Güell 17
Palau March 17
Palau Municipal d'Esports 34, 149
Palau Nacional 18
Palau Reial de Pedralbes 18, 180
Pallaresa, La 131
Paloma, La 158
Panoramica de Noche y Flamenco 200
Panorámica y Toros 200
Paraninf de l'Universitat de Barcelona 149
Parc Atraccions Montjuïc 180
Parc Atraccions Montjuïc, Amfiteatre 185
Parc Atraccions Tibidabo 180
Parc de l'Escorxador 18, 194
Parc de l'Espanya Indústrial 195
Parc de la Ciutadella 194
Parc del Laberint 180
Parc Esportiu del Segre 32
Parc Güell 181, 195
Parc Zoològic 181
Park Hotel 174
Park Putxet 174
Parròquia Santa Maria del Mar 149
Paseo de Gràcia 167
Passadís del Pep 115

Pavelló del Parc Esportiu de la Mar Bella 32
Pavello Mies van der Rohe 19
Pavelló Municipal de l'Espanya Indústrial 39
Pedro Morago 73
Peixerot Barcelona 115
Pelayo 14, 88
Pepa Paper 104
Perla Gris, La 74
Peruomo 74
Pescador, El 115
Pescadors, Els 123
Petit París 116
Pilma 90
Pinus 104
Piscina Maritim 37
Piscina Municipal de Montjuïc 37, 38
Piscina Parc de la Creueta del Coll 37
Piscines Bernat Picornell 35, 38
Pla de la Boqueria 28
Plaça de Berenguer el Gran 28
Plaça de Catalunya 28
Plaça de Espanya 29
Plaça de Sant Felip Neri 29
Plaça de Sant Just 29
Plaça del Doctor Fleming 29
Plaça del Portal de la Pau 30
Plaça Nova 30
Plaça Reial 30
Plaça Sant Jaume 30

Planells Donat 96
Planetari Barcelona 55
Poble Espanyol 19
Poliesportiu Municipal de l'Estació del Nord 37
Polo 74
Polo de Ralph Laurent 74
Port Olímpic de Barcelona 39
Porvenir (Ninot) 98
Prenatal 188
Presidente 177
Primavera 87
Primer Plano 188
Princesa Sofía 177
Principal 170
Puerto 198
Puig Doria 85
Puñalada, La 123

Q
Quartier 158
Quatre Gats, Els 124, 158
Quel Fantástico Lunedí! 127
Quílez 96
Quo Vadis 112

R
Raco d'en Binu 139
Ramada Renaissance see Meridien Barcelona, Le
Rambla, La 197
Reding 170
Regencia Colón 170

Regente 174
Regia 87
Regina 170
Reial Societat de
   Tennis Pompeia 38
Reials Drassanes 19,
   63
Reno 112
Rialto 171
Ribera, La 198
Richart 96
Ritz 177
Rivoli Ramblas 175
Roca 85
Roche Bobois 90
Roig Robí 116
Rosa del Desierto, La
   129
Royal 175

S

Sagrada Família 19
Sala Beckett 144
Sala Cultural de la
   Caja de Madrid
   149
Sala d'Exposicions
   Montcada Caixa de
   Pensions de
   Barcelona 63
Salo de Cent
   (Ajuntament) 149
Saló del Tinell 20, 63
Salvatore Ferragamo
   74
San Agustín 167
Sant Antoni 99
Sant Moritz 175
Santa Eulalia 74
Santa Maria de
   Vallbona 209
Santacana 74

Semon 96
Sendon 85
Senyor Parellada 124
Sert Pavilion 41
Servi-Nens 191
Set Portes, Les 124
Sherlock Holmes 158
Sí Sí Sí 158
Sitges 205
Sitjar 97
Skating 35
Snoocker 159
Soler Cabot 85
Sony Mito 88
Sopeta, La 130
Spaghetti 74
Speedy Pacheco 104
Spleen 75
Sport-Menut 188
Squash 2000 36
Squash Barcelona 37
Squash Diagonal 37
Steak & Salad 125
Studio 54 152, 159
Sugar-Pepe Isus 189
Suite Hotel 177
Suizo 171
Sutton 159

T

Tablao de Carmen, El
   162
Taj Mahal 127
Tambor 187
Tango 159
Targarina, La 116
Tarragona 209
Tastofil, El 97
Taxi Moda 76
Teatre Arnau 163
Teatre Condal 145
Teatre Goya 145
Teatre Grec 20, 145

Teatre Lliure 145
Teatre Malic 183
Teatre Malic, Teatre
   Infantil 185
Teatre Municipal
   Mercat de les Flors
   145
Teatre Poliorama 145
Teatre Principal 146
Teatre Romea 146
Teatreneu-Teixidors a
   Mà 146
Tecmo 90
Teleférico al Castillo
   de Montjuïc 201
Thierry Ashe 76
Tibidabo 195
Tic-Tac 187
Ticktacktoe 135, 159
Tienda Redon 97
Tijuana 128
Tinell, El 79
Tintin 104
Tívoli 97
Tocs 83, 104
Todo Para la Mujer 75
Toledano 167
Tön 75
Tontadas 76
Torrens 75
Torres de Àvila 160
Tragalux 130
Tragarapid 120
Tramonti 1980 127
Tramvia Blau 201
Trapío, El 117
Trau 75
Trecce 75
Tres Tombs, Els 186
Triton 117
Turó Parc – Poeta
   Eduardo Marquina
   181, 184

U

Union Suiza 85
Universal 160
Up & Down 130, 160
Urbe 75

V

Vaqueria, La 133
Vell Sarrià 124
Velòdrom Municipal
    d'Horta 33, 149,
    152, 160
Velvet 160
Venta, La 130
Via Augusta 167
Via Claris 117
Via Veneto 112
Via Wagner 67

Viader 132
Vidosa 105
Vilaplana 97, 132
Villaroel Teatre 146
Vinçon 90, 105
Visita de la Ciudad
    200
Vos Fleurs 100

W

Watch Gallery, The
    85
Wilson 171

X

Xarxa 117
Xix Kebab 129

Y

Yamadori 128
Yashima 128

Z

Z.E. l'Abat Marcet de
    Terrassa, Zona
    Esportiva de l'Abat
    Marcet de Terrassa
    34
Zabriskie 105
Zapata 86
Zara 75
Zeleste 152, 160
Zsa-Zsa 161

10h.30 189